THE TANKS OF TAMMUZ is a dramatic
eye-witness account of the lightning
victory won by Israel's Armoured Corps
during the Six Days' War.

In June '67 tanks were the leading
Israeli land force on every front. They
smashed through the Egyptian defences at
Sinai. They swept the length and breadth
of the peninsula to the banks of the Nile.
They pulverised the Syrian fortress on the
Golan Heights to win the battle for the
west bank of the Jordan.

As a war correspondent who
witnessed these events, Shabtai Teveth
describes the dust, heat and peril of every
engagement – from earliest border incidents
to one of the biggest tank battles of all
time on the scorching sands of the Sinai
desert, when Egypt threw close to a
thousand tanks against Israel's solitary
three divisions.

" . . . an outstanding book, the best I have
read . . . about our wars"

General Moshe Dayan

THE TANKS OF TAMMUZ

The Tanks
of Tammuz

SHABTAI TEVETH

SPHERE BOOKS LTD.
30/32 Gray's Inn Road, London, W.C.1

First published in Great Britain in 1969
by Weidenfeld & Nicolson Ltd.
Second Impression March 1969
Copyright © Shabtai Teveth 1968
Licensed by Schocken Publishing House, Tel Aviv
First Sphere Books edition, 1970

TRADE MARK

SPHERE

Set in Linotype Times

Printed in Great Britain by
C. Nicholls & Company Ltd.

CONTENTS

ILLUSTRATIONS

MAPS

FOREWORD

In recent years the Armoured Corps has played a prominent role in the strengthening of Zahal, Israel's armed forces, and was the decisive factor on every front during the Six Days War: armoured units broke through the Egyptian fortified defences in Sinai and swept through the length and breadth of the Sinai Peninsula; they smashed through the Syrian fortress on the Golan Heights and brought the battle of the West Bank of the Jordan to a speedy decision.

Like the infantry and unlike the air force, the Armoured Corps is open to recruits without special qualifications, but it is unlike the infantry in being a technical force and so requiring a different kind of discipline. Thus, whereas discipline in the Israeli forces has traditionally been based on the individual's understanding and agreement, this is not possible in the Armoured Corps where the maintenance and most advantageous exploitation of the tanks is of paramount importance. The fact that discipline based on blind obedience – so alien to the Israeli people – was enforced and accepted, is an outstanding example of how the undebatable need to survive can change a nation's character.

These two themes – the fact that the Six Days War was a war for survival, and the consequent demands on the country's national service and reserve conscripts – make up the subject of this book. The Six Days War was preceded by the Tractors War and by the Water War over the diversion of the sources of the Jordan in the north. As far as the Armoured Corps was concerned these were a prelude to the Six Days War, for it was during these engagements that tank gunnery was developed and the discipline of the men put to test.

One of the largest tank battles of all times (comparable to those which took place on the Russian front during the Second World War) took place in the Sinai Peninsula, with Egypt pitting close on one thousand tanks against Zahal's three divisions in which there was a considerably smaller number of tanks. In the Six Days War it was General Tal's division which achieved the largest number of break-throughs – within the first twenty-four hours it had to break through five heavily fortified and defended areas. During that period it advanced seventy kilometres and destroyed six enemy brigades; within

13

eight hours its vanguard had reached the rear of the enemy's first line of defence. These are records for tank warfare.

I have given detailed descriptions of General Tal's battles for two simple reasons: his division bore the brunt of the fighting and, as a war correspondent, I was attached to his division. With it I spent three weeks of waiting and uncertainty before the war and then accompanied it in all its battles.

TEL AVIV
31 January 1968

Shabtai Teveth

ACKNOWLEDGMENTS

Many people gave me assistance, and I am unable to list all of them to express my thanks individually. I can only record my grateful appreciation and extend my sincere thanks to the whole of the headquarters of the Armoured Corps, its commanders and armoured units. But I owe special thanks to one who, to my great sorrow, is no longer with us, Lieutenant-Colonel Ehud Elad, commander of 'S' Brigade's Patton Battalion. I met him as a major when he was thirty-one years old, at a time when the people of Israel, its knesset and government were overwhelmed with anxiety at the build-up of the Arab armies and our people were preparing for the war of survival. It was from Major Ehud Elad that I drew faith in our eventual victory. Never have I been so inspired with confidence as by Major Elad. For me he became the symbol of the men of Zahal's combat units whose spirit inspired us all.

PART ONE

THE GATHERING STORM
13 May–4 June 1967

CHAPTER ONE

At midday on Saturday 13 May 1967, Ilan Yakuel, aged twenty-three, parked his father's Peugeot 404 outside the Rehovot home of General Tal. He walked up the mango-tree lined path and knocked at the door. Mrs. Tal and the children welcomed him with pleased surprise. Ilan was always a welcome guest at the house of the Armoured Corps' commander, for although General Tal was known to be a strict disciplinarian, he had taken a great liking to young Ilan, who less than a year ago had been his adjutant.

Ilan was six feet tall, dark and strikingly handsome. It was well known among the officers of the Armoured Corps that the general considered him to be the type of officer of which Zahal's chiefs-of-staff are made. This time, however, Ilan was feeling somewhat apprehensive about his forthcoming meeting with the general. He had come to tell him of his decision to give up his studies in Psychology at Tel Aviv University and to spend several months travelling abroad.

Eight months ago, in October 1966, Ilan's contract with Zahal had come to an end. Armoured Corps H.Q. had asked the general to persuade his adjutant to renew it for a further term, the usual procedure with promising younger officers. General Tal had known that if he asked Ilan he would not be refused, but instead he had backed the young man's decision to study; his feelings in this had been paternal rather than military, as Zahal needs every good man. He had, however, asked Ilan to attend an Armour company commander's course before the end of his service, and for that purpose Ilan had extended his contract until the end of February 1967. He had then been posted to Reserve Armoured Brigade 'K' as a company commander, with the rank of lieutenant. Ilan had begun his studies at the university before completing his military service, and General Tal himself had seen to it that he be admitted to the Psychology Department.

So it was that Ilan was apprehensive. To his amazement the general proved understanding. He even had time to come back to their favourite topic: man's condition and man's destiny.

The general was relaxed. He could see no clouds darkening the political and security horizons. The preparations for the Torchlight Tattoo and Military Parade marking Israel's nineteenth anniversary on 15 May were Zahal's main concern, and at the last staff meeting, General Tal and his officers had been discussing ways of getting rid of the weeds around Base Headquarters.

After lunch the general lit a cigarette and settled down in an armchair in the living room. The walls were lined with books on philosophy and tank warfare. General Tal turned to Ilan. Instead of making himself miserable with his studies, he said, perhaps it would be better if he distracted himself travelling, observing the ways of the world. Perhaps in this way he would gain a better knowledge of himself and so find the purpose of his life. Ilan was delighted. He now found the courage to tell the general about his final oral examination. The lecturer's opening question had been: "What have you gained from my lectures?"

"Nothing," Ilan had answered.

"Then what have you got out of the term?"

"Nothing."

The general laughed. Over Turkish coffee they resumed their talk on Spinoza's philosophy, nature being the cause of itself, its identity with God, the world's lack of purpose and the rule of necessity. Ilan was used to such discussions. In one of their first talks he had been shocked. Nationalism, the general had said, as symbolised by flag, hymn and national tradition, was the cause of wars, evil and disaster. He himself did not believe in Jewish nationalism. But the world was still a society of nation-states and Israel had no option but to be one herself, the more so because its people, who surely had suffered more than any other, were once more threatened with annihilation. In short, men served in Zahal to secure the future of their children. "To save my children," he had told the dumbfounded Ilan, "I am ready to destroy the whole world." The dread of another holocaust was vivid in General Tal's mind, as it is with so many of Israel's Jews. And he had no doubt that the Arab states were intent upon destroying the Jews of Israel.

By the time Ilan left he was feeling much easier in his mind,

18

He drove quickly and confidently to Tel Aviv, then turned towards Ramat Chen, and driving through its tortuous streets, came to a stop before a spacious villa sheltering behind thick foliage. He sounded his horn loudly several times, disturbing the quiet Saturday afternoon.

Mia, who had several friends visiting her, flew to the window.

"Are you out of your mind, Ilan," she called.

"Quick! Come downstairs!" he shouted impatiently.

Eagerly Mia raced down the stairs and out of the house. Three months ago he had said he was no good for her; that she personified the conventional, whereas he still had no idea what he wanted of life. "So go and look for it," she had said bitterly. But they had still kept in touch and now and then would visit each other. Sometimes he would turn up in the middle of the night and sound his horn. Was it possible that he had come to tell her he had decided to take up a profession, to marry, to settle down?

"I've stopped studying," he told her.

Mia was furious. "Look, Ilan," she said, "you're good-looking, intelligent, nice; I think you're the most marvellous man in the world, but tell me just one thing: why have you no faith in yourself? Why?"

"I don't know," Ilan replied.

"What are you running away from?"

"I don't know."

"What are you looking for?"

"I don't know."

They had first met at General Tal's office. She had been a nineteen year old recruit doing her National Service. When he had remarked that he was considering making the army his career, she had said: "Either me or the army." Mia had always known what she wanted, and heading the list was marriage and a comfortable family life. She had by chance once seen the general's monthly pay slip and had been shocked. Her father earned almost three times as much. It had convinced her that a husband with the pay of a regular army officer was not for her. She was a very self-possessed young lady, not inclined to let her emotions run away with her, and a life of hardship was not her idea of living. But now she felt that she would agree to anything, even to Ilan joining the regular army, if this would only put an end to his unhappiness and indecision. She was ready to marry him if only it would bring him peace of mind,

"I want to marry you," Ilan said, "but first I must find out what I want from life."

"In the United States?"

"I'll start off there, yes."

"You're not very patriotic," Mia said.

"Of course I'm not. What is a patriot, anyway? If I'd been born in France, I would have been a French patriot. In England a patriotic Englishman. Patriotism is a myth."

"The trouble is you really believe it," Mia said reprovingly. "If you were only a little patriotic, you wouldn't start with all this looking for things all over the world. You'd stay right here."

Ilan kept quiet, as he could do sometimes for hours.

"Where are you going?" she asked finally, to break the silence.

"To see Oshri."

"The colonel again?" It seemed she always had to share Ilan with the battalion commander.

"He's back from America. He can give me a few hints."

"Then go alone."

"Feel like seeing the parade?" he asked her.

"No, thank you."

Ilan switched his motor on. "So . . . 'bye."

"Will you come and say good-bye?"

"Yes," he promised, and drove off.

On 14 May 1967 a state of immediate readiness was secretly ordered in the Egyptian Army. According to information provided by Syria and the Soviet Union, the Egyptian government believed that Israel had massed three divisions of troops along her northern frontier and that unless prevented, Zahal would attack Syria on 16 May or shortly thereafter.

There was not one iota of truth in the information given Egypt. Israel did not even have two companies of troops along the Syrian border. But the tide of events had begun to flow.

On 15 May the Military Parade was the highlight of Israel's nineteenth anniversary celebrations. That year, 1967, the parade was held in Jerusalem for the first time in many years. A military parade in Jerusalem invariably caused trouble because of the city's contested status. Israel claimed sovereignty over it as her capital, in contrast to the countries who supported the United Nations Resolution on the Internationalisation of Jerusalem. Furthermore, the Armistice Agreement with Jordan restricted the types of weapons allowed into Jerusalem, and Zahal could not display its military might there. So Zahal had to hold its parades elsewhere.

The Nineteenth Independence Day Parade consisted only of infantry units. Neither armoured vehicles nor air force planes took part. The government had made every possible effort to eliminate anything which might upset Jordan and the United Nations, and it was therefore a very modest affair. It did not attract a great crowd, and to some extent seemed to reflect the general mood in Israel, affected as it was by an economic recession and growing unemployment.

General Israel Tal, whose tanks did not take part in the parade, absented himself from the stands. In the company of his wife, Hagit, he spent a quiet afternoon at Nave Magen at the home of his friend, Colonel Moshe Gidron, commander of the Signals Corps. In army circles there was a growing feeling that now more than ever Israel's independence was dependent on its economic efforts. It was thought that Syria, the most troublesome of the Arab states, had been dealt a severe blow on 7 April, when in a few minutes Israeli planes had shot down six of her MIG fighters. Egypt, strongest and most dangerous of the Arab states, was up to her neck in the Yemen fracas and deep in her own economic troubles. Several weeks previously, the chief-of-staff, Major-General Itzhak Rabin, had declared that he did not anticipate an Arab-Israel military confrontation for several years. The official evaluation of the situation was that for the present Egypt was not interested in a confrontation with Israel.

At 1730 hours the telephone rang in Colonel Gidron's house. The orderly officer at Armoured Corps H.Q. wished to speak to General Tal. He informed him that the chief-of-staff wanted the general to contact him at his home without delay.

"Sir," General Tal said into the telephone a moment later.

"Talik," the deep bass of the chief-of-staff came over the wires, "do you remember 'Rotem'?"

"Yes, Sir."

"This is it, Talik."

General Tal at once grasped the significance of what Rabin had said, but he wished to know more. He told the chief-of-staff he was not far from his house and asked if he could come round.

"Rotem" was the code name for a 1960 operation. Its main object had been the rapid deployment of forces for defence against a sudden concentration of Egyptian army units in Sinai. In 1960 General Tal had been a colonel in command of

21

'S' Brigade, while the chief-of-staff had been head of the general staff division at G.H.Q. At 5 o'clock one morning General Rabin had bypassed official channels and telephoned directly to Colonel Tal at his home.

"The Egyptians have entered Sinai with a force of five hundred tanks, Talik."

"I'll get moving at once, Sir."

Within a matter of hours Colonel Tal had had over a hundred tanks in position, ready to meet the concentration of Egyptian forces.

"Rotem" was, therefore, a broad enough hint. General Tal telephoned the home of Lieutenant-Colonel Kalman, operations chief of the Armoured Corps, instructing him to have all staff officers and unit commanders of the corps on telephone stand-by. While General Tal hurried off to see the chief-of-staff, Lieutenant-Colonel Kalman passed on instructions to the orderly officer at corps headquarters to sound the alert.

General Rabin had just returned from Jerusalem where he had attended the official Independence Day ceremonies. He told General Tal that the Egyptians were pouring their entire army into Sinai. There was no knowing whether they intended war, which seemed hardly likely, or whether they were trying some clever ruse to extricate their army from the mess it had got itself into in the Yemen. But whichever it was, Zahal had to be ready. The chief-of-staff ordered General Tal to place all regular units of the Armoured Corps on the alert, but not to mobilise the reserves.

Lieutenant-Colonel Kalman was again contacted by General Tal and instructed to alarm corps headquarters. He was told to report to the general on developments every hour.

Tal himself went back to his friends at Nave-Magen to continue his interrupted social visit. He was used to alerts and alarms and although he had not accepted the view that Egypt's involvement in the Yemen assured Israel of several years of comparative peace, he considered this new situation as nothing more than a 1967 version of "Rotem". The following day, 16 May, the Armoured Corps was to play host to all the former Zahal chiefs-of-staff. The programme for their visit included a tank gunnery show at the Armour School. General Tal saw no reason for cancelling the show.

G.H.Q. now issued instructions and orders to all generals commanding the northern, central and southern fronts, the commanders of the air force and the navy and to commanders of the various forces and services; these went out by runners, telephone and radio.

Later that evening, General Tal telephoned the commander of 'S' Brigade, Colonel Shmuel, who was staying at the Desert Inn Hotel in Beersheba. His brigade was on its way to the Negev from training grounds in the Galilee, for concentrated brigade exercises.

"Remember 'Rotem', Shmulik?"

"Certainly, Sir," the colonel replied.

"This is it."

"Flags up, Sir!" said Colonel Shmuel.

In 1960, Colonel Shmuel had been a major in command of a company of Centurion tanks in 'S' Brigade, the first Centurion company in Zahal. He was then the senior company commander in Zahal. In the 1956 Sinai Campaign he had commanded a company in the 7th Brigade, and his had been the first Zahal unit to reach the Anglo–French ultimatum line, ten miles east of the Suez Canal zone along the Ismailia axis. Shmuel had later been promoted to operations officer of 'S' Brigade, but had agreed to being demoted back to company commander in order to go to England to study the Centurion tank and form the first cadre for its reception in Zahal.

Colonel Shmuel, too, saw nothing extraordinary in this new version of Operation "Rotem". His brigade had been in a constant state of alert during the past few months. Nevertheless he did not go back to bed, though he was suffering from a slight attack of influenza. Neither did he content himself with telephoning instructions to brigade headquarters, but dressed quickly and drove there himself. On the way he thought that of all his units the S/14 Patton Battalion was the most ready for action.

CHAPTER TWO

Major Ehud Elad, commander of the S/14 Patton Battalion, and his wife Hava had spent Independence Day in Ashkelon where they were visiting friends. In the evening, at the conclusion of the day's festivities, they returned to their apartment in Beersheba. Ehud was in love with his Patton tanks and wanted to make a success of his job. General Tal needed officers who besides qualifying as combat leaders excelled in technical knowledge and professional thoroughness, and Ehud had been given command of the battalion even before passing through the Staff and Command College, having been appointed over the heads of several senior officers also eager to command the new Patton tank battalion. In a few months he would attain the rank of lieutenant-colonel, which would make him one of the youngest officers of that rank in Zahal. On 22 May, in a week's time, he would be celebrating his thirty-first birthday. A brilliant military career was ahead of him.

Ehud and Hava had another reason for satisfaction. Both of them were born in Kfar Saba, and both had attended the same school. The difference in age between them was only twelve months and their eight years of married life had been a continuation of their childhood friendship. Hava, a teacher in the lower grades at an elementary school, followed Ehud wherever he went, visiting him even when the battalion was away in the field. S/14 filled their lives, for they had no children. A few days earlier, however, Colonel Shmuel had come into the major's tent up in Galilee and intimated that he would like to discuss a very personal problem, one which concerned Ehud. The battalion commander, an introverted and shy man, told him to go ahead and the colonel then informed Ehud that he had heard of progress made in the Hadassah Hospital in Jerusalem in the treatment of sterility. With Ehud's consent he would talk to General Tal and get his assistance in arranging for treatment. Ehud had agreed; Colonel Shmuel had then informed the general of Ehud's consent and the necessary treatment had thus been assured.

The Gladiator travelled smoothly along the empty highway to Beersheba. The radio was still broadcasting gay Independence Day music; then the eleven o'clock time signal interrupted their conversation. They listened to the late-night news bulletin.

The announcer reported that the Egyptian Army had entered eastern Sinai and that units had marched through the streets of Cairo in a great parade of military strength. Ehud listened intently to the news. Hava stared at him and the fear which was always with her came alive again.

The major pressed his foot down and the army vehicle surged ahead. "Something serious is up," he told Hava, adding, "I probably won't be sleeping at home tonight."

As soon as they reached their apartment in Beersheba, Ehud rushed to the telephone to contact brigade headquarters.

"Sir, did you hear . . ." he began.

24

"Come at once," Colonel Shmuel interrupted. "We're alerted."

Hava was standing next to him, and she watched as he dialled his battalion headquarters. The operations officer had already summoned the assistant operations officer, the signals officer, the supply officer, and the ordnance officer, as well as the headquarter staffs of the different battalions. The deputy battalion commander and all the company commanders of S/14 Battalion had already been called up. There had been some difficulty in tracing the whereabouts of the commander himself.

"I'll be there at once," Ehud said.

Ehud was already at the open door, about to leave. Hava watched him. "Will you phone me?" she asked.

"I always do. You know that."

"I'd like to come and visit you at your headquarters."

"I'll send the Gladiator round to fetch you at the first opportunity," he promised.

Hava stayed awake a long time. At first she listened to the radio broadcasting the Song Festival from Jerusalem. She heard the song "Jerusalem the Golden" presented for the first time, a song that was destined to become the anthem of the war. As the night wore on her fears for Ehud took hold of her. She never had grown accustomed to these sudden alarms and they still worried and frightened her. She burst into tears.

At 0600 hours on Tuesday 16 May, 'S' Brigade held an orders group. The brigade was to be deployed to offer "stubborn and determined resistance within its sector to any attempt by the enemy to invade Israel". It would maintain its high state of alert to use force whether for current security purposes, or for war should the situation deteriorate.

While the various units of the brigade were being deployed throughout the sector assigned to it, General Tal was entertaining Chief-of-Staff Rabin together with all the former chiefs-of-staff at the Armour School. Meanwhile it was learnt that the Egyptians were strengthening their forward positions in eastern Sinai, preparatory to sending additional forces there. Egyptian army units were already deployed throughout their emergency positions and their forward areas were to be augmented by artillery and armour. General Tal's divisional headquarters began to assemble its forces. None of this, however, was allowed to interfere with the visit of the former chiefs-of-staff as they watched the demonstration, which was

25

in their honour. Major-General Moshe Dayan, usually very sparing with his praise, referred to the display as "fantastic" when he spoke to Major-General Rabin, adding that "the Armoured Corps has improved beyond all expectations. I never thought I would see such remarkable progress as this."

When General Dayan had been chief-of-staff, the infantry and paratroops had been the decisive combat forces of Zahal on land. In those days Zahal placed little confidence in the Armoured Corps, so little in fact that during the preliminary planning stages of the 1956 Sinai campaign, General Dayan had visualised the tanks of 'S' Brigade being conveyed on tank transporters in the wake of charging infantry units, while their crews travelled behind them in buses.

At the conclusion of the demonstration, the former chiefs-of-staff saw the tanks being equipped and assigned to their various units. The officers attached to the Armour School began to take over their posts in the units to which they had been assigned in a time of emergency.

Lieutenant-Colonel Abraham, commander of the Armour Officers Cadet Course, now became commander of a battalion of Centurion tanks in 'K' Reserve Brigade; Lieutenant Yakuel commanded a company in that brigade; Captain Amos, who was in charge of the Specialisation Course on Patton tanks at the Armour Officers Cadet Course, became a company commander in the T/01 Reserve Battalion; Major Shamai Kaplan, who headed the Specialisation Course on Centurion tanks, became a company commander in S/10 Battalion, a regular unit of 'S' Brigade.

Shamai telephoned his apartment in Ashkelon. His wife, Nava, was expecting him home.

"I'm in camp, Nava," he said, "and won't be coming home. Nava . . . should your pains come on, don't phone our friends. Do you understand?"

Nava was pregnant, expecting to give birth any day. Her first pregnancy, with her now three year old son, Itai, had been a very difficult one, and Shamai was concerned about how she would find her way to the maternity hospital by herself. Security orders prohibited him telling her there was an alert and that if she telephoned their friends, who were all army men, she would find nobody home.

"I understand, Shamai," Nava said.

"Think of some other way of getting to the hospital."

"Yes."

"Our friends won't be home," he repeated.

"I understand you," she said.

"I'll come home just as soon as I can."

"I'll be all right, Shamai. Don't worry."

"I'll come the moment I can get away."

The day before, Independence Day, Shamai had been at home. His coming home twice in one week was more than she could hope for. Nava, who came from Kibbutz Mishmar Hasharon, had met Shamai in the army when she was doing her National Service. She had been secretary to the commander of S/10 Battalion in which Shamai had been operations officer. Their wedding had been one of the most memorable in the Armoured Corps' history. The ceremony had been held at the battalion base camp, and the canopy had been placed on a platform swung out on the long boom of a recovery tank. The tank, with the bride on top, had stood in the centre of a ring of Centurion tanks shooting confetti through their guns in all directions. A week after the wedding Shamai was already out on divisional manoeuvres and that was how their life together began.

Shamai drove his jeep to S/10 Battalion where he was given command of 'H' Company. At about the same time brigade headquarters received orders to implement "White Radish". Lieutenant Yossi B., the brigade assistant operations officer, went to the safe and opened a plastic envelope on which were the words "White Radish" and "Top Secret". "White Radish" was the code name for the order to mobilise the brigade's reserve transport. In a few hours civilian trucks belonging to haulage companies all over the country were beginning to arrive. Soldiers at once set to loading them with ammunition and cans of petrol.

On 18 May, trucks of 'S' Brigade set out for the last time to pick up the last of its reserve troops. "S" Armoured Brigade was now ready to repel any Egyptian force which attacked its sector of operations in the Negev.

But the Egyptian build-up in the Sinai Peninsula continued. Infantry units and artillery batteries were swarming into Sinai, and armoured brigades were being conveyed there by railroad and tank transporters. On 17 May the Egyptian government began mobilising its reserve forces.

At four o'clock in the morning, 19 May, an army lorry drew up in front of a house in Shikun Dan, Tel Aviv. Two soldiers jumped down and noisily began looking for the apartment of Shalom Cohen. Locating it at last, they banged on the front door. Shalom Cohen, his eyes only half open, was handed a red slip of paper, the mobilisation notice.

Cohen, a clerk with Yardenia Insurance Company, was already acquainted with that red slip. He dressed in a matter of minutes (his olive-green uniform was always ready for use), clipped on his general-service belt, laced up the ankle-high Type 2 boots – compulsory footwear in the Armoured Corps – and, finally, placed his black beret on his head at a natty angle. He slipped his shaving things, a towel, spare underwear and socks into a kitbag and put thirty pounds in his wallet. Five minutes after having been served his call-up notice, Sergeant Shalom Cohen climbed on to the army truck, looking every bit the regular soldier.

Shalom Cohen shared his apartment with his brother, who at the time was not at home. Shalom left him a note reading: "I've been called up". His brother would inform their parents who lived in Kiriat Gat. The note he had left for his brother was not unusual. Since his discharge from National Service in April 1966, he had been called up several times, and as recently as January 1967 he had served two weeks up north.

Shalom Cohen was born twenty-two years ago in Morocco. When he was a year old, his parents had moved to Oran in Algeria The family had immigrated to Israel in 1960 and settled in the new immigrants' town of Kiriat Gat. Six years later Shalom had become the hero of the North African immigrants in Israel. He had been "Mentioned in Dispatches" three times by the general officer commanding the Armoured Corps and was holder of an Israeli record: he had destroyed three Syrian tanks on the northern frontier. On his release from National Service, the North African Immigrants Association had given a reception in his honour. "We are gathered together to do honour to Shalom Cohen, born in North Africa and a sergeant in the Armoured Corps, who has participated seventeen times in military action, displayed exemplary courage, coolness and daring and destroyed three enemy tanks. . . . The Association of North African Immigrants is . . . proud of him and . . . wishes to convey to him their warmest respects, esteem, affection and thanks," was the wording of the Association's official greeting.

Shalom surmised that he would be going north again. That was where his theatre usually was and where all the tension had been during the past few years, and so he was surprised when the lorry headed south. Arriving at brigade headquarters he was summoned to the commanding officer's trailer.

He came stiffly to attention and saluted.

"At ease," said Colonel Shmuel shaking Shalom's hand. After a brief talk he was driven in one of the reconnaissance company's jeeps to S/10 Battalion, 'S' Brigade. Shalom had wanted to serve under Major Shamai Kaplan, in whose company he had done his National Service, but Lieutenant-Colonel Gabriel, the battalion commander, posted him to Captain Amir's company. The quartermaster recognised him as he walked into his store and greeted him with "Welcome home!" He was issued with the best equipment in stock.

"Do you remember my size?" Shalom asked.

"You're a 40," the quartermaster said.

Shalom felt at home, almost as though he had never been away from the battalion. He signed for his things, including an Uzzi submachine gun and set off to meet his tank crew. He had been posted to Platoon Commander Roif's tank, and it was Roif who did the introductions: Popovitch, the driver, and David Shauli, the loader.

Introductions completed, the platoon commander took Shalom to his tent to tell him about the crew. Both men were in their first year of National Service. Popovitch was a good driver, but Shauli – well, Shauli liked to sleep. It seemed that travelling in a tank acted as a soporific. He could sleep even when the Centurion was climbing mountains and sliding from rock to rock. Nothing seemed to disturb him.

"If war breaks out, which I doubt," the platoon commander said, "you'll have to keep a close watch on him to see he stays awake. Otherwise the Egyptians will slap a couple of shells into us before Shauli wakes up."

"How do you wake him up?" Shalom asked.

"Hit him on the head," was the platoon commander's advice.

Lieutenant Ein-Gil (aged twenty-three, head somewhat heavy and square, eyes innocent-looking, body spare and wiry, hands large and practical), from Kibbutz Ramat Hakovesh, was discharged from the Armoured Corps in December 1966; he did not expect to be called up for reserve duty, as he was convinced that Zahal did not have enough tanks. Ein-Gil always seemed to be asking what to do. In the kibbutz he was put to work in the chicken-coop.

His call-up papers reached him half an hour after midnight, the battalion messengers having to wake up half the members of the kibbutz before they found him. When at last he was located Ein-Gil could not remember whether or not he still had his army uniform. "Never mind," his friends said, "you'll be given another one." But Ein-Gil insisted on looking for it; surely it must be somewhere. He did not find it, but still he could not bring himself to board the vehicle.

"I must find someone to take over my job in the chicken-coop."

Although it was the middle of the night, Ein-Gil woke up the other half of the kibbutz, banging on doors and asking who wanted to work in the chicken-coop. The chicken-coop was not the most popular of chores among the kibbutz members, and it was some time before Ein-Gil found a substitute. However, on reflection his replacement did not strike him as being very responsible. He clambered down from the vehicle and began a new search.

"Ein-Gil, the country is in danger, and all you can think of is your chickens and eggs?" his friends rebuked him. They had a long list of men to pick up and had been held up by Ein-Gil for over an hour.

"Well someone must feed the chickens, no?"

CHAPTER THREE

The tanks were already under camouflage nets; their crews carried out whatever exercises could be done under the netting.

Meanwhile the Egyptian army continued to pour into Sinai in ever increasing numbers. Infantry, armour and artillery swept through the streets of Cairo on their way to the Suez Canal zone and Sinai. In Israel many people watched on the television these seemingly endless convoys of Egyptian troops en route for the Israeli borders. *Al Ahram*, the Egyptian government's mouthpiece, announced that Egypt was ready for war the moment Israel attacked Syria, but in Israel there still existed a tendency to view the situation as nothing more than a demonstration of Arab strength. What was rather more worrying was that the armies of Iraq, Jordan and Syria had also been placed in a state of readiness.

The belief that Egypt merely intended to put on a show of strength relied to a great extent upon the people's faith in the deterrent power of Zahal. In every encounter since 1948 Zahal had defeated the Arab armies. The Egyptian Army had been soundly whipped in 1956 and the Syrian forces had suffered heavy losses on land and in the air in every confrontation. Pure logic would seem to demand that Abdul Nasser do nothing which might force Zahal to take action and bring catastrophe upon his head. For that reason, only partial mobilisation was ordered in Israel so as not to disrupt the economic and social life of the country more than appeared warranted.

But on 18 May, U Thant, the secretary-general of the United Nations, agreed to withdraw the United Nations emergency forces from Sinai, in compliance with the Egyptian government's demand. It had been stationed in Sinai and the Gaza Strip in 1957 and had to some extent served as a symbol of non-belligerence, and with its withdrawal Israel's shipping through the Straits of Tiran was in danger. The single benefit retained by Israel after the 1956 campaign had been free passage through the Tiran Straits; the government of Israel was bound to view the blockading of the straits as a *casus belli*.

On Saturday 20 May, the army spokesman announced: "Consequent upon the entry of large Egyptian forces into eastern Sinai, which has been followed by the withdrawal of the United Nations emergency force as demanded by Egypt, Zahal has taken the necessary steps to deal with all and any developments. These steps include partial mobilisation, which has now been completed." This was a placatory statement, containing no admonition to the president of Egypt about the closure of the Straits of Tiran. Every move made by the government of Israel was directed towards assuaging and easing the tension. Israel still had complete confidence in Zahal's deterrent power.

On 21 May the government of Egypt ordered general mobilisation. Cairo Radio reported that Egyptian troops had already taken up positions in Sharm-e-Sheikh at the entrance to the Tiran Straits and that units of the Egyptian Navy had passed through the Suez Canal on their way to the Red Sea. *Al Ahram* stated that "the most modern and up-to-date weapons are ready for action". The newspaper named these weapons "non-conventional"; thus it was as though emphasis was being given to the fact that the Egyptian Army was not to be deterred by Zahal.

The following day, 22 May, President Nasser, accompanied by his deputy president, Marshal Abdul Hakim Amer, visited Egyptian front-line troops in the Sinai Desert. With a broad smile on his face, he made a statement which will be remembered for many years to come. "The waters in the Straits of

Tiran are our territorial waters," he announced. "If Israel's leaders and their General Rabin want war, then *ahalan we-sahalan!* Our armies are expecting them!" The expression *"ahalan we-sahalan"* (a popular form of greeting among Arabs, meaning "welcome") is used by Israelis, and to them it appeared that Abdul Nasser was addressing them in their own language. There could be no doubt about it. The Egyptian president wished to give the impression of being eager for war.

These developments shattered Israel's equanimity. Gone was the power of Zahal to deter aggression if Egypt's president and the commander of her armies could so happily proclaim to the Arabs, to Israel and to the world that they would respond to war with *"ahalan we-sahalan"*.

But words and deeds are not the same, and where Arab rulers are concerned words and deeds are poles apart. Although the severity of the situation was evident, many Israelis still believed that the Tiran Straits would not be closed. The majority of statesmen in Israel, both in government and in opposition, were of the opinion that Egypt would only close the straits if the situation in the Middle East worsened dramatically. The generally accepted view was that the Egyptian president would use the straits as a constant threat. If Israel took military action in reprisal for the Arab guerrilla warfare against Israeli property and lives which was being carried out from bases in Syria, then he would come to the rescue of the Arab world and Arab honour by closing the straits. Should this threat prove effective in keeping Israel's army at bay, Israel would lose the only means she had of safeguarding the lives and property of her people. Israel would be at the mercy of every infiltrator and "Popular War" guerrilla from Syria or any other of the neighbouring countries.

Only one statesman said from the outset that once Egypt had control of the straits she would close the Red Sea to Israeli shipping. On Saturday 20 May, the day after the occupation by Egyptian paratroops of the United Nations positions on the Tiran, Major-General Moshe Dayan, M.K. said that within a few days Abdul Nasser would announce the closing of the Straits. "He will not be able to sit astride the straits and watch Israeli ships pass through," Dayan predicted.

And in fact, shortly after midnight on 23 May the president of Egypt ordered his army to close the Tiran Straits to Israeli shipping and informed the world of his action. At 4.15 a.m. on the same day, General Yeshayahu Gavish, commander of the southern front, informed General Tal: "Abdul Nasser has announced the closing of the straits."

The power of Zahal to deter aggression had proved illusory. Only war could retrieve the situation.

On 19 May Dr. Raphael Mokady received advance warning to be available at all times at one of two telephones; at his laboratory in the Haifa Technological Institute or at his home on the Western Carmel. Dr. Mokady had served in Zahal during the 1948 War of Independence and in Operation Kadosh in 1956. Recently he had been transferred to the Armoured Corps and was now in command of a reconnaissance company in Armoured Reserve Brigade 'A'.

Dr. Mokady was a senior lecturer in soil science. His field of research was closely connected with Israel's most vital problem: the shortage of water and the salinity of the water passing through the National Water Carrier. Together with Dr. Dan Zaslawsky he had carried out research towards mathematical models of salt leaching in various soils.

Since 17 May both scientists had been wondering why they had not been called up and had been telephoning repeatedly to 'A' Brigade headquarters. The invariable answer was – No mobilisation yet for 'A' Brigade. Dr. Mokady was impatient with the government for seeking a diplomatic solution instead of taking action.

Thirty-nine year old Dr. Mokady had already begun to locate the whereabouts of students who belonged to his unit but who had changed their address. He was convinced that his unit would be called up and wanted to do whatever he could to make mobilisation as rapid and smooth as possible when the time came.

On 23 May the orderly officer at 'A' Brigade headquarters telephoned the Technological Institute and informed Dr. Mokady that one of the brigade's trucks was on its way to collect people in his vicinity. It would be at his house that evening. Dr. Mokady returned home from the Institute at 6.30 p.m. He made straight for the kitchen, where his army equipment was kept in a special cupboard. His Armoured Corps boots stood polished on the bottom shelf; he had bought them during the 1956 Sinai Campaign and ever since had worn them when he was called up for reserve duty. Also in the cupboard were two black berets. A few months previously he had been called up and had been unable to find his beret. He had purchased another one, but when he returned he discovered the missing headgear among his four and a half year old son's toys. This time he selected his old beret. He packed his sleeping-bag and wind-jacket. He also took along a spare olive-green uniform and an old battledress with the insignia of his rank permanently attached to its epaulets.

Dressed in the uniform of a major, Dr. Mokady went downstairs with his children to inspect the air-raid shelter. It had become a junk-store for all the tenants of the block and was filled with old beds, mattresses, cupboards, crates, packing cases and stacks of yellowing newspapers. Dr. Mokady asked his neighbours to tidy up the shelter but they were unwilling. "Entirely unnecessary," they said. "Nothing's going to happen." Dr. Mokady, however, was insistent. With the children's help, the shelter was cleared out and cleaned. As they were finishing the job, his parents-in-law arrived to take eighteen month old Dan for a walk. They brought the baby back just in time to see Dr. Mokady climbing on to the back of an army lorry.

Before the lorry had gone far, Dr. Mokady ordered the driver to turn round. "What's wrong, Rafi?" the junior officer asked (Dr. Mokady was "Rafi" to everyone in the army).

"It'll take ages for the driver to find all the addresses," he replied.

Major Mokady took the list of names and addresses from the driver, whom he told to wait with his truck until he got back. He then jumped into his Vauxhall station-wagon and set off round the town to collect his men. Within two hours, by 10.30 p.m., all the men were on board the truck.

Late that night Major Mokady returned to his apartment to give his wife the car keys. The children were already asleep and Shoshana was in her pyjamas. She had been telling herself that nothing would happen, that all the excitement of another Middle East crisis would quickly blow over. She did not accompany her husband downstairs when he left; it was as though this time too he was off on a regular reserve-duty call-up.

While Major Mokady was rounding up his 'A' Brigade men in Haifa, Lawyer Moshe Haviv was at home in Zahala, Tel Aviv, with clients. In the middle of their talk the telephone rang. The call came from the commander of the armoured infantry battalion of Reserve Brigade 'A' of which Advocate Haviv was second-in-conmmand. The battalion commander informed his second that a truck had gone out to pick him up but if possible he wanted him in camp earlier, even before the official mobilisation order reached him.

Lawyer Haviv sent his clients away, telephoned the battalion's company commanders and told them he was coming round presently to fetch them in his car.

Major Haviv's military wardrobe was in the garden shed. He went to get his equipment and discovered that his ankle-high boots had been stolen. Slipping on a pair of suede shoes with rubber soles, he said goodbye to his wife, Gila, and was on his way.

Lawyer Haviv, whom everyone called "Mosh", had been released from the army in 1952. He was only twenty-two and already held the rank of major. He had left in spite of the great future prophesied for him in the army. What had led him to quit was the fact, as he put it, that "anyone with just one pip more than I have can tell me what to do, even though he may be as thick as two short planks". He was a rebel, energetic and very likeable. Naturally an independent thinker, he was inclined to clash with army discipline, which on several occasions had led to his being brought before an army court.

While in the regular army he had served with the Armoured Corps and taken part in Course "B", one of the courses which inaugurated Israel's armoured forces. But tanks were not for him and he retired from the course very early. He did not like sitting in a tank. "I feel I'm choking," he once explained to his wife. "Jews weren't made for tanks, and tanks weren't made for Jews. I simply feel I'm choking. I can't bear sitting in one position, unable to move my little finger."

He was transferred to infantry. "The infantry's fine," he told Gila. "It gives me more confidence. I can see what's going on. I'm not confined and I can move about." Yet he was not to enjoy that pleasure for long. Zahal was being armourised, and he was posted to an armoured infantry battalion. Instead of riding in a tank, he now rode in an armoured half-track .

Lately he had been finding reserve service too demanding. To Gila, his confidante in everything, he admitted that "It's hard to say it, Gila, perhaps it's age, but I find it too severe. Reserve duty is becoming more than I can handle."

Together with the company commanders, Mosh arrived at the Brigade base camp. A driver took his car back home to

Tel Aviv. He and Major Mokady walked into the colonel's office for their first briefing.

"A" Brigade was the last of the reserve armoured brigades to be mobilised, completing the call-up of the reserve armoured forces. At dawn, Lieutenant-Colonel Biro, commander of A/112 Battalion, supervised the issue of equipment at the battalion's emergency stores.

What was happening at that time in the stores of A/112 Battalion of "A" Brigade was being repeated throughout the country. Zahal's reserve forces were swarming into camps all over Israel. The foundations of Israel's reserve army had been laid by Zahal's second chief-of-staff, Major-General Yigael Yadin. Zahal, he used to say, resembled an iceberg. Only its tip was visible, the regular army. Over the years the reserve army had been perfected and had developed into something quite unique.

Lieutenant Nati, of Petah Tikvah, twenty-five years old, six feet tall, 212 lbs in civilian life ("I usually lose ten to twelve pounds on reserve duty"), clad in olive-green uniform, Type 2 boots and black beret, saluted Lieutenant-Colonel Biro. Nati's call-up notice had reached him in Eilat, where he was doing a job for the Israel Insulation Corporation. He was a company commander in A/112 Battalion.

"The company is ready, Sir," he said.

"At ease," said the lieutenant-colonel.

The two officers set out to review the company.

Nati was a head taller than Lieutenant-Colonel Biro but their weight was identical. The battalion commander entered the first hanger like a lion. The crews were about to jump to attention at the sight of him. He bawled out thickly: "Carry on!" Inside the shed were Sherman tanks, reserved for use only in time of war. For exercises and manoeuvres the company used the tanks of the Armoured Corps' Training Depot. Crews of national servicemen were busy all the year round maintaining the emergency tanks, and at set intervals their motors were switched on and they were put through their paces. Whatever adjustments and repairs were then found to be needed were carried out. Each tank had a log-book in which its entire history was recorded. At its far end the hangar was partitioned into supply sections for company, platoon and personnel equipment. Standing on shelves were rows of tank-crew boots, dubbinged once a year; on another shelf were packs containing blankets, tenting, tent pegs and eating utensils. At set intervals these packs and their contents were given an airing. The armoury section contained machine guns and submachine guns which, too, were regularly oiled and examined.

The reserve troops stood in line. Each man was issued a pack, a uniform and a weapon. Most of them had arrived already wearing their Type 2 boots. The men signed their supply forms, then assembled in their platoons. Each tank commander then signed the Indent Card for his tank, after checking that all the equipment and appurtenances mentioned on the card were in place. The crews began their routine inspection and started the motors. The roar and fumes of the motors filled the hangar. The tank company had come to life.

CHAPTER FOUR

On 26 May I too was mobilised and took my place in the Press Liaison Unit of the army spokesman's office. The three days which preceded my call-up were the three most anxiety-laden days of my life, except perhaps for the days when Rommel's Afrika Korps stood at the gates of Egypt.

The government and the Knesset (Parliament) were in a cold sweat. It was clear that the government had not reacted with force to the closure of the Tiran Straits because it was afraid of war. Not that there was any thought of Zahal being defeated; there was no need to go that far. The havoc modern warfare brings is quite sufficient to raise the most serious doubts as to its desirability, and this is particularly true of a small country whose people have had their fill of suffering and disaster.

The opinion prevailing in Jerusalem was that the country would pay dearly for a victory. Some mentioned ten thousand victims, others spoke of a hundred thousand. It was held that Israel's air force would be unable to prevent the Arab air forces from reaching the large and crowded population centres in Israel. Ten thousand dead in Israel is, in proportion, equivalent to about one million in the United States. The destructiveness of war and such loss of life would in themselves be a catastrophe to a small people. And ten thousand was thought to be a modest estimate.

Israel is the haven of refugees from massacres and hatred. There is hardly a family living in Israel which did not lose a relative in Europe, Asia or Africa. If violence and hatred were to overtake the Jews in their own country, what would be the use of a Jewish state? It was for this reason that Israel's government sought a diplomatic solution. The advocates of diplomacy maintained that, after all, the closure of the Tiran Straits was not a death blow to Israel and was not to be compared with war, which might conceivably ruin the country. If it were possible to goad the maritime nations, and in particular the United States, into maintaining passage for Israeli shipping through the straits, it would be preferable to war.

On 24 May Israel's foreign minister, Aba Eban, flew to Paris, London and Washington in an effort to end the crisis through diplomatic means rather than war.

There were two reasons for the government's growing hesitation to use force. The first was that the army chiefs did not lightly dismiss the Arab armies' potential to kill a large number of civilians. The second reason, which had great bearing, was David Ben Gurion's attitude. At so critical a time eyes were naturally turned towards the ageing lion. And David Ben Gurion, that exponent of a tough defence policy, cautioned this time against immediate war. He went so far as to advise the discharge of the reserve forces in order to reduce tension and to make possible the transition to a new phase more favourable to Israel. He maintained that Israel should pick the time for war, when it suited her, and that she must not be dragged into a military confrontation at a time and under circumstances favourable to the enemy. According to Ben Gurion, the present time and circumstances were to Israel's disadvantage because she stood alone and because the Arab states had begun to unite against her, forcing Zahal to fight on more than one front.

Ben Gurion holds one irrefutable axiom, namely: even if Israel were to defeat the Arab states fifty times, they would not cease to exist. But it was enough for the Arab states to defeat Zahal only once, and there would be no Israel. In this he expressed the general trend of public opinion. It was for this reason that Ben Gurion always strove to assure Zahal's success in advance, by strategical surprise or by allies. In May 1967, when the entire Egyptian Army had taken up positions in Sinai and when each day saw another Arab state joining the Egyptian front against Israel, he could not see an easy victory. Ben Gurion was fearful too of the great loss of life even a victorious Israel would suffer. And furthermore, Israel had no allies. He had been very impressed by the international tussle which had followed the 1956 Sinai Campaign. Israel had stood alone then against the demand of the United Nations that she withdraw Zahal from Sinai; both the United States and the Soviet Union had voted against Israel to force Zahal's complete withdrawal prior to a peace settlement.

It followed that even if Zahal were to emerge victorious once again, the victory might well be useless. Ben Gurion's advice, then, was to postpone war until the time and the circumstances were more propitious. Even Knesset member Moshe Dayan, the hero of the Sinai Campaign of 1956 and an ardent man in matters of defence, was of the opinion that this time neither time nor circumstances favoured an Israeli initiative. But, unlike the others, he was of the opinion that war was inevitable. He changed his mind about an Israeli initiated confrontation only a day or so before his appointment as defence minister in place of Prime Minister Levi Eshkol, who had held that portfolio too until 1 June.

Thus there was no member of Israel's coalition government to demand an immediate reaction by armed force to the closing of the Tiran Straits and the Egyptian military concentration in the Sinai peninsula. The dogged tenacity with which President Nasser was conducting his adventure struck dismay into the hearts of the Israelis and their leaders and aroused serious suspicions that he might have sound and valid reasons for wanting war.

It seemed to Jerusalem that there were two possibilities which could explain Abdul Nasser's seeming self-confidence. The one might be a secret weapon, the other the full backing and support of the Soviet Union. The second possibility was the more worrying. If Abdul Nasser's moves were being directed by the Russians as part of an overall plan to establish their presence in the Middle East, the situation was fraught with danger. To parry such an eventuality it was essential for Israel to assure herself of an ally to thwart the Russian designs, and it would be imprudent to rush into war before examining and clarifying every aspect of the situation.

Throughout the entire period during which the government vacillated and hesitated, the general public was kept completely in the dark and thus exposed to the chimera of fears and anxieties. The Israeli population consisted of two distinct entities: those who were still at home and those who had been mobilised into the army. The former, consisting mostly of elderly men, women and children, reacted with the speed and energy of a nation of exiles. Hoarding began, and in a twinkling such commodites as sugar, rice and flour vanished from shops and supermarkets, followed by canned goods, candles and rolls of toilet paper. The hoarders were people with a wealth of experience behind them; some remembered the pogroms, when Jews were forced to hide in their own homes for weeks on end until the mobs got tired. Others recalled the food shortages of the first world war, and a great many had not forgotten the conditions which prevailed in the second. There were also large numbers of Jews for whom the memory of riots and brutality in the towns of the Arab states and North African countries was still vivid.

In the wake of the rumours, the anxieties, the run on the shops, the civilian population became more and more worried and frightened. After 23 May it seemed as though nothing could prevent the war of annihilation which was about to come. The foreign minister's journey to Paris, London and Washington increased the presentiment that this time the Arab armies were superior to Zahal and that the Jewish people were reverting to their traditional defence weapon, crying *"Gewalt"* (literally "have mercy") to the enlightened world.

Meanwhile Egypt was strengthening her position and status as the leader of a united Arab world. On 24 May Jordan permitted the entry of Iraqi and Saudi troops into her territory. Lebanon began mobilising, and Ahmed Shukeiry's Palestine Liberation Army obtained from Egypt heavy military equipment, which was immediately placed in positions along the Gaza Strip border. Against this concentration of Arab armies, the United States and Britain busied themselves with talks about organising an international force which would ensure freedom of passage for ships to Israel through the Tiran Straits, but which excluded Israeli vessels. France suggested joint action by the four Great Powers to solve the crisis over the Straits of Tiran, and on 25 May the Soviet Union flatly rejected her proposal. On 26 May, U Thant stated that the closing of the Straits constituted a menace to peace, and in Egypt, Abdul Nasser announced that "If we go to war against Israel, we are assured of victory!"

On Saturday evening, 27 May, Foreign Minister Aba Eban returned from Washington to Lod and hurried straight from the airport to a late-night cabinet meeting. President Johnson had requested Israel to postpone any military action for a fortnight, the second such request received. Eban had brought with him the hope that during this fortnight the United States would, in a combined operation with Great

40

Britain, effectuate the freedom of international shipping through the Straits of Tiran to Israel.

On Sunday evening, 28 May, Kol Israel radio announced that the Prime Minister would make a statement to the nation. The whole of Israel waited in unprecedented tension. As soon as his weekly cabinet meeting ended, Levi Eshkol rushed to Radio House and broadcast an unrecorded statement.

Eshkol termed the blockading of the Straits of Tiran "aggression against Israel".

Finally, then, a whole week after the blockading of the straits, no reaction by military force was forthcoming except for an official definition of an act the nature of which had been obvious from the start. Following this the Prime Minister said that Zahal stood ready and prepared to defend the security of the state of Israel and that the present emergency would be maintained. "There is no doubt," he said, "that the mobilisation of Zahal and its readiness for all and every test, was and still is a vital factor in expediting international activity" to bring about a rapid end to the blockade. Finally, he said, the government had decided on a diplomatic course of action aimed at spurring on the world powers to undertake action to assure the free passage of international shipping through the Straits of Tiran.

The content of the statement to the nation was depressing. But this was not all; unfortunately, Mr. Eshkol lost his place in the script he was reading from; he began to stutter and stumble. He was actually heard whispering to his aide to ask where his place in the text was. And this was the Minister of Defence.

But it was the contents of his statement which should have worried the public more than the manner of its delivery. The broadcast statement clearly displayed a misunderstanding of the situation. The problem with which Israel was faced was no longer the blockading of the Tiran Straits but the loss of Zahal's power as a deterrent. Without it, tiny Israel could not exist, surrounded as she was by enemies who outnumbered her by forty to one or even more.

The attempt to deal with the blockade as a political – economic problem, with the aid of the Great Powers, was fundamentally wrong. Had it succeeded, the error would have stood out even more clearly. For indeed what would Israel have then looked like, existing by the grace of the Great Powers who had taken the trouble to secure a free

41

passage for her in international waters? In his statement to the nation the Prime Minister said nothing of the Great Powers attempting to assure passage for Israeli ships through the straits, only of international shipping. By doing so he left the statement open to the compromising interpretation that Abdul Nasser might agree to allow free passage to Israel's port of Eilat to any vessel flying the flag of any nation in the world with the single exception of Israel.

The moment Abdul Nasser closed the Straits of Tiran, the moment he welcomed an armed conflict with Israel with *"ahalan we-sahalan"*, the moment he concentrated his divisions in Sinai and gathered round him the armies of Syria, Iraq, Jordan and Algeria, Israel was faced with the identical situation she had faced in 1948. Her very existence hung in the balance. To exist where she is, Israel must be able to stand on its own, not by the grace of others. That is a hard and bitter truth which requires many sacrifices. The minute Israel loses her ability to defend herself, she forfeits all hope of existing as an independent, sovereign state.

In the long history of the Jewish people, miracles have occurred. The mistakes made by the government, their vacillating and weak leadership, was the cause of the miracles which happened to the Jewish people in 1967. The people of Israel began to realise they were again threatened with annihilation and to understand that their lives were in their own hands.

There were hordes of foreign correspondents milling around the Army Press Liaison Offices. Some had been in Israel in 1948 and seen a nation born. Now, perhaps, they had come to see it die. I forced my way to the military correspondents unit. After I had been duly registered and given a sleeping bag – all that was left in the liaison unit's stores – I was told to report on the following morning, Friday 26 May, to Tal's armoured division.

I remember well the night preceding my journey down to the division. The windows of my apartment had already been protected by strips of cloth pasted onto them; the light bulbs had been painted blue, and the children had been told not to be afraid if they heard the air-raid siren.

When I was ready to leave next morning, at dawn, I hugged my children to me. The thought came to me of the feelings and emotions of generations of Jewish fathers over the past two thousand years. "They want your life", would seem to be a fitting translation into words of those emotions.

42

I was sad. Israel seemed like a wounded man, cast out on icy snows, far from civilisation, his strength waning, and with wild animals closing in on him in ever narrowing circles. Egypt, Syria, Iraq, Jordan, Algeria, Kuwait ... every day another enemy joined the circle.

CHAPTER FIVE

From divisional headquarters I was sent straight to 'S' Brigade, and from there to S/14 Battalion. Its Patton tanks were all under nets in the woods near the Magen crossroads opposite the Rafa sector. A sergeant took me to the commander's tank which was under a larger net than any of the others. Major Ehud Elad, dressed in socks and underwear, lay spread out on a stretcher. Behind his glasses his eyes were red from lack of sleep, and his nose, which was also red, jutted out above his moustache.

Somewhat unwillingly the commanding officer sat up on the stretcher and pushed his feet into his high, laced boots. He slipped into his shirt and stood up to his full height.

"What's this I hear – that there's a buying panic in town and they're hoarding sugar? Is it true?" he asked.

"Yes," I answered.

"And Dizengoff Street looks like Tisha B'Av?"

"To some extent, yes."

"The Jews have gone mad; completely mad. And is it true that there are ministers in the cabinet who don't want war?"

"Correct," I said.

"Mad! Ridiculous!" the major said, buckling on his belt. "If only they'd leave it to us, we'd smash them in two seconds flat. But what happens? We sit on our arse doing nothing, while the enemy gets stronger and stronger. Yesterday we had a company opposite us, today there is a battalion, tomorrow a brigade. What's come over the Jews?"

Major Ehud raised a corner of the netting and invited me to come with him to the woods.

"Come along and see the battalion. It'll make you feel better."

The tanks were neatly lined up under their netting, the nets stretched taut, the surroundings clean, with not a soul about. Everything was under nets. "Yesterday I flew over the area in a recce plane," the major said. "It's a great shame but they

43

won't let us cross the border. I flew over the battalion and couldn't spot a thing. Imagine!"

"How long have you been under nets?"

"Ten days. And before that we were three weeks on field exercises."

"Bad luck. And in the heat of the Negev," I commented.

"There's discipline in the Armoured Corps," he said, raising a corner of one of the nets. "The Armoured Corps isn't like all the other Jews."

"Attention!" bawled the sergeant.

The tank crew sprung to attention; the sergeant saluted.

"At ease," the commanding officer said.

The crew had finished greasing the tank. The 0.5mm Browning machine gun had been cleaned; the crew's packs were attached to the turret. Two of the crew were playing draughts, another couple were reading newspapers. A corner of the netting was used as a kitchen and coffee was boiling in a tin on a spirit stove. I asked the men how they felt.

"Fed up waiting," was the sergeant's comment. "Time's come to fight."

"And you?" I asked the others.

"Same," they said. "Fed up waiting."

There was no doubt in their minds as to the outcome. They could not lose.

When we left the tent I said to the major it seemed to be a case of the front line troops cheering on the rear instead of the other way round. I was being given confidence by the same soldiers who might well be going to their deaths tomorrow.

"You're not the only one," the major said. "The Prime Minister and Minister of Defence, Levi Eshkol, too. When he came down here, he asked me why the Armoured Corps was so self-confident. I showed him the Pattons and the lads and he was most impressed. The pity was that at the end he said: 'Zoll mir nur nit bedahrfn' ('Let's hope we don't have to use them'), meaning the Pattons and the lads of course."

The contrast between the mood in 'S' Brigade and that prevailing in the government and in the street was certainly most marked. Everything which contributed to creating doubts, fear or panic among the civilian population only served to heighten the desire for war in 'S' Brigade and to bring into focus the realisation that war was inevitable and that it would be a war for survival.

Gunner Shmuel Bar of Benei Brak, serving with S/10 Battalion, told me: "For me this is a life or death war. If we don't win, my parents will have to leave home."

I could sense the pent-up anger which permeated the brigade; an anger which could be traced back to the Nazi holocaust. It was as if these men in uniform were saying: No more will Jews be driven out; no more shall they be beaten and slaughtered. For years no serious heed had been paid to the threats of Abdul Nasser and the Syrian leaders "to drive Israel into the sea", nor to the diabolic propaganda of the Arabs to annihilate Israel. As long as Israel had Zahal to rely upon as a deterring force, the public had regarded Arab threats as though they were mouthed from behind a high, impregnable wall. Now that the power of Zahal as a deterrent had been impugned, it seemed as though the wall had collapsed; suddenly Arab propaganda and Egyptian troop concentrations in Sinai took on a new and sinister meaning, reminiscent of the holocaust in Europe. And it was this association that was at the root of the soldier's anger.

Time and again Israeli youth had meditated on what had happened, over there, in Europe. How was it possible to round up hundreds of thousands, even millions of Jews, and slaughter them like so many herds of cattle, without the Jews putting up a fight, without them even spitting in their murderers' faces? The answer to it came spontaneously in May 1967. The Jews of Europe had had no guiding and directing frame in which to act. The Jews of Israel do have such a frame – Zahal. Into it have poured all the seasoned exiles from east and west. The reflexes from their sufferings in their dispersion, which in town prompted them to hoard sugar, incited them in Zahal to want war. Those who in Auschwitz had had their arms tattooed, while they stood helplessly before their torturers, were here turned into lions. To be precise, it was not so much Zahal the regular army which gave this focus, but Zahal as a taut, tight frame that included all the able-bodied and fit of the nation. In Zahal one got the impression that the nation had taken a firm grip upon itself. When the Prime Minister was heard fumbling and stuttering in his speech to the nation on 28 May, a sergeant listening over his transistor while under a tank camouflage netting, was heard to say: "Levi, son of Deborah, let us do the talking!"

The will to fight possessed the whole of Zahal and this unanimity of purpose inevitably began to make itself felt among the political party leaders. Its force brought about changes in the cabinet, and a National Unity government was formed,

45

with Major-General Moshe Dayan as minister of defence. Dayan symbolised victorious Zahal. Before his appointment he had visited army camps, dressed in his major-general's uniform, and men and officers alike had welcomed him everywhere he went with cheers and applause. This was the man who had soundly whipped the Arabs: the Jordanians and Syrians in daring reprisal raids carried out by paratroops, and the Egyptians in the lightning Sinai Campaign.

On 30 May Abdul Nasser proved that his bag of tricks was not yet exhausted. Hussein, king of Jordan, and Nasser's arch-enemy, flew from Aman to Cairo in his private aeroplane and signed a mutual defence pact with Egypt; by its terms the Jordanian Army would be under Egyptian command in the event of war. Thus the ring encircling Israel was closed. If Israel still procrastinated and continued to hesitate, even non-Arabs were liable to join the Arab alliance. The entire build-up of Israel's relations with Asia and Africa was in jeopardy. A Druse proverb says: We are with the just who are the victors. This philosophy is shared by all oriental people – and others, too.

The National Unity government was formed on 1 June, and Major-General Dayan received the portfolio of the Defence Ministry. Before he became defence minister Dayan had been inclined to believe that the government and the general public would resign themselves to the blockading of the Tiran Straits, to see it merely as an economic setback, a loss which would eventually be recouped by Jewish resourcefulness and patience. He personally was not prepared to listen to such opinions; it was out of the question for the simple reason that there was a section of public opinion which would never accept or agree to it, the army.

On Friday 1 June Major-General Dayan drove to the Defence Ministry. He was dressed in a white shirt and he drove his green Saab saloon himself. He was on his way to the Ministry to take over as minister even before taking his oath of office in the Knesset. To his friends who welcomed him to the Ministry, he said: "The people elected me."

He was right. His appointment to the Ministry of Defence was the result of public pressure and an expression of the wishes of the people serving in the armed forces. From that point of view it would be correct to state that the people in its hour of crisis took control of its own affairs. The people wanted war, and they wanted to wage it in a white-hot fury.

PART TWO

Itzhak Sade to Israel Tal
1947–67

CHAPTER SIX

The S/10 Battalion of 'S' Brigade was formed in 1948 and was Zahal's first tank battalion. It was established by General Itzhak Sade, the "Old Man", founder of the Haganah Field Companies and Palmach. Its first commander was Major Felix Beatus, who at that time spoke nothing but Polish and Russian.

The battalion consisted of six companies, only two of them tank companies, the so-called "Russian" company and "English" company. The Russian had ten 1935-vintage French Hotchkiss tanks, manned by anyone claiming to have had experience in an eastern European armoured unit. The language used in that company was Russian. The English company had two Cromwell and one Sherman tank, which the Haganah had "acquired" from the British Army when it left Palestine.

The battalion was formed within one week, during the first cease-fire of the 1948 war. Its problems were legion but the most serious was communication. Felix spoke Russian with the brigade commander, General Sade. But Colonel Shaul Yaffe, the brigade's chief of operations, understood neither Russian nor Polish; except for Hebrew he understood only Yiddish. Felix, however, came from an assimilated family and knew no Yiddish. But he did know a smattering of German, so he spoke to the operations officer in German and was answered in Yiddish. Felix did not know one word of English. To command his English-speaking company he had to use an interpreter. No one knowing both Russian and English could be found so Felix had two interpreters, one translating from English into Yiddish, the other from Yiddish to Russian.

The tank battalion's first baptism under fire was the attack on Lod Airport. But its attack on Iraq-el-Manshieh on 16 October 1948, which was defended by an Egyptian company,

47

was a miserable failure. The Russian company never reached its objective because of mechanical and other breakdowns. They all shouted into their radios: *"Gdye Pjechotta?"* (Russian for "Where's the infantry?") and promptly fell into the ditches which the Egyptians had dug as part of their defences. Thus neither the tanks of the Russian company nor the "Pjechotta" which should have been following behind, ever reached their objective. The only two tanks to get there were the two Cromwells of the English-speaking company. The Cromwell's advanced with their commanders standing upright in the turret so as to have a better view of where they were going. Both tanks crashed through the outer perimeter of the objective and continued forwards but at that point one was hit and its gun exploded and the other, which was also hit, had its gearbox put out of action. The tank with the damaged gun drew near to the crippled tank; a Jewish volunteer from South Africa jumped down from his tank and under Egyptian machine gun fire attached a cable to the crippled tank. As he was getting back into his cabin, he was hit. Wounded he entered the tank, set it in motion and towed the crippled Cromwell back to the Israeli lines.

This shaky beginning greatly impeded the tank battalion's progress in Zahal. Felix Beatus was replaced, and Lieutenant-Colonel Shaul Yaffe, a veteran of the Palmach, became the new commander of S/10 Battalion. Yaffe decided that it was essential to infuse "Israeli blood" into the Armoured Corps; in other words to base it on graduates of the Haganah and Palmach who would apply original thinking to defence matters. He first organised Training Course A, at which tank gunnery was taught according to anti-tank gunnery principles. This was followed by Training Course B, and it was this second course which really started Israel's Armoured Corps.

Training Course B lasted a whole year. The main objective of the course was the study of the tank's characteristics. The trainees wanted to discover what its special qualities were. One day, as part of their exercises, they drove their Shermans into the abandoned village of Naana and advanced upon its buildings. The track of one of the tanks came off and only then did they realise that nobody knew the correct procedure for putting it back. To their great delight they then discovered that the tank was able to move on one track, but when a track came off another tank they realised that they had a problem which required careful thought and study. They spent an entire week dismantling and replacing tracks.

They drove their tanks through sands, up mountains, over rocks and against trees. Once, wanting to demonstrate their achievements before a group of officers attending a course for battalion commanders, they drove a tank into a building in an abandoned village but then found that they could not extricate it. The reinforced concrete roof was sitting snugly on top of the tank, which had demolished the pillars supporting it.

The tactics they applied to armour manoeuvres were entirely original, which was not surprising since they had been invented by the trainees themselves. Being infantrymen, their doctrine was based on an infantryman's mentality: to pin down and destroy in formations and timing customary in the infantry.

While the course was in progress, Ezrahi translated an American manual on tank platoon and company training, a manual which contained diagrams giving the Do's and Don't's of the various exercises. Until Ezrahi completed his translation into Hebrew, these diagrams were the main educational material for the trainees who knew no English. To enrich their knowledge and widen their horizons, every evening they were shown commercial films containing battle scenes from the first and second world wars.

The graduates of Course B trained Courses C and D. Sergeant Shmuel attended Course C. He was to become the first commander of 'S' Brigade to rise from the ranks and pass through all the levels of command.

Why did the Armoured Corps have to learn everything by itself from the very beginning? There are perhaps two reasons: The first is simple. The majority of senior officers who stayed in the regular army after the War of Independence lacked formal education and therefore knew no international languages. Their school years had been turbulent ones; there had been the struggle against the British White Paper on Palestine; the second world war; the European holocaust; the illegal immigration activities; and the series of battles which led up to the War of Independence. They had neglected their books and given all their attention to the underground movement.

The second reason is more complex. To begin with, it was not only armour that had to do everything for itself. The infantry too had to make its own way, though undoubtedly it was assisted here by the considerable experience of Palestinian

49

officers from the British and other armies. Palmach units, whose influence upon Zahal is still noticeable, were poor and few in number. Poverty in weapons and the small number of soldiers prevented the Palmach from utilising the experience of other armies. It had to create a warfare doctrine which would minimise their shortcomings in weapons and in numerical strength. Mobility, surprise and night warfare were principles born of scarcity.

The establishment of Zahal did not alter these shortcomings, which were an inevitable part of the predicament of a small, alien Jewish community in a densely populated region; Zahal would never be able to match the Arab armies in quantity of men and weapons. Hence the Palmach doctrine was adopted by Zahal who extended, amplified and improved it.

From the outset, Zahal's combat doctrine was faced with a dilemma: neither Israel's economy nor its industry could possibly manufacture the arms and munitions its doctrine demanded. Thus Zahal was obliged to procure most of its armaments overseas. It was not given the armaments it wanted, but only what was available. And Zahal could not always acquire even what would normally have been available. With the exception of the supplies obtained from Czechoslovakia during the 1948 war, eastern European countries would not sell arms to Israel, and Zahal was restricted to the western world; for political reasons the west restricted the types and quantities of weapons and armaments sold. Until three years ago the United States refused to sell arms to Israel. France began to do so systematically in 1955 and Britain only in 1959. However, these arms, too, were not always those Zahal wanted, as countries manufacture armaments to conform with their warfare doctrine which is not always Zahal's. Quite frequently, Zahal has had to put equipment procured abroad to a different use from that intended by its manufacturers.

In 1951 Lieutenant-Colonel Ben-Ari was appointed deputy commander of 'S' Brigade, which then consisted of two armoured infantry battalions, one tank battalion (the S/10), and reconnaissance, mortar and engineering companies. From the start Ben-Ari became the moving spirit of the brigade. One thing he insisted on was rapid mobility in depth. He noticed, however, that the command vehicles in the brigade were trucks. As trucks cannot negotiate the sort of terrain tanks and half-tracks can they were unable to keep up with their units and were obliged to stay behind. The brigade decided to demand half-tracks for their command vehicles. The request was duly made to Armour Corps headquarters, but Zahal maintained that any available half-tracks would be better employed in the armoured infantry. After a bitter struggle, however, the brigade eventually succeeded in getting half-tracks for its principal command groups.

'S' Brigade took part in the 1952 and 1953 Zahal manoeuvres which took the form of a battle between the southern command (blue force) and the central command (red force). Uri Ben-Ari had read about the armoured battles of the second world war and with these in mind he set off on a non-stop, day-and-night journey in which he penetrated more than eighty miles into red territory. His presence deep in the rear of the red forces aroused the displeasure of the directors of the exercise and the fury of the red forces. A circle was drawn on the map by the umpires and the brigade was not allowed to emerge from it until further notice. Had this not been done the entire timetable of the manoeuvres would have been utterly disrupted.

At that time Zahal did not accept Ben-Ari's ideas and refused to believe in armoured pentration in depth. Its concept of armour's role was that it should progress from objective to objective, taking one at a time and mopping up before moving on. Chief-of-Staff Major-General Yigael Yadin had some harsh words to say about the officers of "S" Brigade in his review of the 1952 manoeuvres.

Nevertheless, Ben-Ari chose to ignore the 1952 rebuke and in 1953 repeated his daring penetration in depth. But this time something happened which affected the destiny of Israeli armour.

This time S/10 battalion of 'S' Brigade surprised and overran a red force infantry battalion at Tel Kunteira near the Faluja highway. Although they were quite aware that it was an army game, the infantrymen were so terrified by the appearance of the assaulting tanks bearing down on them that they threw their weapons away and fled. The sight of infantrymen fleeing from tanks is nothing unusual; but as it happened, standing at the roadside watching the proceedings was none other than the Prime minister and Minister of Defence, David Ben Gurion. He was convinced on the spot that Zahal needed tanks. Up to then it had been generally maintained that the infantry was the queen of the battlefield and in budgeting the slender means at Zahal's disposal it had invariably gained priority whenever the need arose for priorities to be established.

Now the Armoured Corps was promoted in the list of priorities.

The Armoured Corps now really began to grow. But Zahal's top brass still had little faith in its armoured Units. First and foremost this was due to the units always being held back by mechanical breakdowns. They could not be relied on to carry out daring thrusts such as Ben-Ari had demonstrated and this problem was to dog it for many years to come. The paratroops contributed in no small measure to this lack of faith in the ability of armoured units for they had successfully carried out every reprisal raid entrusted to them. Yet when they needed the half-tracks of the Armoured Corps, the vehicles would get bogged down on the way and the paratroops would have to complete the journey on foot.

Zahal really began to appreciate the value of armour during the 1956 Sinai Campaign. Then, for the first time, an Israeli armoured formation went into action and demonstrated its potentiality as a mailed fist which could move non-stop and make deep penetrations at great speed. It was not that these qualities were unknown until then, but it was only then that they were actually demonstrated in warfare.

The preliminary planning for the campaign provided 'S' Brigade with a minor role. They were assigned the task of the dupe: a false offensive on the Jordanian front to divert Egypt's attention from Zahal's main activities on the Sinai front. General Laskov and Colonel Ben-Ari enlisted the aid of the general officer southern command, the late General Assaf Simhoni (who was killed in an aeroplane accident after the Sinai Campaign) and in a joint effort they succeeded in persuading the chief-of-staff to assign 'S' Brigade a more significant task on the Sinai front. According to the new plans which were then drawn up, 'S' Brigade was to travel on tank transporters and buses behind the 9th Infantry Brigade, who had been assigned the mission of attacking and breaking through at Kusseima.

This plan was not altered to any great extent but at the last moment the general officer southern command changed it on his own initiative. In his book, *Diary of the Sinai Campaign** Moshe Dayan himself refers to it thus:

"Yesterday I had a row with the General Officer

*Weidenfeld and Nicolson, 1957.

Southern Command who, contrary to G.H.Q. orders, threw 'S' Armoured Brigade into action before the time set for it. Notwithstanding explicit orders, which stated that the armour would not go into action before 31 October, and in spite of the explanations giving the reasons for this order, the G.O.S.C. persisted in his own point of view that no time should be 'wasted and that concurrent with the commencement of operations the initiative and surprise element must be exploited to advance and capture whatever possible."

The plan disrupted by the G.O.S.C. was that the 4th Infantry Brigade was to have attacked the Kusseima defences and taken them. The armoured brigade should have moved into Sinai twenty-four hours later.

Opinion is still divided on whether the 4th Brigade completed the break-through of Kusseima by itself, before the Armoured Brigade burst into Sinai like a whirlwind, or whether the Armoured Brigade supported the attack and in fact decided the outcome of the battle. Those who state that even in 1956 an assault and break-through operation could be made by armoured forces, support the version of 'S' Brigade commanders that it was they who bore the brunt of the assault.

There were few battles in the Sinai Campaign. 'S' Brigade controlled the main axis to Ismailia after bypassing the Abu Agheila region, and in vain did they seek to make contact with the 1st Egyptian Armoured Brigade. The latter reported to Cairo that they were locked in fierce battle with Israeli armour, and even said that they had inflicted damage and knocked out Israeli tanks; but the truth was that the Egyptians evaded making contact and it was with the utmost difficulty that the tank company, commanded by the present Colonel Shmuel, was able to catch up with the fleeing Egyptians and tweak their tail.

The bypassing of the Abu Agheila region and the penetration of the entire brigade as far as the central Sinai axis was carried out in a most original and daring manner. Colonel Uri Ben-Ari conceived the idea that it would be possible to bypass the region by using the Deika road, which passes through the Deika Wadi and reaches the Abu Agheila–Jebel Libni highway behind Abu Agheila. At that part of the route the wadi forms a narrow canyon and at both ends the Egyptians had built fortifications manned by guards. Thus they were safeguarded against surprise attacks from the rear of the Abu Agheila region. As soon as the brigade went into action, Colonel Ben-Ari dispatched a reconnaissance party to see if the way to Deika was negotiable. They discovered that the Egyptians who should have been stationed at Kusseima had fled to the Egyptian rear through the Deika and that their panic-stricken flight had infected the guards who had been stationed to defend the Deika pass and block it. This information decided Colonel Ben-Ari to advance his entire brigade, except for the force fighting at Um Sihan, through the Deika to the Abu Agheila front, before the Egyptians had time to refortify the pass. It was this plan which brought the bulk of the Armoured Brigade to the Deika defile, straddling the central axis in the rear of Abu Agheila.

While the main force of the brigade was making its way through the Deika, a combat team was busily engaging the Egyptians at Um Sihan, the south-western "suburb" of the Abu Agheila defences. Spearheading that team was the company commanded by the officer who today is Colonel Shmuel. The moment they were sighted, a barrage of artillery fire descended on them and the first casualties of the brigade were recorded. The tank in which Shmuel was riding got stuck in the sand, its tracks were hit and Shmuel was wounded in the arm. He was losing blood but managed to dress the injury himself and continue fighting until the battle ended. He was then rushed to hospital, suffering from advanced blood-poisoning.

"S" Brigade operated in central Sinai like a division. Combat teams were spread out over a wide area, far beyond the range of the radio-communication equipment then used. Colonel Ben-Ari commanded these teams by using runners, sometimes acting as his own runner.

The dazzling war of mobility waged by 'S' eclipsed the 27th Brigade which fought under the command of Colonel (today Major-General) Haim Bar-Lev along the northern axis (to Kantara). That brigade, too, entered the battle on the heels of an infantry brigade which attacked and captured the fortified area of Rafa. Its entry on to the northern axis had also been accomplished at a crucial moment in the battle between the infantry and the Egyptians in their fortified positions.

Zahal thus really discovered the tank in the 1956 Sinai Campaign. Like other armies, Zahal too was late in appreciating its importance and capabilities and had to learn from its mistakes the hard way. But unlike some other armies, Zahal learned these lessons quickly and thoroughly. After the Sinai Campaign a new Zahal arose in which armour was the deciding force on land.

Immediately after the 1956 Sinai Campaign, Zahal began transferring senior officers from the infantry to armour, the first being Colonel Israel Tal. When the campaign was over, the chief-of-staff, Major-General Moshe Dayan, asked Tal, who was then commander of Zahal's Officers Cadet School, when he would be ready to transfer to the Armoured Corps as deputy commander.

Tal: "In two to three weeks?"

Dayan: "No, no. I meant what time today?"

The build-up of armoured brigades was soon under way; it became a constantly growing undertaking, for Egyptian armoured strength had grown dramatically and Israel was now able to procure armoured fighting vehicles and improve its existing equipment. Colonel David Elazar was the next to be transferred to armour; after a lengthy period of apprenticeship and study he was appointed commander of 'S' Brigade. From the Paratroops came Major Biro, to be followed by Lieutenant-Colonel Man. The most senior of the officers to be transferred to the Armoured Corps was General Haim Bar-Lev, who in actual fact was a dedicated and experienced armour man but who until that time had been considered "too good" for the Armoured Corps. He became general officer commanding Armoured Corps after the brief tenure of Colonel Ben-Ari.

The organisation of the Armoured Corps as the decisive land force and its expansion were carried out between 1957 and 1964, when General Haim Bar-Lev was G.O.C.A.C., followed by General David Elazar (Dado). There were two stages in Zahal's approach to armoured warfare. In the first, the lessons of the 1956 Sinai Campaign were examined and it was found that Israeli armour had proven its ability to outflank and penetrate to the enemy rear if the objectives which it was outflanking or bypassing were thinly dispersed or deployed, enabling the armour to pass through without disturbance. In 1956 the Egyptian forces had not been large enough to enable them to heavily defend positions covering a wide area. Hence the thought was that armour should outflank the objectives and penetrate deep into the enemy rear, on the assumption that the appearance of an armoured force, from the rear, would cause the Egyptian defences to collapse. Dealing with the "pockets" themselves was considered of secondary importance. Assault tasks were still reserved for other forces, mainly the infantry at night (as was the case at Kusseima and Rafa in 1956). This was to preserve the freshness and vigour of the armoured force for its main role – that of penetrating in depth, foiling the reorganisation of the enemy forces and dislocating its logistical system.

However in the second stage, particularly during the early 1960s, Zahal's thinking changed; this was due to the increase in Russian-made armour being acquired by the Egyptian Army. Although Zahal still persisted in its adherence to by-passing and outflanking tactics, it realised that armoured break-throughs could not now be avoided as the Egyptians were now deployed in Sinai in accordance with Russian doctrine, placing fortified positions between natural obstacles to block the passage of armour. A system of fortifications had been created in Sinai which obliged a force wishing to penetrate to the enemy rear to break first of all through the first-line defences.

In his period as G.O.C.A.C. General Elazar worked out and refined the tactics of breaking through fortified defence positions. He initiated the forum which came to be called Brigade Commanders Conferences, where the commanders were presented with subjects and problems for study and thought. Their ideas would be expounded at these sessions and Elazar would evaluate them. A committee was set up, headed by Colonel Abraham Eden (Bren), whose task was to edit the discussions for publication in text-book form. Colonels Shmuel, Motke, Albert, Mandi and Herzl all participated in writing the chapters.

For the 1964–5 manoeuvres the Armoured Corps practised breaking through Russian-model fortified positions. Zahal had not completely abandoned the idea that the cutting through of fortified positions was a job for the infantry in night battles, but the idea was taking hold more and more that this task should be given to the Armoured Corps.

CHAPTER SEVEN

On 1 November 1964, after three years of study (philosophy and political science) at the university in Jerusalem, General Israel Tal was appointed general officer commanding Armoured Corps. On the same day the outgoing G.O.C.A.C., General David Elazar, became general officer northern command.

During the six months which preceded the change in command at Armoured Corps headquarters, the situation on the Syrian sector had deteriorated. The disputes which were to be termed "the war of the tractors" had been augmented by another and potentially more dangerous quarrel – that of the National Water Carrier, which could quite easily be the cause of the outbreak of war between Syria and Israel and as a result, of a full scale war against the Arab states.

The National Water Carrier, a conduit which carries water from Lake Kinneret to the Negev, had been put into operation in July 1964. This operation had cost about a hundred and thirty million dollars, and was not only intended for the agricultural development of the parched Negev but also for the settlement of immigrants there which Israel had taken in from its early beginnings. The Arab states objected to the undertaking in spite of efforts made by President Eisenhower to proportion the waters of the Jordan, which feed Lake Kinneret. The Arab states' first summit conferences decided to prevent by force the operation of the carrier. Syria demanded war, but Abdul Nasser argued that they were not yet ready for a military confrontation with Israel and that they should start a war only when victory was certain. As an interim measure they decided to divert the sources of the River Jordan, and in particular the Banias springs, so as to nullify from the outset the purpose of Israel's water carrier. Israel for her part declared that she would not remain indifferent to the diverting of the Jordan sources and it soon became clear to all that the water dispute could lead to war. But for the time being both sides wished to avoid it and took restrained measures in border disputes.

Syria now began making plans to build a carrier of her own, which would divert the waters of the Banias springs to Mukheiba, a joint undertaking with Jordan. At the same time the perennial disputes over rights of cultivating soil along the armistice line between Syria and Israel continued. The Syrian Army, which had a topographical advantage, being dug in in fortified positions on top of the Golan Heights, fired at Israeli patrols protecting the tractors working in the valley on fields which Israel put claim to. Israel had cleared and prepared the patrol route as near to the frontier as possible and the fields were worked right up to the border.

Border incidents usually flared up after a Syrian position had fired at a patrol or a tractor. The Israeli response would first result in an exchange of fire with automatic weapons, and if the incident developed artillery would join in, with the Syrian gunners in most cases having the upper hand because of their commanding position. United Nations truce observers would eventually arrange a cease-fire but after a short interval a new incident would break out, either at the same place or somewhere else along the disputed frontier.

One area prone to such turbulence was that near Tel Dan. The Jewish national fund had laid a dirt track there and the kibbutzim had prepared the land with tractors for planting. This area was vulnerable from two Syrian positions, one in Nukheila village and the other in Tel Azaziyat, a tall hill dominating the valley. The G.O.C.A.C., then still General David Elazar, contended that tank guns capable of hitting point targets could silence the Syrian fire, which was directed from dug-in tanks more efficiently than had been the case until then. Some expressed their reservations as to the ability of the Armoured Corps to handle these incidents without them developing into a situation bordering on war. However, the chief-of-staff, Major General Rabon, gave his consent.

One week before General Elazar took up his new post as general officer northern command, 'S' Brigade was ordered to send a company of Centurions to the Syrian sector.

The Centurions were stationed in an area concealed from the Syrian positions across the border. Within a matter of minutes they would take up firing positions to silence the Syrian guns at Nukheila should the Syrians fire upon the tractors clearing a pass for the road.

Captain Shamai, who had been put in charge of the operation, stayed with the platoon. He had already issued battle priorities to his men: "The first thing is to knock out their tanks. There are two; one on the east side of the village and the other on the west. This job comes first. After you've knocked the tanks out, get their anti-tank guns and artillery. Only when you've done that are you to fire on the Syrian headquarter's position and their automatic weapons. I'll do the fire observation. Is that clear?"

"Yes, Sir," said the platoon commander, Second-Lieutenant Kahalany.

Night fell, the keen chill of the Galilee made the men shiver, though perhaps they were trembling not only from the cold,

Should there be an incident, it would be their first experience of combat, the first in six years for the Armoured Corps, and the platoon was apprehensive. Shamai brought his accordion. "Lads, let's sing a bit. It'll warm us up!" At first he sang alone in his pleasant voice while the subdued men gathered round to listen. Gradually the members of the platoon joined in.

"Men!" the sergeant called out, "liven it up! Pretend you're having a picnic on the beach!"

The voices grew livelier. Shalom Cohen, Dahan, Haim Levy, Shitreet, Mishla, Joseph Albaz (known in Signals as Buloz 1), Yehuda Albaz (known as Buloz 2), Menashe Manzur, Guata, Avner Goldschmidt, Moshe Rabinowitz, Itzhak Shabazi and the others sang together; voices from Morocco, Iran, Turkey, Europe, Iraq, the Yemen and Israel.

When dawn broke on Tuesday 3 November, the tractor harnessed to the road-levelling equipment went to work and slowly neared the spot where it would bypass the source of the Dan River. The reconnaissance half-track drove in front of it. Army engineers walked ahead of the half-track and the tractor, prodders in hand, checking for mines. Captain Shamai watched through his binoculars from the observation point. The reconnaissance vehicle gradually drew near to where the path curved. Through his field-glasses, at a range of eight hundred metres, he could see the Nukheila position. Two tanks, German Panzers, were in their dugout emplacements, only their turrets and guns revealed; there were also two recoilless guns placed in the shadow of some houses. Shamai noticed that the emplacements of the anti-tank guns had not been changed since the previous day and that the 81 mm mortars, the machine gun nests and the riflemen's foxholes were also exactly as the day before.

His watch showed 12 noon when the Syrians opened machine gun fire on the reconnaissance patrol and on the engineers walking ahead. To enable them to get back, the Syrian position would have to be silenced. That was his job. Shamai gave the command over the wireless. "On vehicles!"

Within five minutes the Centurions had taken up firing positions, dispersed within less than fifty metres. The tank on the left was the first to open fire, aiming for the anti-tank gun emplacement. Then the commotion started. The air was filled with flying shrapnel, screaming shells, clouds of smoke and dust. The Syrian 81 mm mortars emplaced in Tel Hamra; the tank and light weapons located on the Banias Heights; the 120 mm mortars from Tel Azaziyat and both the tanks dug

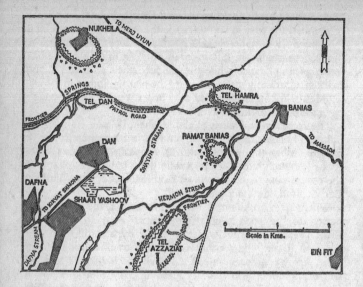

1 *The frontier sector of the first and second Nukheila incidents (3 and 13 November 1964).*

in there, all joined in with the Syrian position at Nukheila as it fired upon the dirt track and Tel Dan. Israeli artillery also went into action.

The Centurions fired non-stop, each shot raising a thick cloud of dust in front of the tank caused by the air blast and escaping gases. Armour-piercing shells travelling at 1,470 metres a second shot out of the 105 mm gun. If they hit their target they reached it within half a second, before the dust of the shot had settled. Before long the air was thick with smoke and dust and the strong smell of gunpowder. Mortar shrapnel burst over Tel Dan and the hail of metal mingled with the fly-ing stones and rocks.

The duel lasted an hour and a half before United Nations truce observers managed to organise a cease-fire. Zahal suf-fered eight slight casualties and two tractors and a bulldozer had been damaged.

General Tal, who only two days ago had taken over as G.O.C.A.C., hastened to the Galilee. He reached Tel Dan a few hours after the cease-fire. "How many Syrian tanks were knocked out?" was his first question.

"None, Sir," said Lieutenant-Colonel Oshri.

"None?"

"One might have been slightly damaged, Sir."

"Did their tanks fire all the time?"

"We didn't silence a single tank, Sir. The Syrians were still firing after we stopped."

"How many shells did we fire?"

"Eighty-nine, Sir."

"There will be an investigation!" Tal stated.

In Zahal circles, the incident at Nukheila was definitely considered a failure. Chief-of-Staff General Rabin told his friends that those who claimed that enemy fire could be silenced by the accurate flat-trajectory fire of the Centurion gun had been wrong. Here General Tal stepped in.

"Your strictures have been very severe, and to my mind misguided," he said to his friends, the generals. "It is most certainly possible to silence enemy guns with the flat-trajectory fire of the 105 mm British gun of the Centurion, which is highly accurate. What has been proved at Nukheila is that *Zahal* cannot silence the enemy guns."

The investigation concluded that in spite of its superiority in number of tanks, in accurate and zeroed guns, in pre-calculated firing-range, the platoon had achieved very limited results, and that the blame lay in the human element, and mainly in deficient leadership.

General Tal called a meeting of Armoured Corps officers, from lieutenant-colonels upwards. This was his first meeting with his senior officers as G.O.C.A.C. He lectured the assembled officers on the lessons of the Nukheila incident. His main point was; the enemy tanks are the prime objective of our tanks.

Captain Shamai returned home on Friday evening. Nava, his wife, ran to greet him with open arms, but his embrace was cold. He hurried to the cot of his son, six month old Itai. The baby was asleep and Shamai stood looking at him a long time before taking his clothes off and washing. When he returned, the baby was awake and he picked him up in his arms. Nava felt something was wrong.

"What happened, Shamai?" she asked.

"Nothing," he said.

He played with the child and showed no signs of going to visit his grandparents in Ramat Gran. Normally, Shamai went every Friday evening to his grandfather's house, even when he was just back from the field and worn out from lack of sleep.

"Not going to grandma and grandpa?"

"No," he said.

Shamai had been eighteen months old in 1940 when his father, Shmuel Kaplan, a member of L.E.H.I., had been arrested by the British police. At first his father had been imprisoned in the Mazraa detention camp, later at the Latrun camp, and after that in Acre prison. Finally he had been deported by the British to Eritrea. During the war his family was wiped out by the Nazis in Poland. He had been released in 1947, when Shamai was eight and a half and Shamai had been brought up by his mother and her parents. He was very attached to his grandparents.

"What happened?" Nava asked.

"Nothing happened," he said.

He did not even want to go round to visit friends and play gin-rummy. He went to bed early. On the Sabbath he went for a walk with Itai and on Sunday went back to his unit.

Everyone in the brigade knew about the Nukheila incident. Some shook his hand on his return and said the person to blame was the one who had chosen the tank positions. Others blamed the Centurion, which for some time now had been growing steadily more unpopular.

"It's no tank, Shamai," they said.

"That's right," Shamai said, "it's no tank. Too complicated."

There were also those who were pleased at his failure.

CHAPTER EIGHT

General Tal's blunt appraisal of the Nukheila incident was a foretaste of things to come. To an outside observer it might have appeared that the corps and General Tal had fused together harmoniously from the very beginning, but in actual fact his assumption of that office caused quite an upheaval. The general is one of those who wish to put their stamp on whatever they undertake, and who believe that there is always plenty of room for improvement.

General Tal was born in Mahanayim in 1924. His father, Ben-Zion, was one of the founders of Mahanayim. In 1917 General Allenby's expeditionary forces reached there in their pursuit of the Turks. The Australian scouts asked Ben-Zion Tal whether the B'not Yaakov Bridge was in sound condition. Ben-Zion did not understand a word of English. He ran home, fetched his English–Yiddish dictionary and asked the British officer to point out the words of his question. When Ben-Zion saw that the question concerned a bridge, he immediately grasped that it must concern the B'not Yaakov bridge over the Jordan River. He pointed to the word "bridge" in the dictionary, then said most convincingly "BOOM!" Nowadays when he tells this story he is fond of adding: "So you see, Talik was born into a family with a strong military background and tradition . . ."

In 1930 the Tal family moved to Moshav Beer Tuvia which had been rebuilt (in 1929 it had been destroyed by Arabs). There Israel Tal was brought up until at the age of seventeen he volunteered for the British Army. He served in the 2nd Battalion of the Jewish Brigade in the Western Desert and fought in Italy. He was discharged with the rank of sergeant, and immediately joined the permanent staff of Haganah headquarters as an instructor in medium machine guns. In the 2nd Battalion he had been considered an outstanding machinegunner.

Israel Tal was blessed with some technical talent. At the age of sixteen he had invented a weapon against moles (it was called a "gun"). The moles had been damaging the potato crops, and already seemed immune to arsenic. Israel Tal then produced his tube loaded with shot which was placed as a trap. As the mole pushed up the earth, the tube's trigger was released and the creature received a blast of shot. His invention was actually produced commercially. There was another story told about him which illustrated his technical expertise. When in the Western Desert Sergeant Tal liked to carry out experiments with explosives. Together with a friend he would fill a cave with whatever explosives he could lay hands on and then from a distance blow up the cave. On one occasion the explosion was so violent that the battalion commander in his headquarters fell off his chair.

Tal's exterior sternness cannot hide his sensitivity. From the neat and well-ironed uniform of a general still peers the face of the Jewish scholar. Short and lean, when he is bent over the artillery and logistics charts of the Armoured Corps one cannot help forming a mental picture of his grandfather swaying over a page of the Talmud. Tal even has the habit of twisting a finger around the spot where his sidelocks should be;

he is actually touching a small splinter which buried itself under the skin of his cheek and which never stops irritating.

When Tal took over from General Elazar his plan of action was already prepared. While at the university in Jerusalem (where he studied Spinoza and Aristotle) he had given some deep thought to methods of warfare and to the optimum use of armoured forces, and had attempted to pinpoint those factors which served as negative influences upon the quality of Israel's Armoured Corps.

At his first meeting with his staff and command officers, he had given a lecture in which he had outlined his plan of action. To those of his officers who had read the letters of General Patton to his daughter, General Tal's enthusiasm for the arena and for tanks reminded them of the American general's glee upon seeing terrain which was suitable for tank operations. "The arena is ideal tank country," General Tal had said enthusiastically. "An excellent arena which provides opportunities for deploying great masses of armour. That is why Zahal maintains a large Armoured Corps."

Nor had the fact that the arena was good tank terrain been lost on the commanders of the Arab armies, and the armour element in their military forces had steadily grown. The existence of large masses of armour in the area could not help but draw attention to the size of Israel, which prevents effective defence; at its narrow waist, between Natanya and Tulkarem, it is a mere fifteen kilometres wide. In terms of mobile warfare the country's size is of minor consequence. Israel could never defend in depth, but since its inception Zahal has always contended that in all cases the war must be carried into enemy territory. Hence all Zahal defensive plans are based on assault into enemy territory.

General Tal had no argument with that. His idea was to carry Zahal's maxims still further. His predecessors too had spoken of employing armour in large masses moving together, and had been opposed to splitting armour into narrow fingers. Tal, however, had also considered another factor. It seemed that as the armoured force grew larger, its quality deteriorated. At that first meeting with his officers Tal had enumerated four factors which tended to lower quality: quantity, national and reserve service, heterogeneity and lack of discipline.

Zahal's need for a large force, and the fact that this force is mainly an army of national service and reserve men, leads to a certain difficulty. If Zahal wishes to double the number of its armoured brigades, it must double the number of na-

1. Major Shamai Kaplan as a
Captain commanding a company.

2. Major Felix Beatus in 1948.

3. General Itzhak Sade (*right*), and Lieutenant-Colonel Shaul Yaffe.

4. General Israel Tal with one of the Egyptians' Russian-made T/55s knocked out by Major Haim.

5. Lieutenant-Colonel Binyamin Oshri in 1964.

6. Lieutenant Ilan Yakuel.

7. General Tal when he took command of the Armoured Corps in November 1964.

8. General Tal at the end of the Six Days War with the girl soldiers of his staff; from left to right, Varda, Liora and Ziva.

tional servicemen and reserves serving in it, but these men cannot be employed beyond the absolutely essential security requirements without seriously affecting Israel's economy. Another factor, relating to the tank corps, is that because it is a technical force it requires, ideally, a regular cadre of superior quality to run it. The air force is mainly composed of regulars, and the armoured forces in other countries, including those of the Arab states, operate and maintain their tanks by means of regular army personnel, many of whom are on the permanent staff. Such is not the case in Israel.

The main function of the regular army in Zahal is to supply trained soldiers for the reserve brigades. At first sight it is not possible to make a professional tanker out of a national serviceman, at least not during the period of his compulsory national service. If a battalion could train recruits for its own use only, its efficiency would be greatly enhanced, but apart from the fact that its recruits do not continue their reserve duty with that unit, they do not even do the whole of their national service with it. A national serviceman who is not actually designated to become a tank commander serves only a few months of his thirty months of national service with a tank unit, and after this short time has to make room for another recruit. If regular battalions wanted to keep their national service recruits with them for a longer period, Zahal would be obliged to increase the number of its regular army units, but Israel's economic resources render this out of the question. The regular army, apart from its training function, can hope to do little more than delay an attacker until the reserves have been mobilised.

After deducting the periods of basic training, tank crew trades, and platoon and company training, only a short period remains for the average national serviceman to serve in a tank unit as a tanker. The tank is a complex weapon, consisting of mechanical, hydraulic, optical and electronic systems. To use it skilfully, specialisation is essential. But nevertheless, the national serviceman soon has to make way for the next man and spends the rest of his national service in the servicing units. There is a very detailed yearly programme which accompanies every recruit from the day he joins the army to the day of his release and there is a similar programme for every tank. Such detailed planning and intensive exploitation of manpower and material are necessitated by Zahal's shortages.

These two factors were accepted by General Tal as being part of Israel's situation. The third factor, which also had to be accepted, was that of heterogeneity. Whether for economic or political reasons, Zahal could never procure the arms it needed at the right times and in the right quantities, and the Armoured Corps had gradually come to possess a variety of tanks. If Zahal had one type of tank throughout, its maintenance, the training of its technical personnel and its equipping would be made much simpler. As it is, a particular type of tank necessitates the maintenance of a regular army unit in order to train tankers for the reserve units equipped with that type of tank. For example, the Sherman tank is outdated but the Armoured Corps is obliged to maintain regular units of Sherman tanks simply for the purpose of training tankers for the reserve brigades equipped with it. The same applies to the light French AMX/13 tanks, which entered service with Zahal at the end of 1953.

Had General Tal wished to introduce more uniformity in equipment, he would have had to recommend the removal of the Sherman and AMX/13 from the service, leaving only the Centurions and the Pattons which are newer, but by doing this he would also have made the Armoured Corps smaller – a cure worse than the disease.

Nevertheless General Tal did find limited solutions to the problems arising out of the national and reserve services and from the variety of equipment. He found a way of extending the tanker's period of service in tanks, while cutting down the more technical subjects into narrower areas of specialisation, in which even national servicemen could achieve good results. And by a certain amount of juggling, both at corps and general headquarters level, larger units were able to be fitted out with standard equipment, while throughout the corps standard weapons were fitted into the various types of tank, all helping towards a certain lessening of heterogeneity.

The fourth factor, that of defective discipline, General Tal was not willing to accept as an inevitable result of Israel's situation. He launched a continuous and forceful campaign to impose good discipline throughout the Armoured Corps. His aim was to knead his corps into a community, uniform in appearance and behaviour. On his first day he prohibited all crews and units to zero their tank guns, and made the rule that zeroing was to be done by a uniform method and by authorised personnel only. There were those who commented that he was overlooking Jewish individualism, and that this would be his undoing. When he next began to insist upon uniform procedures and conduct, others commented that the

66

general was after robotisation. Imposing a uniform discipline was General Tal's hardest battle by far.

When General David Elazar was commanding the Armoured Corps he had noticed the colourful appearance of his officers. None of them would wear the same colour of socks. In 'A' cadre on one occasion, when the officers had sat down and hitched their trousers up as they crossed their legs, they had revealed socks encompassing the entire spectrum of the rainbow.

It is possible that these individual tastes in hosiery were an expression of Jewish revolt against discipline and uniformity. But General Elazar decided that an army should wear one colour of socks. In September 1962 the blow fell. General Elazar issued an order intended to "establish uniformity in matters of footwear and legwear". The order stated that a soldier on duty under field conditions was obliged to wear Type 2 boots (black, laced-up boots, supplied by Zahal) and woollen army socks. Concessions were made for soldiers in barracks or on leave, when General Elazar would permit them to wear other shoes and other socks provided: 1. that the shoes were black, plain and without embellishment; 2. that the socks were black.

General Tal did not stop at black socks. He imposed dress routine in general. In order to set the Armoured Corps apart he even wanted to design a special hat for the girls serving in it, in place of the Women's Corps hat. However, Colonel Stella Levy, commander of the Women's Corps, refused her consent. Colonel Levy won and General Tal capitulated. Two months after becoming G.O.C.A.C. he dropped the matter of the girls' hats and did not revert to it again. But he won the battle of the khaki. He wanted to see all his men in one khaki, and banned the use of Zahal's elegant uniform made of Dacron in a light khaki colour. He permitted only the olive-coloured khaki dress uniform issued by Zahal. In the field, fatigues type 8 was the only clothing permitted and not the two-coloured denims worn by the paratroops nor any other of the various types of uniform seen in Zahal units.

The general next began to indoctrinate the men of the Armoured Corps in carrying out an order because it was an order. Nothing, it seems, so aroused public opinion against him as this requirement. At first the complaints were mild enough, and only from the soldiers themselves. They felt imposed upon, they said, for in other units nobody bothered to check how belts were done up or shoe-laces tied. Soon, however, the revolt against General Tal was coming from higher-ups who objected to his concept of Zahal's mission and the education of its men.

Israeli society includes a large and powerful community which was weaned upon and influenced by the kibbutz ideology. The kibbutz is a free society with a collective will based on an appeal to the understanding of each member, on gradual and patient explanation, and finally upon conviction. The kibbutz stands for inner discipline which leads to unity of action through the consent and understanding of each individual, and shrinks back from any form of coercion. The Haganah, as the main stem from which Zahal emerged and developed, was indoctrinated in this ideology of the collective society. Many of the Haganah officers were members of kibbutzim or favoured the kibbutz way of life. The Palmach, the shock troops of the Haganah and later of the magnificent brigades of Zahal during the War of Independence, grew up and was educated in the kibbutzim. In many a Zahal unit the kibbutz members proved themselves successful commanders and left behind them the imprint of their spirit and temperament upon their units and subordinates.

General Tal's point of view that operational discipline, administrative discipline and ceremonial discipline cannot be divided, and his insistence on an order being carried out simply because it was an order, aroused displeasure and alarm both within the army and outside it. The protagonists of inner discipline, particularly, feared for the character and mission of the army, and General Tal had to explain his way of thinking most thoroughly. First, he explained, he did not consider the army inherently valuable. That was an important point, and a surprising one. For in Israel it had become customary to look upon Zahal as a national and social asset. When David Ben Gurion had been minister of defence the army had been called on to give help in settling new immigrants in camps, in educating the ignorant and teaching them the A.B.C. Even today Zahal provides teachers from the Women's Corps to give lessons in reading and writing in new immigrant villages. Zahal has always been lauded most highly for these activities. And here was General Tal saying that the army was only a means for national security, and that there was not the slightest justification for its existence apart from national security. Even in the opinion of his critics, it was agreed that General Tal was joking when he said he would agree to humiliate and starve soldiers if it could be proved to him that it would serve the security of Israel. But as he put it to them: "*If* it serve the army's purpose, I would be in favour of it, because in my opinion the attitude towards the individual is of secondary importance to the security of Israel. However, for an individual to really feel that he is an important part of an organisation he must have morale, a sense of identification and a feeling of participation, just as much as he must have food, water and clothing. This is why we do not want an individual who will fulfil his duties unwillingly but prefer an active individual, who carries out his security assignment with enthusiasm. It is this that makes the morale of the unit important to us, and of particular importance to this morale is the soldier's knowledge that there is justice in the army."

CHAPTER NINE

General Tal extended the scope of his discipline to encompass matters of combat doctrine, incurring in this almost the same hostility as if he had interfered with religious freedom. Again the general had to explain himself. "Where there is no discipline in this field," he said, "everyone invents doctrines. If a commander discovers by pure chance that he can fire accurately by moving the telescope instead of correcting the lens surface he immediately thinks he has discovered a new system and in no time at all he is indoctrinating an entire generation of tankers with it. A young commander of that sort cannot understand that what seems to him a new 'discovery' is merely applicable in a certain situation, and that his particular 'discovery' was already known to those who wrote the official doctrine." General Tal would wind up his remarks on that subject by saying, "There are as many doctrines as there are Jews." In the same way as he had forbidden tank crews from zeroing their own guns, he prohibited the dissemination of private doctrines, and this he did shortly after assuming his post. He issued orders that an officer making any changes in the doctrine of the Armoured Corps would be summarily dismissed. "Inventions and initiative? By all means. But only through Armoured Corps headquarters."

Although General Tal only forbade the questioning of an order, to his critics it seemed as if he was trying to clamp down on freedom of expression. He was denounced for trying to robotise Jewish youth. This reaction was yet another aspect of the dilemma in which the Jews of Israel had found themselves since Israel became a sovereign state, fighting for its existence. A people reared in a tradition of individual freedom and the absence of a hierarchy, for whom social justice is a supreme value, suddenly found themselves plunged into confusion. For the sake of their existence they must strike at the other side which sought to destroy them. The maxim "Arise and kill him who comes to slay you", is not a rule of justice but of instinct for survival; and although the Jews have repeated it for many hundreds of years they had never carried it out except in Israel. In most cases in the past the Jews valued faith above existence. General Tal's forefathers had given their lives for their religious beliefs – hurled themselves into the flames of a blazing synagogue – and never even lifted a kitchen knife against those who persecuted them during the pogroms in eastern Europe. Faith took precedence over survival. But their son, General Tal, was resolved to defend life and was prepared to subordinate values held sacred by his forefathers to the skilful use of the tank.

Those imbued with the ideology of the kibbutz claimed that discipline should spring from understanding and identification, and not be the product of fear and sanctions. They saw no essential connection between ceremonial discipline and operational discipline. In their opinion a soldier was capable of superior combat discipline even if his shirt was unbuttoned, and could attack an objective with tenacity and courage even in red socks.

General Tal explained to them that the Armoured Corps was not an exclusive society for the few who wished to belong to it, but a mass technical force, made up of operational units, not of individuals and their specific wants. He too, the general said, stood for understanding and persuasion; he had directed that commanders were to explain their orders time and again if necessary. But the army could not wait until every individual had been made to understand why the gun had to be fired like this and not like that; or why certain ammunition behaved as it did and not otherwise. It had taken hundreds of years to evolve a doctrine of gunnery, and it would be useless to attempt to convince each individual of its validity.

Meeting with members of a certain kibbutz who had censured his principle that an order be carried out because it was an order, the general could not contain himself. "Last week I attended the funeral of a tanker at one of the kibbutzim," he said. "Your people eulogised him as a hero, but I could only

70

feel the pity of it all. That boy did not die a hero. He was killed accidentally during a simple training exercise, merely because he was not brought up on the principle that an order should be carried out because it is an order. The Armoured Corps rules that shells must not be stored in tanks without their safety clips, for the simple reason that the static electricity inside the tank might set the shell off. Therefore the order is quite categorical. Shells are to be stored in tanks in no other way, and this order must be carried out regardless of whether or not a soldier is convinced of its logic. This particular soldier did not do this and was killed as a result."

He was obliged to press the point time and time again that: "One cannot expect a large and constantly changing group to think all the time and to educate itself. That is why there are orders of commission and omission. These orders are the product of the experience of many generations of men in many armies; they are the result of scientific considerations and empirical knowledge."

Another factor was that a mass technical force necessitated a form of discipline which Zahal had never had before. The deep-rooted inner discipline of the paratroops, which the proponents of inner discipline cited as the perfect example, could not work in a technical corps. As General Tal told both his supporters and critics: "A paratrooper with a deep sense of inner discipline is capable of fighting bravely and tenaciously, even when he is hungry and when his shirt is torn. But no tank will function, even given the most rousing Zionist orations, when there is no fuel in its tank or when it has thrown a track."

In trying to bring home his point of view, General Tal would often repeat the same object lesson. "When a gun fails to fire, the order states that the gunner shall wait a given time before opening the breach and removing the faulty shell. Those who designed the gun found that sometimes the firing action is delayed. If the gunner fails to wait, as laid down in his orders, there can be an accident. But you cannot expect everyone to understand exactly how the primer and its chemistry operate."

The imprinting of this discipline upon the Armoured Corps was planned by General Tal as an operation in which each phase was worked out in detail, almost as though the objective was the capture of a fortified, topographically complicated country. He was not alone in planning and executing the campaign. Senior officers of the Armoured Corps willingly responded to his ideas. Colonel Shlomo, Colonel Herzl, Colonel

Moussa, Colonel Albert and Colonel Uri, as well as other offi-cers, took part in consolidating the disciplinary patterns, in preparing a code, and later in conducting a programme of in-formation and elucidation among officers and men, prepara-tory to the forthcoming changes.

There was one aspect of Zahal's discipline which General Tal refused to tolerate. This was "*Tirturim*" in army jargon, or bullying. In the absence of conventional discipline this plague had spread. Junior officers would ignore army regulations and order after-midnight parades, or order their men to run round the camp, or to bury a cigarette butt with full honours, this last being one of the most popular forms of *tirturim*. In fact there were no limits to the soaring imagination of some of the section, platoon and company commanders, sometimes only a year or two older than their men. Some contrived "horse racing" as a punishment for units which had failed their platoon tests; a soldier would be harnessed up and compelled to gallop across the square with a corporal holding the reins behind him. Another form of punishment for disobedience was to make the culprit carry the "pocket wrench" of the tank around with him for a few days. It weighed eleven pounds. Several years ago there was the case of the company commander who made a soldier wear a barbed-wire con-certina around his waist. He had sentenced him to what he called "mobile imprisonment". Things went from bad to worse until eventually queries were raised in the Knesset after the son of a Knesset member had told his father that his platoon commander had extinguished a cigarette on his body. The Knesset investigated the case and the officer was dismissed.

From the very beginning G.H.Q. had endeavoured to eradi-cate "*tirturim*", but with only limited success. For complete success headquarters needed the goodwill and cooperation of junior officers, and these were reluctant to give up what they strongly felt to be a means of imposing their will upon their men. The surprising thing was that junior officers insisted that it did not lower morale, but on the contrary helped to raise it. An exemplary major claimed that he himself had served in a company in which it was prevalent. Bullying, he had said, was part of a military tradition which the men later recalled with nostalgia.

As soon as he assumed office, General Tal set about estab-lishing Standing Orders of rights and duties for the Armoured Corps. Characteristically he first analysed why bullying was in no sense beneficial to the Armoured Corps. He argued that only discipline, the purpose of which was the obeying of an order because it was an order, could ensure the eradication of this disregard for army orders, as exemplified in the maltreatment of soldiers. In the absence of discipline the commander became an absolute despot. He could go wild and still the soldier would have no redress, because in the absence of discipline the sergeant-major would not report deeds and misdeeds, as Orders demanded that he should, purely on the strength of a soldier's complaint. General Tal was aware that Israelis have a strong sense of justice and that the Israeli soldier was ready for any assignment or burden provided that what he did was apportioned fairly. When the distribution of assignments was just, and seen to be so, the Israeli soldier was willing to make any sacrifice. His identification with his army was then complete. Bullying damaged the army because it exemplified injustice, degraded the soldier and precluded his identification with the army.

When Colonel Tal had been commander of "S" Brigade, Major Moshe N. had been the brigade's personnel officer. It was in "S" Brigade that Colonel Tal had made his first attempt to impose a single pattern of discipline. Through his personnel officer, he had drawn up Standing Orders for the guard room and Orders for the reception of new recruits. When Tal became G.O.C.A.C., Major N. was promoted to lieutenant-colonel and became the corps' personnel officer. General Tal instructed him and other senior staff officers to prepare drafts for two sets of regulations, one dealing with the rights and duties of the soldier, and the other with dress routine, inspections and parades.

Both sets of regulations were a digest of General Staff Orders. But in editing the Orders into regulations more was involved than abridgements and additions. These Standing Orders became the code of the soldier's rights. From his own experience General Tal knew that often people made mistakes because they did not know the rules and regulations. He therefore ordered that the Standing Orders of Rights and Duties be encased and prominently displayed in every unit of the corps, both in barracks and in the field. Showcases made of wood and glass, painted in the corps' colours of green and black, contained a placard listing the rights and duties of the soldier. One of the first orders listed made it a duty incumbent upon every soldier to read army regulations, and at the new recruits depot the code of rights and duties was given as a subject for study, examination and grading.

The basis of a soldier's rights was his right to fair treatment and respect from his officers. He also has the right to complain against his officers; to be granted leave and to apply for a transfer to another unit. These rights were formulated as obligations upon the officers, underlined by a warning that officers who failed to fulfil these obligations would be prosecuted. A detailed timetable was provided for dealing with a soldier's applications to his commanders and steps were taken to ensure that the soldier's application received proper attention. The soldier's right to leave was also clearly worded, to preclude it being withheld or shortened.

The duties of the soldier began with saluting. The code contained twenty-one orders dealing with saluting and specified situations in which a soldier must salute or need not. The foremost duty read: "It is the duty of every soldier to carry out any order given him by his commander. The order shall be carried out to the letter, with dispatch and without delay." But because memories of the Nazi regime pursue the Jews of Israel like a phantom, an immediate reservation was added: "However, a soldier shall not carry out an order when it is clear and evident that the order is illegal."

The third and last section of the code dealt with the powers of officers, commissioned or non-commissioned, up to the rank of platoon commander. The code implicitly denied them the right to arbitrary punishment by the thorough and precise definition of the soldier's rights. It was also forbidden to penalise a soldier by cancelling or shortening his leave. Discipline was placed under keen observation by the opening of a quick route for complaints with a time limit for dealing with them, and an address for an appeal to high authority over the heads of the unit commanders.

To buttress the authority and status of junior officers, sugar was given them to replace the whip. After first obtaining confirmation from his superior officer, the platoon commander was entitled to award his men with Saturday leave, after-duty leave, relief from orderly duty, to recommend promotion to the rank of lance-corporal, and to recommend the mention of men in dispatches. Certain minor disciplinary measures were left to the discretion of sergeants and platoon commanders; to cancel permission to leave camp after duty; to cancel permission to attend an entertainment event of the unit, to impose extra guard, kitchen and sanitary duties. Instead of the former collective punishment, such as moving camp in the middle of the night, or two or three bed parades a night, junior officers were given the power to impose an "additional exercise", aimed at "bringing the unit up to the required performance standard of that exercise. This extra drill is in no sense a punishment, but a methodical means of improving the unit's performance."

The draft of the other code, that of uniform, inspections and parades, was given to a study committee headed by Colonel Shlomo and the corps' personnel officer, Lieutenant-Colonel Moshe N. The committee's suggestions were brought up for discussion before the commanders of the armoured brigades, and their conclusions were reviewed by the committee and finally by Armoured Corps H.Q.

The Code of Rights and Duties and the Code of Behaviour became subjects in the curriculum of the courses for tank commanders, section commanders, N.C.O.'s commanding reconnaissance units, armour officer cadets and company commanders. Gradually, bullying came to an end and a discipline unique to the Armoured Corps was consolidated. The soldiers of the corps began to look and behave so differently that it was said in their praise: "The Armoured Corps is a different army." Gradually, too, it became less and less necessary to educate the soldier to adapt himself to these norms as outgoing generations of national servicemen passed them on to the new recruits as an accepted tradition.

CHAPTER TEN

The inculcation of this new discipline needed a lot of hard work. However, the Armoured Corps soon had more important matters to attend to. The situation along the Syrian border was getting worse. The springs of the River Dan have their source near the Israel–Syrian frontier; these springs had been part of the British Mandate, and the United Nations observers had ruled that they flowed within Israeli territory. Syria refused to accept this ruling, and to safeguard her rights Israel had cleared a track leading to the springs, which Israeli troops patrolled. The Syrians regularly opened fire on these patrols.

It was this situation which had brought about the first Nukheila incident, after which General Tal had ordered all regular Armoured Corps officers, from company commanders upwards, to be informed of the shortcomings which the incident had disclosed. Major Shamai Kaplan's main error, it was decided, had been in failing to withhold his fire when he could see that it was having no effect, and in failing to switch to ammunition of a type more suitable to the circumstances. Also, he had not dispersed his tanks over a wide enough area, and the flashes and dust in such a confined space had interfered with the crew's accuracy. Armoured Corps headquarters began to impress upon its officers that the decisive element in tank warfare was accuracy; that one must know who was firing and at what target. Patience, accurate fire observation, and effective fire correction were more important than the number of tanks firing.

Three days after 3 November, General Elazar and General Tal began to teach the lessons learned from the first incident and to decide upon the operational policy for the future. In order to prevent failure in any future engagement which might take place over the track to the Dan springs, a platoon of Sherman tanks was brought to Tel Dan. A platoon of Centurion tanks was given a secondary role, that of joining the battle only if the Sherman platoon could not handle the situation. Zahal considered every border incident as an engagement whose value to morale was as important as its practical purpose. In its role as a deterrent force Zahal could not allow itself to fail. By now, experience of the Shermans had accumulated and modifications had been introduced in its engine and gun. In spite of the fact that the calibre of its new gun was smaller than that of the new 105mm British gun on the Centurion, and that its ammunition was inferior, it was very accurate at short and medium ranges and allowed good fire observation. At a range of eight hundred metres it was capable of piercing the armour of Syria's old German Panzers, although they, in turn, were able to pierce the armour of the old Shermans. If there should be a battle, conditions would be equal.

The commander of both platoons was Captain Shimon, and the commander of the Centurion platoon was Lieutenant Avigdor.

The second Nukheila incident came earlier than had been expected. It occurred only ten days after the first and became one of the oustanding incidents along that frontier. It was Friday, 13 November 1964. The routine Israeli patrol was passing along the track leading to the springs, and walking in front of the patrol's half-track were sappers checking the track for mines. At 1325 hours the Syrian position at Nukheila opened fire on the patrol. The men on foot were picked up by the half-track which continued patrolling, now under Syrian fire from heavy machine guns and a recoilless gun. Captain Shimon ordered the Sherman platoon out of hiding and into firing positions. These were more or less the same positions as in the previous incident except that this time their dispersion was wider. He next allotted each tank's assignment and prepared himself to direct and control their firing. From the Israeli observation post, the two Syrian tanks in their dug-outs on the east and west of Nukheila presented a target less than 60 centimetres high and about 120 centimetres wide.

The Syrian tanks opened fire on the patrol.

From the moment Captain Shimon gave the order until the Sherman tanks actually took up their firing positions less than three minutes elapsed. But one tank had a mishap. Climbing out of the woods in the valley towards the firing position above, it brushed against an oak tree. Branches fell on to the turret and covered it, obscuring the telescope. The driver could not see where he was going and the Sherman began to slide down the steep and rocky slope.

Here was the opportunity for the platoon of Centurions waiting in reserve inside the woods. Earlier the Sherman crews had been poking fun at the Centurion crews; "You've muffed quite enough. Just you wait here quietly while we finish the job off", and orders stated that the Centurions were to join in the battle only if the Sherman platoon was unable to silence the Nukheila position, or if heavy fire was opened up from other Syrian positions. Lieutenant Avigdor saw the Sherman sliding down and immediately ordered his Centurion to occupy the vacant position. Shalom Cohen, the platoon commander's gunner, was ordered to open fire.

The Syrian positions at Tel Azzaziat, Tel Hamra and the Banias hill now joined in the battle, but instead of aiming at the Israeli positions they began to pound away at Kibbutz Dan and Kibbutz Shaar Yishuv with 120mm heavy mortars and later even with 122mm artillery guns. The kibbutz members ran to collect their children from the nurseries and get them into underground shelters. Within a matter of minutes everyone was underground.

Medium mortars, recoilless guns and tanks had now opened fire upon the Israeli force at Tel Dan. Lieutenant Avigdor called over the intercom: "'Gunner, Shot, 800, Tank, On!" Shalom Cohen began to sight his target. He completed this by elevating the gun and lowering it again, "so the teeth get a proper grip," he explained to his team-mate in the Centurion.

"On!" called Shalom Cohen.

"Fire!" ordered Avigdor.

"Firing!" called Shalom Cohen.

And he fired. The Syrian tank to the east burst into flames.

Captain Shimon now ordered the sergeant to turn his attentions to the Syrian tank to the west.

"Gunner, Shot, 750, Tank, On!"

"On!"

"Fire!"

"Firing!"

The second Syrian tank went up in flames.

The Syrian fire from Nukheila began to die down, but they stepped up their artillery bombardment, which had been ranged in advance in the event of Israeli counter-action. Most of their shots were fired at the two kibbutzim and the chief-of-staff, Major-General Itzhak Rabin, finally decided to silence the Syrian artillery by bringing in the air force. At 1455 hours, about one hour after the Syrians had first opened fire on the Israeli patrol, the air force planes made their appearance: Vautours, Mystères, Super-Mystères and Mirages III, which silenced the Syrian artillery. Mig 21s of the Syrian Air Force hurried to the scene but were chased off by the Mirages. At 1530 hours a cease-fire, negotiated by the United Nations observers at the request of Syria, came into effect.

The chief-of-staff justified the intervention of the air force on the grounds that Zahal could not tolerate the Syrian bombardment of Israeli settlements from where there had been no shooting, simply because they were at a topographical disadvantage and hence more vulnerable. It was also the beginning of a lesson, the A.B.C. of ethics in border disputes, which Zahal decided to teach the Syrians – that bombardment of settlements would be countered by the air force.

Zahal casualties in the second Nukheila incident were three dead and eleven soldiers and kibbutz members wounded. Kibbutz Dan and Kibbutz Shaar Yishuv both suffered serious damage from the Syrians' heavy mortar bombardments. The following day Radio Damascus announced that Syrian Army losses had been seven killed and twenty-six wounded.

"Were the Syrian tanks destroyed?" was General Tal's first query.

"Destroyed and burnt out, Sir," said the brigade commander.

"Then it's a victory," said General Tal.

The crews of the Centurion tanks who had participated in

the Nukheila incident were invited to the offices of the brigade commander. He shook hands with them, asked them to be seated and offered them hot coffee. Lieutenant-Colonel Oshri and Lieutenant Ilan Yakuel as well as the crews were delighted, not merely because they had won a tank battle, but because they had taken the first step towards building up faith in the so greatly slandered Centurion tank. However, as Lieutenant-Colonel Oshri was leaving the brigade commander's offices, he met the commander of another battalion.

"What makes you so happy, Benny?"

"Haven't you heard how our Centurions performed?" asked Lieutenant-Colonel Oshri in surprise.

"Don't be too optimistic. Summer will soon be here and then you'll see how hot they get."

"Not with me, they won't," said Lieutenant-Colonel Oshri. "I've already had experience of them in summer."

"You saw them at the end of summer. Wait until you've had Centurions for a whole summer. You'll be able to fry eggs on them for the entire corps."

The delight of S/10 Battalion was denied to one man. The success of Captain Shimon on this second Nukheila incident could not help but emphasis the failure of Captain Shamai Kaplan on the first. The lessons learnt then and the defects in leadership displayed by Captain Shamai Kaplan were now common knowledge throughout the Armoured Corps. General Tal himself was well aware that Captain Shamai Kaplan's failure would be generally known, in fact this had been his purpose, for he had assembled all the officers of the corps from platoon commanders upwards and read out to them the findings of the investigation commission. But the thought of the reprimanded platoon commander perturbed him. During a routine visit to 'S' Brigade he quietly asked the brigade commander to point out Captain Shamai Kaplan to him. Later, during an interval, he drew Shamai aside. The battalion was stationed in the Negev.

"Let's sit down," said General Tal.

They found some stones to sit on, out in the field.

"Border incidents, Shamai, have both national and strategic implications. I want you to understand that. The Armoured Corps must examine every error and learn what lessons it can from it. That was why such wide publicity was given to the incident at which you were in command."

"I understand, Sir. I'm not angry."

"I have heard, and I can see, that you are depressed. You should know that the success of Captain Shimon was due in no small measure to your failure. It was mere chance that you happened to be commander at the first Nukheila incident, and he at the second."

"I am O.K., Sir."

"The Armoured Corps itself cannot look upon one failure as a mere episode, Shamai, but for an individual this is what it is. Do you understand?"

"But I failed, Sir."

"Officers before you have failed; it has even been known for them to go completely to pieces in their first battle. I know you are a good officer, and I do not want you to feel too depressed."

"I am all right, Sir."

"Those who know how to overcome their depression, to better themselves in anticipation of their next battle – for these officers their first failure really will be a passing episode. Those who do not have the strength to anticipate the next challenge will really fail."

The general went on to tell Captain Shamai Kaplan of some of his own experiences. "Some of our most admired officers failed in their first battle. I want to give you the opportunity to prove yourself."

"Sir, I have a request."

"Yes?"

"I don't want to serve in Centurions any more, Sir."

"But even the Centurion was given a second opportunity to prove itself at Nukheila, and it proved itself to be a good tank. You will prove yourself to be a good commander."

"How, Sir?"

"I'll make a deal with you. Every time there is a state of alert, you will command the force. Agreed?"

"Agreed, Sir."

"With Centurions," said General Tal.

CHAPTER ELEVEN

In spite of its success in the second Nukheila incident, the Centurion tank was still a long way from gaining complete confidence. Memories of exercises in the not so distant past were still fresh in the minds of the tankers. They remembered how rapidly one Centurion had slid down an escarpment, with the crew powerless to brake it, and that on another occasion not all the Centurions had reached the finish of a 120 kilometres course in the Negev.

In fact, there had been good reasons for every breakdown, which could mainly be traced to faulty maintenance. Conditions in the desert, too, were another factor. Dust is the enemy of all machinery, and the dust of the Negev is among the worst. It shortens the life of engines and mechanical parts, and fuel dross, oil and dust would coagulate in the partitions of the radiator, preventing the air from making contact with the metal surface and reducing the efficiency of the radiator, thus causing the engine to become overheated. The causes of the breakdowns were not traced immediately. It took some time before the crews realised that the radiator had to be scraped every day, hard work for the crews. Until this was discovered it was generally understood that the high temperature of the Centurion engine was inevitable, and there were officers who would allow them to be driven even when the indicator on the thermometer had passed the danger mark.

Officers such as Lieutenant-Colonel Oshri, who had a feeling for machinery, did not accept the assumption that the Centurion breakdowns were inevitable, and demanded full and detailed information on every Centurion mishap in their battalions. When on one occasion the bearings of an engine burned out, his investigation discovered that a mechanic had let the tank take to the road when the oil pressure in it had been too low. He had the mechanic tried and sent to prison, a fact which drew the attention of the battalion to the importance of good maintenance.

It was obvious to General Tal that correct tank maintenance was dependent on the understanding and personal ability of the unit commander and the priorities he established in his own unit. When a man like Oshri was in command of a Centurion battalion, maintenance standards would rise and the tanks would perform well. But his successor might be an officer with a different set of priorities, and the meticulous standards of maintenance which existed when he took over would be relaxed; again low standards would soon prevail. The problem was how to make good maintenance institutionalised, independent of the idiosyncrasies of each commander. General Tal maintained that the answer lay in applying strict discipline to the observance of Ordnance Corps' instructions concerned servicing, repairs, tuning and synchronisation of tanks, both in the units and in the workshops. Similarly, he made officers of all ranks accept direct and professional responsibility for all ordnance matters. To assume such responsibilities, unit commanders required the close collaboration of qualified ordnance officers, and to that end Ordnance Corps directives were drawn up and presented in a form very similar to that of the Code of Rights and Duties, as had been done in the case of the forgotten General Staff Orders. Lessons on maintenance and servicing were given to officers and technical staff, and commanders were given refresher courses by Ordnance Corps officers. Besides this, General Tal began appointing commanders who had an inclination for strict discipline and a bent for thoroughness. These two qualities became the basis of General Tal's promotion policy. He would note down in his notebook the names of candidates for advancement. His attitude in this respect was severe and uncompromising, so convinced was he of the need to instil a feeling for discipline and maintenance which would go right down to the roots, and in one or two cases he nominated officers whose personalities he did not admire at all, but who had the inclinations he wanted.

Singlehanded, he worked on instilling an atmosphere of studiousness and professionalism into the Armoured Corps, which soon became one of its vital characteristics. Directives followed fast upon each other: Suspend the use of a particular fuse pending its examination by the Ordnance Corps; examine the possibilities of reducing the length of tank commanders' courses, with a view to extending the time the men serve on tanks; examine the possibility of shortening reserve officer courses to enable more men to attend them; and check the feasibility of separating company commander courses into two specialisation sections, one covering tanks and the other armoured infantry.

But above all, headquarter's main preoccupation was gunnery. In his very first week on the job the general had mentioned that he was considering issuing a book on gunnery which would bind every armour officer to a single gunnery doctrine. At first he had thought it would be possible to prepare such a book in a few months. But two and a half years of study and experimentation (and considerable expense and exasperation) went by before the book was completed.

It was the policy of the Syrian government to show itself the most hostile to Israel of all the Arab states, while Egypt sought to present herself to the world as being the most restrained of Israel's neighbours. At first it seemed that Syria was the motivating power behind the scheme to divert the sources of the River Jordan, but gradually it came to light that Egypt's restraint merely camouflaged her real intentions, and that she was in fact encouraging the Syrian government to carry out the Jordan diversion scheme, a policy decided upon by the Arab states at their first summit conference.

Egypt's calculations were shrewd. If the Syrian government succeeded in diverting the sources of the Jordan, thus depriving Israel of vital, life-saving water, so much the better. But Israel could not sit back and do nothing; she would be obliged to retaliate with force. World opinion would then condemn her as the aggressor (for the international community tends not to go into details, but satisfies itself with the obvious facts) and Israeli aggression would give the Arab states a certain moral advantage. What was more important, in Egypt's evaluation of the situation, was the enormous strength of Syria's steel and concrete defences on the Golan Heights. Israel's forces would, it was hoped, wear themselves out in a long and difficult battle. This gradual erosion of Israel's strength was the rationale behind Egypt's so-called restraint. The wearing down of Israel's strength was also the aim of the "People's War for the Liberation of Palestine" which Syria began to direct against Israel in the name of the Arab states and with the blessing of Egypt. This People's War consisted of sending saboteurs into Israel to kill and destroy; the "People's Soldiers" were described as Palestinians, but they were in fact Syrians, trained by the Syrian Army.

It was the chief-of-staff, Major-General Rabin, who found the answers to these Syrian–Egyptian policies of attrition. Zahal had always been against a policy of retaliation in kind – the dispatch of Israeli saboteurs into Syria in revenge for the sending of Syrian saboteurs into Israel – mainly on moral grounds. The Syrians attacked civilians but Israel objected to its soldiers killing Arab civilians and reserved its reprisal actions for the Syrian Army. This policy, however, tended to deprive Zahal of its advantage, for its true strength lay in a direct confrontation with the Arab forces which at that stage was out of the question.

In consultations with the northern command's General Elazar and the G.O.C.A.C., the chief-of-staff outlined a plan which would exploit Zahal's advantages and yet would not result in a dispute deteriorating into war. Zahal began to use its strength like a honed razor instead of an axe. Following a border incident in which the Syrians killed an Israeli tractor driver, the chief-of-staff requested the approval of the minister of defence to retaliate by hitting the Jordan diversion project. General Elazar and General Tal argued that within the limits of a local border incident the tank gunners could hit point targets more than two kilometres away – the distance of the Syrian earth-moving equipment at the foot of Mount Hermon. In other words, there would be no need to employ either the air force or artillery, both of which would aggravate the chances of the incident leading to open war. The very next day, when the Syrians opened fire on an Israeli patrol which was travelling along the road to the Dan springs, Israeli tanks shot up the earth-moving equipment and set it afire.

It seemed that the war along the Syrian frontier had entered a new phase, that of tank gunnery. And indeed, during the next two years, until the Six Days War, Syrian belligerence and the Armoured Corps' gunnery developed side by side.

At first it was not clear to the Syrians whether the heavy mechanical equipment for their diversion project had been destroyed by accident or deliberately. The location of their diversion works was close to Nukheila, to the Banias Heights and to Tel Hamra, and it was from these positions that they fired on the Israeli patrols travelling along the Dan springs road. Gradually it dawned on them that the diversion project equipment was a target in itself. In May 1965 the Syrians moved their work on the Jordan waters diversion scheme from the foot of Mount Hermon, which was in an exposed area and near to Israel, to a distant and concealed location. Here, above the B'not Yaakov bridge, the Syrians had a topographical advantage. High above the Israelis in the valley, they were defended by a dense line of fortified positions. They also transferred the scene of their provocative onslaughts to this new location, and from here they soon began to fire at Israeli patrols and civilian workers in the fields close to the border.

The advantage the Syrians now enjoyed disconcerted Zahal. Israeli retaliation was met with heavy fire. There were those who suggested employing artillery to thwart the Jordan diversion undertaking, but two major considerations negated this suggestion. One was that in an artillery duel the Syrians had a decided advantage, both in guns and in topography. Their guns were positioned in unpopulated areas, in elevated and fortified positions, while the Israeli guns could only be positioned in densely populated areas. An artillery duel could bring disaster upon the settlements in that part of Galilee. The second consideration was the danger of an artillery duel developing into a major battle, bordering on full war, particularly as artillery salvoes over a wide area cannot ensure accurate hits on small targets unless the salvoes are extremely heavy, and this would mean a deviation from the policy of locally restricted incidents.

Israeli observers closely followed the progress of the water diverting works and discovered that the Syrians were working from both sides of the Customs House above the Binot Yaakov bridge, along the watershed, which was at the crest of the mountain. On the northern side the Syrians were working along an exposed line which covered a considerable distance. From the point of view of the Armoured Corps this was the ideal sector for carrying out its difficult mission of hitting a small target at a range of six kilometres. South of the Customs House the Syrians held the advantage because it was a concealed area where the digging operations ran through a gorge. The southern side was also further away from the Israeli tank emplacement. Defending the distant earth-moving and digging works were the larger and more fortified Syrian positions, which were equipped with large quantities of armaments, including tanks. It was apparent that if a battle ensued it would develop along two levels. On one the Israeli tanks would have to strike at the earth-moving equipment, and on the other they would have to silence the Syrian positions.

When it was decided to dispatch the regular patrol along the border, Captain Shamai Kaplan was ordered to hurry to the Galilee. At that time he was already commander of the Centurion Specialisation Section of the Armour Officer Cadet Course. On the strength of his arrangement with General Tal he was given command of a combined unit of Sherman and Centurion tanks. The tank crews, men from his former company, greeted Captain Shamai Kaplan with rousing cheers. Swarming around him like bees, they shook his hand and struggled with one another to stay by his side. Kaplan realised at once that the preparations being made were not for a conventional retaliation. The operations officer, Lieutenant Ilan Yakuel, explained to Captain Shamai what it was all about. The captain was excited. At long last success might be within his reach. He felt somewhat ashamed when he found himself hoping the Syrians would fire at the patrol, to enable the Israelis to retaliate. But several days went by and the Syrians did not fire at the squads patrolling the frontier.

On 13 May 1965 considerable movement was seen to be taking place inside the Syrian positions near the Customs House. The first thing to be noticed by the Israeli observers were the black-overalled Syrian tankers, providing a clue to the Syrian intention of bringing in tank gunfire. Also seen were Syrian artillery observation officers scanning the Israeli sector. The Israeli intelligence officer immediately reported these movements, which brought two very important visitors to the Israeli tank unit – General Elazar and General Tal.

The patrol which set out at dawn completed half the route without incident, but when it neared Shaiyun, the Syrian positions opened fire with machine guns and mortars; another border incident.

"Take positions!" Shamai ordered, while he himself made for his Centurion. Quickly the crews began removing and folding the camouflage nets. The crews took their places and within three minutes the tanks were in their firing positions. But the commander's Centurion was delayed. Thick smoke was pouring out of it. For a moment Shamai's voice could not be heard over the radio, and when it did come through it sounded nervous and high pitched. While Shamai's crew had been removing the camouflage netting, a smoke grenade had dislodged itself from the tank's smoke-discharger, and had exploded. One of the crew was badly injured and the rest were stunned by the explosion and smoke.

Two minutes later the voice of Captain Shamai Kaplan was heard coming over the radio, clear and calm. He dispelled the panic of his crew and organised first aid for the wounded man and his speedy dispatch to hospital. Now he could turn his attention to controlling and directing the tanks' fire. The Centurions engaged the Syrian positions, aiming mainly for the Syrian tanks dug in high above them. With their first shots the Centurions disclosed the sources of the Israeli fire to the Syrian positions, and a rain of mortar fire was directed at the Israeli tanks. The battle was joined.

The Shermans aimed their shots at the Syrian earth-moving equipment, six kilometres away. However, their observer was disappointed. The Syrian tractors could not be seen in the works sector north of the Customs House, while southward everything was quiet, the scenery only being disturbed from time to time by something which appeared and disappeared at regular intervals. After studying it carefully through binoculars, the Israeli tank commanders came to the conclusion

86

that it was nothing more nor less than the scoop of a dredger, hidden in the gorge. Using a high trajectory, they took aim. Two tractors and a dredger were hit in this way; a third tractor managed to escape behind a hill.

The Mishmar Hayarden incident, as it was called in the records of the Armoured Corps, was considered a success from Israel's point of view. Before taking his leave of the unit, General Tal shook Captain Shamai's hand and congratulated him on his success.

"What have you got to say about Centurions, now?" he asked.

"Excellent tank," replied the captain.

"And you were an excellent commander," said the general.

"I don't know why you should say that, Sir. I didn't do a thing."

"Take a look. Look around you. Such peace! You have silenced the Syrian positions, and we have no casualties."

"Sir, it was easy. There was nothing to it. At that range it was almost impossible for the Syrians to touch us."

"They could hit us just as we hit them."

"Their tanks didn't even shoot, Sir."

"O.K., we'll give you another opportunity; against tanks that do shoot. Meanwhile I want you to know that you carried out your job very well."

General Tal felt that Captain Shamai Kaplan still had doubts about himself. For some reason this disturbed him. To some extent he felt a personal responsibility for the public admonition Captain Shamai Kaplan had experienced. He too wanted that failure erased, to be drowned in success. He felt that the Mishmar Hayarden incident had indeed compensated for the Nukheila failure. Yet here was Captain Shamai Kaplan refusing to consider this incident and his leadership in it as warranting success, and declining to accept remission for that earlier misfortune.

As the Syrians moved their diversion project further and further away from the border, the tank battles became more complex and demanding. Other armour officers demanded from General Tal that they too be given the chance to take part in the engagements, both because it would give them their first taste of fire and because of the battle experience they would thus gain. These demands hampered the agreement between General Tal and Captain Shamai Kaplan, and it was not until the Six Days War that Shamai got another opportunity to command a tank battle.

CHAPTER TWELVE

These long-range battles flared up and died down in various sectors of the border. To some extent the battles resembled a catch-as-catch-can match between two giants, with the whole of northern Galilee as their arena. Sometimes one would blast away from a mountain top or the other let loose from the depths of the valley; sometimes both would thunder away from the ravines, or exchange shells from the crests of the mountains. These were sniping battles, for the tanks never attempted to move into the assault, but merely changed positions.

In one battle the rivals opposed each other from the same elevation and at a range of 1800 metres; on one side the Centurions and on the other the dug-in Panzers of the Syrian Army. On another occasion they fought it out at a range of 2200 metres. In the former engagement a Centurion hit a Panzer with its second shot, and set it ablaze with three more shots all of which hit the target. In the latter a Centurion struck a Panzer dead on with its second shell.

Another place, a change in positions. The Syrian tanks were now at 3000 metres range, Russian T.34s, dug-in and difficult to locate. Suddenly a T.34 left its dug-out and began to race away; a Centurion fired a shell which exploded ahead of the fleeing tank. The driver panicked and for a moment stopped his tank. The next shell reduced the T.34 to flames.

The Syrian tanks emplaced themselves at higher and higher altitudes; another time battle was joined with the Centurions positioned 80 metres above sea level and the Syrian Panzers at 180 metres above sea level at a range of 3000 metres. The Centurions' gunners could see only the Syrian tank's gun and part of its turret. The first two shots from the Centurion missed their target, the third scored a direct hit and the next two set it on fire.

The Syrian tanks continued to climb higher and retreat to more distant positions. The next engagement found the Centurions not far from the Lake of Galilee, 140 metres below sea level. The Syrian T.34 and SU. 100 were dug in at a height of 350 metres above sea level and at a range of 3900 metres. At this vantage point the Syrians had one disadvantage. It was difficult for them to point their guns downwards, and they were obliged to leave their dug-out emplacement. In front of their tanks, however, they erected a sandbag wall; thus the Centurions' crews down in the valley could see only the gun and the front part of the turrets of the Syrian tanks. The Centurions opened fire. The first shell fell short, the second overshot. The third fell very near to the T.34 and the fourth set it on fire. The other Syrian tanks were then hit and set ablaze.

Lieutenant-Colonel Oshri was not happy. His tanks had now participated in many battles and the results of his leadership were really beginning to show. The Centurion had at last gained the confidence of the Armoured Corps, but he himself had not taken part in a single action. He put pressure on his brigade commander, Colonel Shlomo, and finally requested an interview with General Tal.

"Sir, if there should be another engagement, I want to take part in it."

"Your battalion participates in quite enough action, Benny."

"But I've not been under fire myself. It's ten years – the Sinai Campaign – since I have fired a shot in anger. Sir, I can't look my men in the eyes. Sergeant Shalom Cohen has already knocked out two Syrian tanks and has more experience than I have."

"I cannot endanger commanders unnecessarily," said General Tal.

"Sir, I request permission to take part in an engagement."

"Permission refused."

To Lieutenant Ilan Yakuel, his operations officer, Oshri poured out his heart. "I send men into battle and to their deaths, and I am never with them, I am always at some observation post. I can't go on like this. If they won't let me take part in a battle, I'll tell them to go and look for another battalion commander."

"Oshri, take it easy," said Lieutenant Ilan.

"What? Take it easy? I trained the battalion. I'm the one who puts them through their paces with all sorts of disciplinary and maintenance demands. But when it comes to the great moment, to the battle, where am I? In the rear!"

Oshri was angry. He also realised that Ilan's army service would soon be coming to an end. In a few weeks time he would be leaving the army and Oshri would be left alone in the battalion. His resentment grew. He looked at Ilan. The young man's coal-black hair fell over his ears. Ilan did not like haircuts.

"When did you last have a haircut, Ilan?"

"Benny? Not again."

"You know the regulations. Haircuts every ten days."

"Benny, your obsession is showing!"

"Go and get one."

"Now, really, Benny."

"Look, Ilan, how do you expect me to maintain discipline in this battalion if you, the battalion's operations officer, known to be a personal friend of the O.C., goes around looking like a beatnik?"

"And you're the chap who asked me to extend my term in the regular army. Honestly, Benny!"

"Get a haircut, or I'll put you in clink!"

"Ah, well. They won't let you sit inside a tank during a battle, so you cry like a baby and then suddenly take a great interest in my hair. Such is life, Benny."

"Sir, not Benny! Get a haircut or I'll cut it myself."

"I'd be nuts to sign up for another term in the regular army. I'll study law and grow my hair as long as Ben-Gurion's."

The next engagement took long in coming. The Syrians had learnt a lesson. Realising that even at a distance of six kilometres from the Israeli positions they were not invulnerable to Israeli tanks, they moved to a new scene of operations much further away. They were now opposite Kurazim, about eleven kilometres from the Israeli frontier. There they could work without fear of their equipment being destroyed while they plotted border incidents. Until then every mine explosion and each attack upon Israeli patrols had been met with a two-fold retaliation by Zahal who attacked both the Syrian border positions and their earth-moving equipment. Now they could comfort themselves with the thought that their equipment was beyond Zahal's reach and that they were free to do as they pleased along the border.

Certainly, at a range of eleven kilometres it appeared most difficult to destroy this equipment and for a time it seemed that the Syrians would be able to carry out their scheme of depriving Israel of the Jordan waters. But General Tal did not give up. He believed that with the Centurion's 105mm gun it would be possible to achieve complete success. He announced that the Armoured Corps was ready to put a stop to the water diverting operations even at that range.

General Elazar decided to station a tank unit above Kurazim, opposite the locality where the Syrians were digging the new river bed, at a range of eleven kilometres. When it was seen that the Syrians were preparing a new border incident, General Tal paid a visit to the tank unit. Lieutenant-Colonel Oshri led him to one of the Centurions standing under its camouflage netting. The unit was located inside a ravine on top of a hill. He invited General Tal to enter the tank whose crew was one of the best and whose gun was looked after by an excellent gunner. The general wished to fire the gun himself in order to check his doctrine in practice. They were expecting a flare-up because members of the border settlements had begun to work their fields near the borders. It was the usual practice of the Syrians to interfere with any work done along the border, and there was no reason to believe this time would be an exception.

Commanding the tanks was Colonel Shlomo. Colonel Mandi set up the large field binoculars on a tripod at a suitable spot close to the tanks. To correct the firing, he would use his field telephone, the wires of which stretched to the Centurion tank in which General Tal was the gunner. Colonel Mandi was not in favour of his commander taking part in an engagement. In his opinion General Tal was endangering himself unnecessarily, and he had plucked up enough courage to tell him so. But the general, who had already heard similar remarks from his superiors and even from the chief-of-staff himself, argued that outside of books this was the only way a G.O.C.A.C. could learn about warfare in peacetime.

Colonel Mandi's fears were certainly justified. If a battle developed it would be fierce, for it would involve the strong Syrian positions on the Golan Heights. The Israeli positions could expect heavy shelling from Syrian mortars and artillery, besides tank gun-fire. The observers had already noted four Syrian tanks on Hill 62 (also known as Observation Hill) as well as anti-tank guns and considerable artillery.

The two forces faced each other at a range of 2000 metres. The Israeli unit occupied positions in a ravine between two stone walls along the bed of the old conduit, above Kurazim and some fifty metres above sea level. Should an incident flare up, the tanks would have to move to firing positions which were exposed to the Syrian positions on Observation Hill. The Syrian targets stretched across terrain shaped like an S. In its frontal, elevated section was the observation Hill position, and in its exposed sector the Syrian tanks waited in their emplacements, revealing only their guns and the upper part of their turrets. That sector was at a range of 2000 metres from the Israeli ravine in which the Zahal tank unit waited. The Syrian fortified position rose 300 metres above sea level. On the slopes of the S, hidden from sight, waited the heavy mortars and guns of the Syrian artillery. In the upper and more distant sector of the S, eleven kilometres away, two tractors and earth-moving equipment were levelling the terrain for the Jordan diversion project.

Colonel Shlomo detailed the crews. There were two main tasks. In the event of an incident, the Centurions were first to engage the enemy tanks on Observation Hill and set them ablaze, and then to fire at the tractors working on the diversion project. The task of the Shermans was to block the escape of the tractors while the Centurions attempted to hit them. On the orders of General Elazar the Israeli artillery was to silence the Syrian artillery. A final observation revealed three dug-in tanks on Observation Hill. A fourth tank which had been spotted there on previous occasions seemed to have disappeared. Hence the three Syrian tanks were divided among the Centurions. Lieutenant Ilan Yakuel was in command of one of the tanks.

As usual the unit was gripped with tension. In all probability the other side was experiencing the same feeling, though perhaps somewhat less, for the Syrians knew what they were going to do, while the Israelis were obliged to wait.

When morning came, the Israeli tractors went down to plough the fields near the border. A minor breakdown delayed their work but by 10.30 they had resumed operations and one of the tractors began ploughing long furrows extending right up to the border. From a distance the tractor looked like a beetle, drawing ever closer to the Syrians and then at the last moment swinging away to start a new furrow; back and forth and back and forth. From experience the tankers knew that the Syrians' nerves would not hold out for long; that they would soon open fire. The entire unit was on full alert.

At 10.45 a.m. the Syrian positions opened fire on the Israeli tractor, wounding the driver. A rescue squad which rushed to extricate the man was also met with machine gun fire from the Syrian position. Immediately the crews whipped the netting off their tanks, and the drivers drove them at a brisk pace into their firing positions.

Lieutenant-Colonel Oshri, half his body exposed above the turret, handled the Centurion's gun rapidly and expertly. While still traversing the turret, he called: "Gun, shell, 1800, on!"

The loader called out: "Loaded!"

General Tal turned the ammunition selector to gun position, set 1800 metres on the sights, called: "Shell, 1800" and began to locate the target.

The second Centurion tank, delayed by a sudden mechanical failure, failed to reach its firing position in time. The third Centurion, in which Shalom Cohen was gunner, and Oshri's

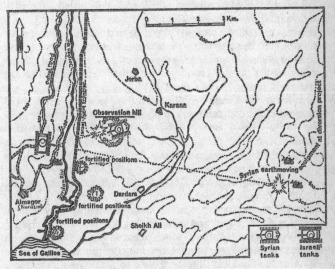

2 *The battle of 12 August 1965, in which General Tal and Lieutenant-Colonel Oshri took part.*

tank reached the firing position together, almost as though the two Centurions were involved in a race.

"On," called General Tal the moment his gun was on target.

"On," called Sergeant Shalom Cohen in his tank.

"Fire!" called Lieutenant-Colonel Oshri.

"Firing!" called General Tal and pressed the trigger.

"Firing!" called Shalom Cohen, pressing his trigger at the same moment.

General Tal hit his Syrian tank with the second shot, as did Sergeant Shalom Cohen. However, Lieutenant-Colonel Oshri was a quicker tank commander than the commander of Shalom Cohen's tank, and realising that the second Centurion was still held up, he took on the Syrian tank earmarked for it

93

and traversed his turret in its direction. The Syrian tank, which was further away than the others, had already begun to flee from its emplacement as soon as it saw its two neighbours ablaze. Oshri traversed his turret towards the fleeing Syrian tank, and at 3000 metres General Tal stopped it with a long shot which fell ahead of it. Again the driver seemed to panic for a moment, and stopped the tank. Oshri pinpointed gunner Tal on to the Syrian tank. "On," called Tal, and "Firing!" and the shell scored a direct hit.

Within three minutes the three Syrian tanks had been set ablaze. But the Syrians now laid on a heavy bombardment, and the opposing artilleries began to exchange fire. The Syrian shells were drawing nearer to the Israeli tanks, some falling extremely close. As the three Syrian tanks were on fire the Israelis excluded the possibility that these accurate shots could be from tanks and came to the conclusion that they were mortar shells. The Shermans with their French guns began to block the retreat of the Syrian tractors, eleven kilometres away, as they had been detailed. But their success was only partial. The Centurions with their new 105mm British gun began shooting at one of the tractors, but to correct the fire Colonel Mandi and tank commander Captain Ori had to wait what seemed an age, for many seconds went by between the shell leaving the gun and its arrival at the target area. Hence the job of the Centurions which silenced the Syrian tanks on Observation Hill was completed long before the Centurions firing at the far-away tractors began to place their shots close to their targets.

Oshri now ordered his driver to bring the tank to its new firing position against the tractors operating on the diversion project. The driver began to move the Centurion out of its position. At that moment Oshri discovered where the accurate Syrian shots were coming from. It was no mortar, but a tank, the fourth Syrian tank, which the Israeli observers had not yet noticed. A shell homed down on him.

Colonel Mandi turned his head away from the big field binoculars to watch the approaching Centurion, the noise of whose motor could be heard above the din of the bombardment. Startled, Mandi noticed that the turret of the Centurion was black, and that the commander's cupola and the aerial were gone. What surprised him even more was that nobody seemed to be in the turret. Realising immediately that something had happened he ordered first-aid to the spot immediately. He could see that the Centurion had been hit but still did not know by what, for the shots from the Syrian tank had rained down with the mortar bombardment. From Colonel Shlomo's command post officers ran out under heavy shelling towards the damaged tank. With the help of General Tal inside the tank, they pulled Lieutenant Colonel Oshri out. His overalls did not hold the injured commander's weight properly, and he fell from their hands on to the ground. General Tal climbed out of the tank, his clothes red with Oshri's blood.

A shell fragment had pierced Lieutenant-Colonel Oshri's skull. He lay on the ground unconscious, a gurgling sound in his throat. He breathed with great difficulty.

"Free his intercom harness," someone called out.

Hearing the order, Oshri instinctively moved his hands to his chest as though wishing to pull open the hook on his harness. But it was only a convulsive movement. A jeep removed the wounded. The gunner of another tank was wounded in his chest, Lieutenant Zeital had a leg injury. Oshri was flown by helicopter to hospital.

Meanwhile the Centurion commanded by Captain Ori finished off its task. The Syrian tractor eleven kilometres away was hit and burst into flames. After three hours, at 1340 hours, the shooting ceased.

General Tal, together with some of his officers, rushed to the hospital. The gunner with the wound in his chest died after surgery. The surgeons who had operated on Oshri did not believe he would live. On a bench near the operating theatre, General Tal saw Lieutenant Ilan Yakuel weeping. "Benny, I promise you: if you live, I'll sign up for another year. It's a vow, Benny."

When Oshri regained consciousness, Lieutenant Ilan Yakuel told him: "Well, Benny, I'll have to keep the vow I made. You're alive and I shall sign on for another year in the regular army."

"What terrific armour those Centurions have," Oshri said. "In any other tank we would have been blown to pieces."

News of Ilan Yakuel's vow reached General Tal and he asked that the young officer be invited for an interview with him. A short while later Ilan became the general's adjutant.

By now the Centurion had attained full rehabilitation. Confidence in it was so high that its earlier faults were spoken of jokingly. Officers who had been sceptical of the British tank's capabilities and had claimed that it was a complicated piece of British machinery, suited perhaps to England's lawns but not to the Negev dust, became its most enthusiastic champions.

CHAPTER THIRTEEN

And so border incident followed border incident, and it seemed inevitable that there would be another war. Less than a year later the whole army was under canvas, waiting. In General Tal's division the tension was rising. In the division's war room information had been received of a steady strengthening of the Egyptian forces in the Rafa region, of minefields being extended and of movements of Egyptian armoured units. Each increase in enemy strength necessitated bringing up to date the plans of the division and its units.

On 27 May 1967 an armoured half-track of one of the reconnaissance patrols touched off a mine near Kerem Shalom, a sector in which the Egyptians had been constantly building up their strength. The half-track got stuck and an enemy unit of armoured personnel carriers prepared to attack the damaged Israeli vehicle. The commander of the Israeli reconnaissance patrol, Lieutenant Avi, had a broken shoulder, and the party was having difficulty extricating the wounded from the half-track. In the division's war room it was believed that an Egyptian intelligence force wanted to kidnap members of the Israeli patrol for intelligence purposes. The divisional commander was most anxious to prevent this, but the orders he had been given were clear: Avoid serious border incidents. Hence he was looking for a way of recovering the damaged half-track and the wounded without having to involve many men. In the meantime he ordered the patrol commander not to abandon the damaged half-track and to prepare to defend it. After three hours the Egyptians gave up hope of an easy snatch and retired. All wireless and radio transmissions had been shut down and orders were given by means of field telephones and runners.

Egyptian provocations along the Gaza Strip continued to increase. In the intelligence room there was speculation as to what were the Egyptian high command's intentions. Were these provocations intended to bait Israel into open warfare, so that later Egypt could accuse Israel of aggression, or were the provocations locally inspired actions of the para-military Palestinian units, such as the "Liberation Army" of Shukeiry, aimed at pushing both Israel and Egypt into an armed confrontation? Extreme caution was essential and General Tal's

directives were strict; no one was to open fire under any circumstances unless specifically ordered to do so by him.

On 29 May at 12.35 p.m. the Egyptians opened fire on an
Israeli patrol under the command of the commanding officer
of the 22nd Brigade. The commanding officer had gone out
with the patrol in order to see for himself the situation along
the inflamed border. The attack occurred near Kibbutz Be'eri.
The Egyptian force was considerably superior in numbers
and was carrying mortars as well as automatic weapons. The
brigade commander, fearing for the safety of his men, requested permission to open fire with the artillery of his brigade support unit. A runner left the war room and made for
General Tal's caravan.

The commander's caravan was covered with a net; nobody
was allowed to come near it in a vehicle of any sort, but had
to make his way to the general on foot from a parking lot in
a nearby copse. When the runner arrived the general was having a quiet academic discussion with a professor of chemistry
from the Hebrew University, who had been mobilised. The
general had made his acquaintance while at the university in
Jerusalem and meeting him in one of his units had invited
him to his caravan for a chat.

The messenger from the war room entered the caravan,
stood stiffly to attention and saluted. From where he sat,
leaning on a couch, the general acknowledged the salute.

"Sir, the commander of 22nd Brigade requests authority to
use artillery in order to extricate his patrol," the runner said.

"Permission refused," replied the general.

The runner saluted and hurried out.

The professor asked if the general thought that the Egyptians would drop gas bombs near the border, although on their
side of it there was a dense Arab population. The prevailing
winds blew in the direction of the Gaza Strip as well and were
liable to carry the gas into the Arab populated centres there.

The general's clerk lifted the receiver of the telephone.
"Division's operations officer Kalman wants to speak to you,
Sir," she said.

"Kalman? Tal here."

"Sir, the Egyptians have extended their area of bombardment. Be'eri and other settlements are now being shelled and
many fires have broken out."

"Open radio networks for listening purposes only, repeat,
not for speaking, for listening only, and stay by the tele-

phones," the general ordered. He went back to the sofa and sat down. His eyes were red from lack of sleep, and his finger circled round and round his cheek in a movement reminiscent of somebody curling his sideburns.

The runner entered again and saluted. "Sir, the operations officer informs you: The commander of the 22nd Brigade has managed to extricate the patrol without artillery fire. The operations officer asks whether the radio networks can be closed?"

"Permission given," said the general.

The runner saluted and departed.

Colonel Herzl, the division's chief-of-staff, came into the caravan and saluted. He sat on a chair and reported that an S/10 Battalion tank had touched off a mine. The brigade commander, Colonel Shmuel, had investigated and found that it was one of our own mines. There were no casualties. One track had been damaged. Colonel Shmuel had ordered: 1. To make it known in his brigade that a Centurion tank had touched off a mine and that its crew had escaped unharmed, and 2. the appointment of an enquiry commission to establish the blame. After General Tal and Colonel Herzl had had a brief discussion, the colonel left the trailer.

The general and the professor returned to their business. The professor was dressed in a light, worn, khaki shirt. His trousers were too wide and were held up by a narrow leather belt which went around his waist almost twice. He wore shoes and purple-coloured socks. His face was pale.

When the professor got up to leave, the general asked him if he had been given somewhere to sleep. The professor replied that somebody had given him a sleeping-bag and that he would sleep on the ground.

"Out of the question," the general said and issued orders to equip, clothe and accommodate the professor.

In 'S' Brigade war room, a tent covered with camouflage netting, staff officers and unit commanders were seated on benches in front of a large wall map pinned to a huge board. Intelligence officers had clipped a transparent sheet of nylon over the map and using coloured chinagraphs they marked in the dispositions of the Israeli forces and those of the enemy. Colonel Shmuel, the brigade commander, and his officers had just returned from an Orders Group at divisional headquarters, where the brigade intelligence officer had been furnished with information at the divisional intelligence room. This was now being recorded on the map by his assistants, as forecasts, graphs and tabulated information.

The military policemen on guard duty at the entrance to the war room stiffened to attention and saluted.

"Attention!"

Everyone came to attention. Colonel Shmuel entered with quick, decisive steps, his gait somehow creating the impression that he was struggling upstream against a strong current. He was of average height, his rump protruding somewhat in his tight trousers, and with a slight paunch so that in profile his figure resembled the letter S. He was muscular, without an ounce of flaccidity, and as tensile as a ball.

"Be seated!"

Colonel Shmuel removed the black beret from his head and threw it on to the only chair in the war room, his own chair, standing next to the maps. His hair was close-cut and his face shining with the cleanliness of a close shave on a tough beard. He was wearing spectacles.

"Who marked this?"

"I did, Sir," said Major Casey, the intelligence officer.

"Rub it out. It's incorrect. That axis takes a left-turn to that thicket, not a right-turn."

The intelligence officer picked up a duster dipped in benzine and erased the offending line. He did it very carefully so as not to touch or smudge other lines.

"Erase it all," barked the brigade commander.

Major Casey began to wipe out all the markings.

"Quicker!"

Meanwhile he had caught sight of the plan showing an estimate of enemy minefields. With a quick, almost imperceptible movement, he tore the plan off the board, crumpled it up in his hand and threw it into the centre of the tent.

"How long does it take to draw up such a plan correctly?"

"Fifteen minutes, Sir," said Lieutenant Mike.

"Get it here in ten minutes," said the brigade commander and turned towards his secretary, a junior officer. "Make a note of that, Tzipi. Ten minutes."

Major Casey had finished redoing the chart and had begun to tabulate the estimated strength and make-up of the enemy forces in the brigade's sector.

"Where's this information from?" Colonel Shmuel asked in a cold voice.

"Divisional intelligence, Sir," said the intelligence officer.

"And you remember it by heart?"

"Yes, Sir," said the officer. He was tall and stout and beads of perspiration were rolling down his chin.

"Didn't you write it down in your notebook?" the commander asked.

"It is written in my notebook, Sir, but I've worked on it so many times that I remember it."

"You don't remember a thing. And what you have written is incorrect."

The major looked at the list he had tabled. A hush fell upon the war room. Nobody moved from where they were sitting, not even to take a swipe at a bothersome fly.

"Open your notebook and take another look at it," said the brigade commander.

The major flipped his notebook open and immediately saw where he had made a mistake. He had mixed up the number of tanks of one enemy unit with that of another unit. He began to erase the two incorrect lines, again doing it very carefully. Colonel Shmuel took the duster from him and roughly wiped out the entire tabulation. The nylon was now as clean as new. Glancing through the pages in the intelligence officer's notebook and then through his own, he started drawing a new tabulation with a sure and precise hand. When he had finished he picked up a long pointer and stood at the side of the maps.

"The situation is worsening. The Egyptians are laying mines. New minefields have been laid here, and here, and here," he indicated each position on the map with his pointer. "Minebelts have been added here, here and here. In our sector armoured units have been added, mostly T/34s. Two brigades of Egyptian armour are deployed in our sector and Egyptian artillery dispositions are still being reinforced. It is possible that other tank forces are also located in our sector. Those are the changes. The rest remains as previously. The intelligence officer will later provide you with the corrected deployments.

"We have two problems: Mines and artillery. We shall try to move along the axes and so avoid the mines. The air force will attend to the artillery. An attack at brigade strength, not at battalion strength, will be made on Rafa. During the last few days the Rafa opening has been considerably reinforced."

A lieutenant appeared at the entrance to the war room, puffing and blowing. He walked over to the colonel. "Sir ..." he began, but got no further.

"Who taught you not to salute?" demanded Colonel Shmuel.

The lieutenant left the tent, returned, came stiffly to attention and saluted smartly. The brigade commander acknowledged the salute. "Sir," said the lieutenant, "the General wishes to inform you 'Grasshopper 1', Sir." The lieutenant again jumped to attention and saluted. As he walked out of the tent he saluted once more.

Disappointment showed on the colonel's face as he returned the pointer to its place in the corner. At that moment his secretary, Tzipi, said: "Ten minutes, Sir." The words were hardly out of her mouth when Lieutenant Mike came into the war room, saluted and gave Colonel Shmuel a chart.

"You must understand, Mike, that when you indicate a minefield you have to be precise; show exactly where it begins and where it ends. What's more, you must note down each and every change. *You* won't be attacking with the spearhead company; *you* won't be the one to touch off a mine. You'll be sitting at main headquarters. But the battalions will be attacking, and perhaps someone will get killed because of your error. Very good. You managed it in ten minutes and the chart is precise. Sit down."

The colonel turned to his officers.

"T.T.T." he said.

"Attention!" cried the war room duty sergeant.

Everybody sprang to their feet. The colonel saluted and left, followed by his company of officers. "T.T.T.", the initials for "Total Tail Tucking", was repeated over and over again, with bitter disappointment. If there had been a plan to counter the steps taken by the Egyptian Army and those of other Arab countries by military confrontation, it had been shelved.

The brigade commander returned to his caravan. "Georgy," he said to his personnel officer, "can you at least organise a hot shower?" Georgy knew the colonel was displeased; "T.T.T." was not at all to his liking, and if he was thinking of a hot shower it meant he thought it would be some time before another incident occurred which might result in war.

"I'll ask Kibbutz Tzeilim for a hot shower, Sir."

"Ask for two," the colonel said. "One for yourself as well."

The colonel sat in his caravan, his fingers tapping on the table in front of him, and humming to himself the one and only tune he knew, ya ba ba ba bim-bom. Suddenly he brought the palms of his hands down on the table with a bang, stood up and said: "There will be war. There's bound to be war. It's unavoidable."

When Georgy returned with the news that a shower had been arranged, the colonel said: "Georgy, I feel in a better mood now. It's quite clear that there's going to be war. It just can't happen otherwise."

Colonel Shmuel climbed into the driver's seat of the jeep. Tzipi joined them (the trip would take them past the paratroops camp at which her boy-friend was stationed) and sat at his right. Behind them sat Georgy and the brigade commander's signalman, earphones clamped to his head. An escorting jeep armed with a machine gun led the way at the prescribed distance ahead. All the men in the escorting jeep wore steel helmets. It was already dark and the two jeeps switched on their small, blue-painted lights. Ahead of him all the colonel could see was the red tail-light of his escorts' jeep. He deliberately slowed down to check if his escort would notice; Brigade Commander Shmuel's movement orders were among the strictest in the Armoured Corps. The escorting jeep began to draw away, but then quickly slowed down. Colonel Shmuel stopped his jeep and switched the motor off. At once the escorting jeep swung round and raced towards the vehicle.

"Anything wrong, Sir?" asked the sergeant excitedly, though obviously also somewhat relieved to see the colonel was all right.

"Nothing wrong. Very good. Drive behind now."

The route was a mass of troops, with enormous trucks loaded with ammunition, fuel, food and military supplies parked along the sides. Two jeeps driven by paratroopers passed the jeeps of the battalion commander and his escort. They were moving fast, with their head-lights on so that the bright beams lit up the roadway and the troops and supply lorries. They had no shirts on and their heads were uncovered. The sight of the carelessly dressed paratroopers and their disregard for strict security regulations always raised Colonel Shmuel's hackles. He repeatedly claimed that the Armoured Corps, which was not a volunteer force, was equal in every respect to the paratroops, which was a volunteer force. This time the two paratroopers infuriated the colonel for an additional reason. He had found out about Tzipi's boy-friend in the paratroops and that particular paratrooper was immediately put into his black books.

102

"What do the paratroop boys have that armour doesn't?" he demanded of Tzipi.

The question embarrassed the charming young officer, but her reply, "I simply met a nice fellow and later he volunteered for the paratroops," did not satisfy Colonel Shmuel.

"All right, Tzipi. So what? He can apply for a transfer to armour, can't he?"

"But Sir, he's a platoon commander. He has responsibilities."

"So drop him, Tzipi."

"Drop my boy-friend, Sir?"

"Why not? I'll introduce you to a thousand nice fellows in the brigade, superior to your paratrooper in every respect. Or perhaps you are one of those girls who fall in love with their spotted uniforms?"

"No, Sir. Uniforms are of no importance to me at all."

"Or perhaps the red beret attracted you? Don't tell me now that red is nicer than black?"

"The black is very nice," Tzipi hastened to assure him.

"Or do you find that the red boots of the paratroopers are nicer than the boots of the armoured corps?"

"Not at all," Tzipi said.

"Ah, Tzipi. A lovely girl like you, a high-school graduate, well-read, shouldn't fall for a uniform."

Tzipi explained once more that it was not the uniform which attracted her, nor did mere outward appearances impress her. Her boy-friend was an excellent student and intended to become a doctor. He had volunteered for the paratroops to be with his friends.

"All right, Tzipi," said the brigade commander jovially. "First love is not necessarily true love. You'll grow wiser and fall in love with a tanker. Am I right, Georgy?"

"Correct, Sir."

"On that understanding," said the colonel, stopping his jeep near the paratroops camp, "I allow you to get off here. Leave granted until 2100 hours."

"Thank you, Sir," said Tzipi.

When they drove into the kibbutz, Georgy directed the colonel to the apartment of one of the members. The whole family was waiting for the brigade commander. They all wanted to see him. The father, mother and three children were waiting in the dining room and the table was laid with refreshments, fruit and coffee, as though the colonel was their weekend guest. The electric boiler had been switched on and there was now plenty of hot water for the colonel's shower.

Kibbutz Tzeilim is near the Gaza Strip border which meant that if the Egyptians attacked it would be right on the front line. The farmers went about their work armed. There was much coming and going in the kibbutz yard, and the youngest of the three children had escaped from his mother to see what was going on. His mother was furious with him for vanishing from her sight at such a tense time, and told him to go and do his homework, which he did, with obvious reluctance. While the colonel was taking his shower, the family waited in hushed silence, as though participating in some ceremony. He was in the bathroom for a considerable time, removing with difficulty the Negev dust, of which there were several days' layers encrusted on him.

When he reappeared he examined the children's knowledge of the Bible, much of which he remembered by heart, and then sat down to discuss defence matters with the elders of the family. He assured and reassured them that if war broke out, and even if the Egyptians struck first, the war would quickly be carried into enemy territory.

Back in his caravan, Colonel Shmuel reached a decision. He asked Tzipi to connect him with the divisional commander. When the field-telephone had made contact with General Tal, the colonel requested another intelligence officer to replace Major Casey. The divisional commander agreed. Lieutenant-Colonel Zwicka would report to Colonel Shmuel the following day.

That was General Tal's approach; always support Number One. If Number One is no good, replace him, but as long as he stays on the job he is entitled to the full confidence of his superiors. On one occasion, Colonel Shmuel's operations officer requested an interview with General Tal and asked to be relieved of his post; he had felt that his and the colonel's characters were incompatible. He was told: "Had Colonel Shmuel asked me to replace you, I would have done so at once. But the fact that your natures are incompatible is completely irrelevant. It is your job to adapt yourself to Colonel Shmuel and not he to you."

"But, Sir, I cannot work with him."

"That is an impertinence. As brigade commander he is the one to decide with whom he can work and with whom he cannot."

"But surely, Sir, a person's nature can also be taken into consideration. Isn't that so?"

"Nature has nothing to do with it. Only orders. You receive an order and you carry it out, that is all. The army is not a debating society nor an institute for matching off compatible couples. Get back to your job. Leave it only when Colonel Shmuel orders you to."

"Yes, Sir!"

CHAPTER FOURTEEN

Colonel Shmuel drove his jeep through the darkness. Ahead was only the red rear-light of the jeep escort. Lying beside him was a Thompson submachine gun, its spare magazines close to hand. He was not partial to the Uzzi submachine gun. In his opinion its 0.9 calibre was too small. This was to be his last visit to his units before the war.

Colonel Shmuel was born in Vilna, Lithuania, on the eve of Passover 1930. His father was an upholsterer and a Talmud scholar, who believed the Messiah would come not riding a white donkey but in the form of Israel's independence. When Shmuel was three and a half years old the family emigrated to Palestine and settled in Givat Shaul in Jerusalem. The father opened a furniture shop there but it was not a success, and he went back to working as an upholsterer. During its hard times the family – father, mother, three daughters and three sons – lived in one room. To support the family, the mother also worked. She was employed in a metal foundry which in 1940 began manufacturing mines for the British Army.

Shmuel grew up in an atmosphere of restrictions: in Cheder, at the Yeshiva and at home. The constant question, is it allowed or is it forbidden, stood in his way at every turn. His father demanded discipline, respect and no nonsense. In some ways this was a remarkable preparation for Shmuel's future in the Armoured Corps. Until he was sixteen, he studied at the Etz Hayim Yeshiva and was an excellent pupil. At the Yeshiva he became accustomed to thoroughness and tenacity of purpose, and learned to overcome fatigue. His teacher, Rabbi Yedler, made it a practice that each day at a certain moment, usually ten minutes before sunset, the students should begin studying with redoubled vigour. At a given signal, the tired and hungry boys would conquer their lassitude and renew their studies with enthusiasm.

At one time he had been a zealous champion of the sanctity of the Sabbath Day ("But for the Arabs and the wars I would most probably have become the commander of the Sabbath Day Zealots in Jerusalem instead of commanding a tank brigade," he once said). But one day he had turned up at the Yeshiva with his sidelocks shorn. His head was unshaven, and a lock of hair curled up over his forehead. His father did not upbraid him, believing in the maxim: "Better they should sin in ignorance than sin knowingly." His father died a year before Israel's independence, when Shmuel was already an active member of the Haganah in Jerusalem area.

When he was thirteen, Shmuel volunteered for service in a religious youth unit of the Haganah. Now, twenty-four years later, he reflected that this would be his third war in Egypt.

They were now nearing his battalions, but there was not a light visible nor a sound to be heard. He felt proud of the strict discipline he had instilled; he turned to his personnel officer.

"A nation such as ours, Georgy, must always be prepared for war. Otherwise it will perish."

"Yes, Sir."

Colonel Shmuel hummed as he used to in his childhood. Ya-ba-ba-bim-bom. He was very tired. For several days he had not slept. But when he saw shadows materialising out of the darkness, he became wide awake. As he parked his jeep next to that of his escort, a tall silhouette approached him, Major Ehud Alad, commander of the S/14 Patton Battalion.

"The battalion is ready, Sir."

"Good work, Ehud. I drove through the battalion's deployment area and neither saw nor heard a thing. The discipline is perfect."

Major Elad accompanied the colonel. It was not every day that one got a compliment from the brigade commander, Ehud was pleased. They walked in complete darkness until they came to a spot marked with whitewash, and stopped.

"Attention!"

Two jeeps stationed by a long rectangle of troops, seated on the ground, who sprang to attention at the command, switched on their headlights and caught the brigade commander and the battalion commander in four intersecting beams of light.

"The brigade commander will speak to you," Ehud told his men.

106

"Be seated," said Colonel Shmuel, his voice more gentle than usual. The rustle of movement and the dull thud of submachine guns knocking against the ground was heard and then – complete silence. The lights blinded Colonel Shmuel and he could not see the faces of the men in front of him.

"You may smoke," he said.

Several matches were struck. The faces of the men were briefly illuminated. Then the sound of the first exhalation was heard, like a sigh of relief. Gradually the darkness became flecked with sparks.

Colonel Shmuel knew that in the brigade it was jestingly said that they were more scared of him than of the war; to which he would reply that he did not mind what the men thought of him as long as they obeyed his orders. He wanted discipline, and the Standing Orders drawn up by General Tal had been made even more severe in his brigade. The One Kilometre Order, as it was known, gained him high notoriety among Zahal drivers. The order stated that drivers of 'S' Brigade were allowed to drive at the speed laid down in General Staff Orders less one kilometre per hour and less ten k.p.h. in the Beersheba area. Thus he was able to try offending drivers himself. He would also give advance notice to the Military Police of movements of brigade units so that they could set up road traps in good time. There was soon a drop in the number of accidents involving the brigade's vehicles, until one month not a single accident occurred – an achievement which was praised by the chief-of-staff.

Colonel Shmuel found that accidents also resulted from driving vehicles when they were not in good condition. He maintained that the Armoured Corps had sufficient workshops to make sure that the brigade's vehicles were in good condition. He would send inspection squads to make surprise checks and any vehicle which lacked water or oil, or had a shaky steering wheel, or any other deficiency, was taken away from the unit and sent to a workshop for repair. The brigade's unit commanders grumbled that because of this system they were unable to carry out the tasks assigned to them but Colonel Shmuel was uncompromising and demanded absolute obedience. Within three months vehicles were in better condition. Unit commanders quickly formed the habit of checking them most carefully to avoid their vehicles being caught by the brigade commander's inspection squads. Sometimes Colonel Shmuel himself would catch and sentence offenders, for driving in a jeep without a steel helmet, for failing to lace

107

their boots in the brigade's prescribed manner, or for buckling their belt with the clasp on the left side.

Deep in his heart Colonel Shmuel wanted his troops to like him, and he believed that when the real test came they would appreciate his sternness. In this he relied to some extent upon the reputation he had as a fearless fighter, for troops respect a brave and able commander. Occasionally he would compete against the brigade's best gunners and tank drivers. He had already told his unit commanders that in the event of a battle he would fly a large black flag from his tank, so the men would know where their commander was, in the thick of the battle.

"Men," Colonel Shmuel said, "all the Arab armies have now taken up arms against us: Egypt, Jordan, Syria, Iraq and Kuwait, Saudi Arabia and Algeria, and who knows who else will join them tomorrow. Many against one. That is good. That is very good. That way we shall be able to smash them all in one good blow. In our sector we have Egyptians. I know them well. I have fought against them three times, twice in Sinai. This time also, I promise you, we'll light a few bonfires in their tanks, a little Lag B'Omer, and they'll run."

A murmur of satisfaction was heard passing through the rows of seated men.

"We shall have a war like the war of 1948. Maybe even greater. We'll thrash them as we did in 1948 and in 1956. Because you are better soldiers than they are. Better trained and braver. After all I know you personally, and if the politicians let us, we shall be in El-Arish within twelve hours."

A wave of contentment rode through the ranks. More cigarettes were lit.

"And if they let us, we shall reach the canal, and at long last be able to wash our feet."

Laughter. The pressure of three weeks of waiting escaping.

"No, I am not just being funny. You know well enough that when I promise something I keep my word. And when you get to that canal, I must ask you to remember one thing – that one kilometre of ours."

The laughter rose and was now hearty, that of an intimate gathering of friends.

"And if you behave yourselves, I might even let you exceed the speed limit. But only when you're travelling in the right direction. To Cairo. Abdul Nasser says he'll be in Tel Aviv. I promise you this, you'll be in Cairo first. You'll replace him with another Egyptian; one who respects the rights of other nations and shows respect for the Jewish people."

Ripples of satisfaction and pleasure flowed through the ranks. Colonel Shmuel's words had relieved the tension and sown confidence to such an extent that the men forgot where they were and began talking to one another, exchanging impressions, as though their formidable commander was not standing in front of them.

"However!"

Complete silence.

"I will not tolerate lawlessness."

Utter silence enveloped the darkened field, with Colonel Shmuel and Major Ehud looming out of it like legendary giants. The soldiers thought he was referring to their conduct; that the slight liberty they had taken in talking among themselves was considered anarchy.

"And these are the things I mean by lawlessness. The wrong use of ammunition. That is lawlessness. Do not fire your guns at unarmoured vehicles or at troops. For these 0.5 and 0.3 machine guns will do, and on troops use your Uzzis. Not machine guns. It's a waste of ammunition. And now for one last word."

Again, complete silence.

"Men, if we do not win, we have nowhere to come back to."

An officer stepped into the beams of light. "Men, now all together, give it everything you've got. Aleh!"

"Krav!" answered the whole battalion with one rousing voice.

"Aleh!"

"Krav!"

"Aleh!"

"Krav, Krav, Krav!"

The echoes died away in the distance like the thunder of guns.

"Attention!"

The battalion stood up. The brigade commander and battalion commander saluted and the headlights of the jeeps were extinguished. Immediately complete darkness prevailed. The men returned to the tanks which were dispersed in the open beneath camouflage nets. Their receding footsteps could be heard as they trod on their rubber soles in the soft sand.

The officers gathered in the operations tent, where they were served black coffee and sandwiches. Colonel Shmuel was given a bottle of Scotch whisky and asked to autograph it, then Ehud and the other officers added their signatures. On this occasion they would drink only half the bottle; the other half would be drunk on the day of victory. The bottle was passed from hand to hand as each one signed it, then given to Colonel Shmuel to take the first sip.

"In actual fact we are already at war. Remember that we in Israel are only the vanguard of the Jewish people. If we are weak, if we don't stand fast, our generation will be to blame for the destruction of the Third Temple. General Tal says that the outcome of the war depends upon the success of our division. And I say the success of the division depends upon the success of our brigade," said Colonel Shmuel.

Later he inspected the battalion's operational plans. In his relations with the battalion commander, Major Ehud, there was respect and understanding. He found the plans good, made a few more remarks and left the tent accompanied by the battalion commander. A group of soldiers swarmed round the brigade commander's jeep, each wanting to shake his hand, to remind him where they had served and shared experiences together. Suddenly a soldier whose long sidelocks stood out from a pale face, burst into the closed circle surrounding Colonel Shmuel, threw both arms round him and kissed him on the cheek. He mumbled a blessing, and finished it with: "May God look after you."

Colonel Shmuel stood transfixed with emotion. Never before had a soldier kissed him. "Who was that?" he asked when only Major Ehud remained with him.

"The sergeant from the Army Rabbinate Service."

"Clean-shaven?"

"Have you forgotten, Sir? You ordered all beards shaved off. For the gasmasks."

"Of course. Well, Ehud, I won't say 'be seeing you', because before that we'll be hearing from one another."

The brigade commander's jeep and that of his escort were swallowed up in the darkness, on their way to the next of the brigade's battalions. Again Colonel Shmuel spoke about the war having already started the moment Abdul Nasser blocked the Tiran Straits, that it was a good thing there was going to be war, when all of Israel's enemies would be trounced once and for all. Again the cry "Aleh Krav!" rang out in the Negev night.

Finally he arrived at the S/10 Battalion, to the Centurions, the first of which he had brought to the country. He hardly recognised Major Shamai Kaplan, who had shaved his beard. The battalion commander, Lieutenant-Colonel Gabriel, and his deputy, Major Eli Globus, passed the autographed whisky bottle from mouth to mouth.

Then off went the jeeps of the brigade commander and his escort on their way to another unit. Some of his men, among the best and bravest, he would never see again. When he returned to his caravan he was called to the divisional commander and by the time he returned the night was half over. Colonel Shmuel called the headquarter's cook and asked for some hot soup.

"Sir," said the cook who had dressed hurriedly and was still half asleep, "I don't have any hot soup. We waited for you and warmed it up and warmed it up until it got spoiled."

"And you're not ashamed to let your commanding officer go to sleep without having anything hot?"

The cook's face reddened. "I'll make fresh soup for you, Sir."

"Ten minutes?"

"Sir, you can't make soup in ten minutes. The potatoes alone...."

"Make a couple of omelettes for me then."

"Yes, Sir."

"And a salad."

"Yes, Sir. What would you like to drink?"

"Hot-and-cold."

In other words cold soda-water and piping hot black coffee. After his meal Colonel Shmuel fell into a sound sleep.

CHAPTER FIFTEEN

On the eve of the war the Egyptians had already completed their emergency dispositions in Sinai. They had seven divisions, nine hundred and fifty tanks and about ninety thousand troops. A large force was concentrated at the Rafa Opening and a special mechanised force under the command of General Shadaly threatened to link up with Jordan and cut off Eilat. Against the Egyptian Army Zahal concentrated three divisions in northern Sinai. The southernmost was the division of General Ariel Sharon, the central division was under General Abraham Yaffe, and the northern division deployed against the Egyptian infantry and armour at the Rafa

Opening was that of General Tal. On the Israeli side of the border there were neither fortifications nor natural barriers. The only protection against Egyptian attack was Zahal, not dug in, but mobile. On the Egyptian side were strong fortifications barricading a series of passages between natural obstacles – sand dunes and mountains – which were impassable to motorised transport and tanks. Behind these impressive fortifications ranged the Egyptian Army, ready to strike.

Since the 1956 Sinai Campaign the Egyptians had adopted a defence system known as "linear dispositions", which is basically a Russian system. These dispositions were designed to defend and block the axes of advance, and in this case were bordered on both sides by obstacles, a natural one and an artificial one – minefields. A linear disposition is not a single line but extends in depth and consists of three sections: the forward defence line where the main fighting force and weapons are assembled, a deep rear defence line which serves as a second holding line if the first is overrun and also as a base for counter-attacks in support of the forward line. Both these lines consist of continuous trenches which run the full length of the disposition. Between these two lines – forward and rear – is the anti-tank locality, which contains the men and weapons – mostly tanks and anti-tank guns – whose task it is to destroy whatever force penetrates the lines and to provide covering fire. The basic strength of this defence system is that it cannot be outflanked. Any force attacking such a disposition is obliged to attempt a frontal assault, and advance upon its objective under heavy artillery bombardment. And even if it gets through the first line, although inevitably weakened by the assault, the anti-tank locality still awaits it. And if it overcomes that obstacle, there is still the rear line to deal with.

If the Egyptian Army were to break through into Israel first, the tank battles would then be mobile. If Israel broke through into Sinai, its first encounters would of necessity be break-through battles. Since its establishment, Zahal has adopted the principle of carrying the war into enemy territory, and the Armoured Corps was trained and prepared for break-through engagements. When General David Elazar was G.O.C.A.C., the doctrine for breaking through fortified objectives had first been laid down, and the subject had been further developed by General Tal, who maintained that break-throughs must be made in daylight, with tanks, while the air force destroyed the artillery. Other Zahal officers held different views. General Ariel Sharon preferred night attacks by infantry sup-

9. Pattons of S/14 Battalion entering Khan Yunis.

10. Two S/14 Battalion Pattons ablaze at the Rafa Junction.

11.   An S/14 Patton engaging a dug-in Egyptian T/34 at the southern wing of the Rafa Junction. Egyptian anti-tank guns are concealed behind the ricinus plants.

12.   The Rafa Junction: Lieutenant Avigdor Kahalany signals to Colonel Shmuel.

13. An Egyptian Stalin Mark III after the battle with Lieutenant Ein-Gil's company at the southern wing of the Rafa Junction.

14. The evening of Monday, 5 June at Rafa Junction: an Israeli helicopter evacuates the wounded.

15. The morning of Tuesday, 6 June: General Tal (*left*) and Colonel Shmuel plan the attack on Bir Lahfan, on General Tal's command half-track.

ported by armour, with the artillery being destroyed by paratroopers. (Both Generals Tal and Sharon were successful with their methods.)

In the war room, at a divisional orders group, General Tal discussed the division's position in the event of war. His division was the largest and most powerful, but against it were ranged the strongest Egyptian forces and dispositions. If his division was to break through into Egypt it would have to breach the fortified positions at the Rafa Junction, at Sheikh Zuweid, at El-Jiradi, El-Arish and Bir Lahfan. The Jiradi is a narrow defile between shifting sand dunes, stretching for eleven kilometres and defended by a series of deep and elaborate linear dispositions. Facing his division, therefore, was a formidable enemy force.

As land and air reconnaissance had been forbidden, General Tal did not have precise information on the locations of the Egyptian minefields or their network of trenches and fortifications. Hence he could only set down the general principles of his plan, which were: movement and assaults along those communication axes utilised by the enemy themselves, so as to avoid mines as much as possible; outflanking and assaults from the rear at locations where it was possible to pass through the sand dunes; and the silencing of Egyptian artillery by whatever means the air force would provide for the division.

The general prepared his commanders for a battle of attrition. The traditionally accepted ratio if success was to be assured was three to one, even five to one, for the attacker when the enemy was dug-in, fortified and ready to counter-attack, and his division was actually numerically inferior to the enemy. At best he could hope that with correct manoeuvring he would be able to engage the enemy forces at a ratio of one to one.

"It's ten years since we last met the Egyptian Army," he told his unit commanders. "If war breaks out, the first land battle will also be a test between ourselves and the Egyptian Army. Other countries, other armies, can afford to lose the first battle. Large armies can sometimes even afford to lose the second and the third. They have strategic depth in which to retreat, to recover, to learn the lessons from their defeats, to reorganise and return to the attack. We do not. We must not fail in the first battle. Remember: the side which emerges victorious from this first encounter will not only conquer a physical objective, it will achieve a psychological and a moral advantage. The winner goes over to the attack, the loser into retreat. We have nowhere to retreat to. Therefore this first battle will be a test, the outcome of which will have an immeasurable influence upon the fortunes of the war as a whole, and thus upon the fortunes of the state.

"The major offensive in the assault will be undertaken by our division, which has the best brigades in Zahal. Obviously, therefore, if our division cannot carry out the job assigned to it, it means that Zahal itself will be unable to fulfil the task that national security imposes upon it. Therefore, if war breaks out this first battle will be a battle for life or death. We will attack till the end, no matter what the cost. Officers will explain to every soldier in the division that the first battle will be the decisive one of the whole war. Only in the battles which follow, after we have won the first assault, can we take a breather."

General Tal watched the unit commanders: tankers, paratroopers, gunners, engineers, doctors. All were tense and serious. Only on the peeling face of the paratroopers' commander, Colonel Raphoul, was there a fleeting smile. Zahal did not have a commander more battle-experienced than he. It was said of him that by rights he should have been killed several times already. He could recall many occasions when it had been said: "No matter what the cost."

The Orders Group dispersed.

The term "No matter what the cost", was first introduced into Zahal by Moshe Dayan when he was head of the General Staff Branch, shortly before becoming chief-of-staff. That was in 1954 when infiltration from neighbouring Arab countries, aimed at robbery, murder, and the undermining of morale in border settlements, was at its height. Traffic to these settlements was stopped by the laying of mines and shelling from across the border. City dwellers feared to leave the precincts of the towns and the youngsters stopped going on hikes. The general public turned to Zahal, but Zahal was unable to control the situation along the borders and in the outlying areas. In the Knesset and in the press, criticism and resentment mounted at the helplessness of Zahal to put an end to the terror, and at its inability to safeguard the civilians. Zahal itself was in the middle of reorganisation, building up its formations and changing over from the combat methods of a partisan army – as it was in 1948 – to the methods of a regular army. Most of its regular troops were new immigrants who had not yet been integrated into the life of the country, and the senior officers had no confidence in their men and could not rely on the junior officers.

Nevertheless, Zahal began its reprisal actions, a policy which reached its climax in the Sinai Campaign of 1956. However, serious restrictions were imposed upon these reprisal operations – the use of shells was forbidden and sometimes even hand grenades were excluded – to avoid injury to Arab civilians. These restrictions could not help but further expose the Israeli fighter in an enemy attack. Courage and a great sense of devotion were required of the Israeli soldier to accomplish his assignment successfully, and only a few were capable of it. Time after time Zahal units returned without fulfilling their missions, when the officers would repeatedly justify themselves by saying: "Four or five of my men were hit."

To Israel's Jews after the Nazi holocaust an individual life seemed more valuable than almost anything, even national security. Zahal had to launch an intensive campaign to explain to the officers that avoiding danger to a few soldiers would in the long run endanger entire communities. But this verbal exhortation, true as it was, did not penetrate the minds of the officers and was unable to change the situation. Zahal failed in many operations. In one such case General Dayan met the officer who had failed in his assignment and asked him straight out: "How many casualties did you have?" The number did not seem to Dayan to warrant the failure of the mission and he cashiered the officer. Dayan then took it upon himself to go from command to command, assembling before him all officers from company commanders upwards. He neither lectured nor explained, but read out an unequivocal order: "Any officer in Zahal who shrinks from completing his assignment before the majority of his troops, or at least half of them, have become casualties, will be cashiered from his post."

When Dayan became chief-of-staff he assigned current security matters to a volunteer unit, which later grew into the Paratroops. Here, under the leadership of General Ariel Sharon, an extraordinary fighting spirit was created. These were soldiers who would never return without carrying out their assignment to the letter. Courage, devotion, dedication and daring became standard in this fine unit. For three years the Paratroops bore the burden of Israel's current security and carried out all the reprisal operations. During those three years they aroused the envy of the whole of Zahal. In the Paratroops it was the officers who led the assault, and their battle-cry was "Follow me!"

Major-General Dayan and the Paratroops gave Zahal yet another important rule in operational discipline: It is better to err in doing too much than too little. In his *Diary of the Sinai Campaign,* Dayan describes the disciplinary lapse of the G.O. southern command who, contrary to his orders, threw the 7th Armoured Brigade into battle twenty-four hours earlier than planned, and his anger at him for doing so. But at the end of the chapter Dayan says: "I could not deny the sympathy I felt for the premature entry of the armoured brigade into operations before being authorised. It is better to struggle with a stallion when the problem is how to hold it back, than to urge on a bull which refuses to budge."

The Paratroop Corps, which was used by Major-General Dayan as an instrument to foster the fighting spirit of Zahal, was a commando corps, and this spirit was soon to be imbued into other Zahal formations. Now, when General Tal stated that the first battle must be won "No matter what the cost", his intention was not to spur his officers on but to inform them that from the command aspect there should be no holding the stallions back.

PART THREE

THE WAR
5 June – 10 June 1967

CHAPTER SIXTEEN

Lieutenant Yossi B., the assistant operations officer of 'S' Brigade, twenty-two years old and a graduate of the Officers Cadet Academy, "stocked" his jeep in preparation for the war. Although he was used to being under fire and had aspired from boyhood to a military career, had even been wounded in border incidents, he still looked like a boy scout about to set out on a Passover hike.

Because of the prolonged state of alert, his initial supplies had run out and he had just sent his driver to Beersheba for replenishments. Lieutenant Yossi felt quite certain that war would break out and that the brigade would carry it into Sinai. He had no intention of being cut off too long from the things which made life bearable, and as his money too had run out, he had sent a note to his bank manager in Beersheba requesting him to give his driver IL.200. With this sum the driver purchased, according to the shopping list given him: films for a camera, condensed milk (sweetened) in tubes, cans of beer, bottles of dry red wine, anchovy fillets in tins, sausages, milk chocolate and butterscotch. "In a war," Yossi liked to say, smiling like a mischievous boy, "there is no need to live like a barbarian."

A lump of butterscotch was already melting in his mouth as, with the help of his driver, he loaded his private supermarket on to the rear of the jeep, a load so variegated and large that it took up the whole rear section, leaving only the two front seats free. He put the films in a haversack together with his camera. Now and again he would look up to the sky. Jet planes screamed overhead, southward, towards Egypt. After so prolonged a ban on flying over the area, they indicated a decisive shift in the situation.

"Sir, the brigade commander wants you," Colonel Shmuel's runner called to him.

"Watch the jeep, and stay on the ball," Yossi shouted to his driver. "It's started." He ran towards the brigade commander's caravan. Colonel Shmuel sat on a bench, his arms leaning on a folding table which, during the day, occupied the place of his bed. Yossi saluted.

"Yossi, organise the forward command group. Wait for orders. Who's listening in?" he called out towards the doorway of the caravan.

"I am, Sir," Tzipi replied.

"Stay next to the telephone, don't move from it."

"Yes, Sir."

Wave after wave of planes passed overhead. Colonel Shmuel had not the slightest doubt that the war had started. Any moment now he expected a phone-call from divisional headquarters informing him of "Red Sheet", the code-word announcing the end of the radio blackout. After "Red Sheet", he would begin to receive orders from the division via the division's radio network, and would be able to pass orders to his units through the battalions' radio networks.

"Are you keeping an ear open for that telephone?" he called out again.

"Yes, Sir," Tzipi replied.

His deputy, Lieutenant-Colonel Pinko, entered the caravan and saluted.

"You called for me, Sir?"

"Sit down. Pinko, I would like you to prepare a second forward command group, just in case. You understand?"

"Yes, Sir."

"I don't want you to remain with main headquarters. The operations officer will attend to that and will move the echelons up. Prepare a second forward command group for yourself, Pinko, and be ready for action at any moment."

"Yes, Sir," Lieutenant-Colonel Pinko saluted and left the caravan.

It was as though everyone sensed battle orders were imminent. Tension had been high ever since 16 May but it seemed now as if a new spirit pervaded the brigade. Every morning the engines of the tanks had been revved up, but this morning they seemed to have a new and more powerful roar. The H.Q. vehicle compound was filled with noise and smoke. Commands became brief, incisive. Things were done at the double. There were no soldiers idly resting. Every voice seemed raised a semitone.

In the brigade commander's half-track the driver warmed up the motor. Ruby, Colonel Shmuel's signals technician, wrote out twenty postcards. On each he wrote "I'm fine. How

118

are you? Yours, Ruby." He was afraid that during the war he would not be able to write home and was preparing a supply of ready-written cards. Next to him, nervous and excited, sat Shambico, the radio operator. This would be his baptism under fire. He knew that Colonel Shmuel's orders would be given at a murderous pace and that he would have to be accurate, no matter what. Deep down Shambico prayed that the order to operate the networks would be postponed. At that moment Colonel Shmuel emerged from his caravan.

"Red Sheet!" he shouted. "Open networks!"

Major Israel, the signals officer, immediately began opening the signals networks of the brigade to the division, the battalions, the companies. Runners who had been waiting all the time near the colonel's caravan jumped into jeeps, written "Red Sheet" orders in their hands, and headed for the brigade's various units. "Red Sheet!" the runners called excitedly as they handed the envelopes to the unit commanders. In a twinkling the crews had folded the camouflage netting from their tanks and taken up their battle stations. The brigade's lead units began to move forward. To the roar and smoke of the motors was added the crackling of the signals stations and the hum of their receivers. Colonel Shmuel sprang into the half-track and took his place on the raised seat, clamping headphones to his ears, one connected to the divisional network and the other to that of the brigade. The radio equipment began to crackle like the chirruping of new-born chicks breaking out of their shells in a giant hatchery. A code language only few understood blanketed everything.

"Calling all Tirah stations: This is Tirah. Sunray speaking," came the voice of General Tal over divisional radio. "Do not move before I give the order. Over."

"Prepare the command group for the move," said Colonel Shmuel.

"Get ready to move," called Yossi to the command group units. These were already marshalled to take up their position at the head of the column, with tanks bringing up the rear. In front of the rearguard tank were the jeeps, Yossi's jeep being the last before the first rearguard tank. Behind the lead tank were the command half-tracks, sprouting wireless aerials like a mobile forest.

"I'm going in the half-track," Yossi told his driver. "Drive carefully, and don't forget to collect a bayonet for me."

"Sir, you've forgotten something," the driver called out handing Yossi the haversack with the camera and films.

"Thanks." He looked down once more to make sure his load was properly secure on the back of the jeep, then after due consideration pulled out a package of butterscotch from one of the parcels and slipped it into his pocket.

Colonel Shmuel sat in the half-track, higher than the others, map in front of him, binoculars round his neck, goggles on his forehead, and headphones on his ears. He waited for the order to move. This would be the third war in his life, and he recalled what General Tal had said: "In war nothing goes according to plan, but there is one thing you must stick to: to the major designation of the plan. Drum this into your men."

The task assigned to 'S' was to take the Khan Yunis and Rafa fortified positions, to engage Sheikh Zuweid, to be ready to capture Sheikh Zuweid when ordered, to plan the capture of the El-Jiradi fortifications in a daylight attack, and to advance southwards. It was to cross the border opposite Kibbutz Nir-Oz, and its movements towards Khan Yunis and the route to the Rafa area via Gaza Strip territory were so planned as to avoid coming within radius of the enemy's concentrations of artillery fire. General Tal had assumed that the enemy would not lay down a heavy artillery barrage on to built-up and residential areas in which were Egyptian and Palestinian army units and which were densely populated. At all events he demanded a swift and silent approach, and for that reason forbade his tanks to open fire until explicitly ordered, which would be only when they were very close to their objective. For the same reason he also barred the divisional artillery from opening fire until the last moment. The general was determined not to give the enemy the slightest hint regarding his possible moves.

"Calling Tirah stations: This is Tirah," came the voice of Colonel Herzl, divisional chief-of-staff. "Do not open fire unless ordered. Over."

Colonel Shmuel's plan required S/14 Battalion to lead the attack and break through via Khan Yunis while S/10 Battalion was to enter enemy territory in the wake of S/14, part from it before Khan Yunis, turn south-west, and make gunfire contact with the Rafa fortifications at long range. Colonel Shmuel wanted to see as many enemy tanks as possible hit from a distance, so as to begin the battle with this blow to their morale. The armoured infantry battalion was to follow in the wake of S/10 and capture the outer defences of the Rafa fortifications.

The driver of the half-track switched on his transistor radio,

It was 0800 hours, Monday 5 June 1967. The news reported that enemy planes had been spotted on radar screens but that they had been driven off by the air force. In the coastal towns air-raid warnings had been sounded and the inhabitants had gone down into shelters. Following the news was the soft early-morning music of the Light Programme interrupted occasionally by the commercials.

"Calling Tirah stations. This is Tirah," came the voice of General Tal. "Do not move until I give the order. Over."

South of Colonel Shmuel's group, Colonel Raphoul's 'Z' Brigade waited for its orders. 'Z' Brigade, with the support of the T/01 Patton Battalion, had been assigned the task of taking the Rafa Junction fortifications south of the El-Arish road, and of destroying the Egyptian artillery which was in their rear. Thus the division would advance in a pincer movement on the Rafa Junction, with 'S' Brigade the western prong and 'Z' Brigade the southern. 'M' Brigade was to be held as a divisional reserve. This would be 'Z' Paratroop Brigade's first assignment acting with armoured infantry. The paratroopers would be conveyed to their assignment in half-tracks preceded by tanks opening the way for them. General Tal believed that Rafa Junction was heavily defended on both its eastern and western extremities and had directed 'Z' Brigade and T/01 Battalion to attack from Dekel in the south and to attempt to push through the sand dunes to the Egyptian defences from the rear.

"Shamir and Zebra. This is Tirah. Sunrays to the mike. Over," came the voice of General Tal to the half-tracks of Colonel Shmuel and Colonel Raphoul.

"Tirah. This is Shamir. Sunray speaking. Over."

"Tirah. This is Zebra. Sunray speaking. Over."

"Shamir and Zebra. This is Tirah. Move now and Good Luck. Over."

The time was 0815 hours.

"Calling Shamir stations. This is Shamir. Move. Move. Over," Colonel Shmuel announced over the brigade's radio network.

"Calling number two stations. This is number two. Move! Move! Over," Ehud announced over the battalion's network.

Company commanders called over their networks: "Move. Now. Follow me!" They held their flags up high, then lowered them until their arms were horizontal with the ground. Instantly a cloud of dust rose up into the morning air, engulfing the Patton battalion. A crew from the reconnaissance company,

121

and after it Lieutenant Kahalany's company, which included S/14 Battalion command group, raced for the border. The rest of the battalion crossed the border in a second column. "Move, move," cried the battalions' commander, Ehud, over the radio network from where he was standing in the commander's cupola. Civilian traffic on the roads and dirt tracks was diverted to the roadsides. The Pattons gained speed.

"Shamir. This is Tirah. Calling Sunray," came the voice of General Tal. Major Israel, the signals officer, plugged Colonel Shmuel into the divisional network.

"Tirah. This is Shamir. Sunray speaking," Shmuel said.

"Shamir. This is Tirah. Sunray speaking. Inform me the moment you cross the green line. Over."

The green line was the frontier. Colonel Shmuel ordered his command group to catch up with S/14 and move forward with it. "Stick to S/14's tail," he told Yossi B. Yossi began directing his driver, who swung the half-track into a stubble-field and began overtaking the tanks of S/10 Battalion which were moving forward in single column. The command group raced across the field, its tanks and jeeps following.

The countryside was obscured by a thick cloud of dust. The tanks left such heavy vapours in the fresh air that it was becoming difficult to breathe. Only above the trees was the air still clear. Small, fleecy clouds floated in the sky and the bright sun moved steadily in its orbit, until suddenly here too there was commotion. The sky trembled and became filled with trails of grey smoke as Fouga-Magister jets, their wings loaded with rockets, swooped down and passed in a flash, heading for the Egyptian artillery concentration in the rear of the Rafa defended zone.

At 0837 hours, when S/14 was nearing its first objectives, the divisional commander announced he had ordered the division's artillery to be ready to open anti-battery fire. The first range-finding shells had already been fired by the Egyptian artillery at the Pattons which were approaching the frontier. Colonel Zvi now ordered the artillery battalions to lay down a barrage for S/14 and the self-propelled guns began to bark; the forward observation officer advancing with S/14's armoured infantry company sent back fire corrections. By 0847 hours there were already pauses in the Egyptian artillery bombardments, and at 0848 Colonel Shmuel informed General Tal that the lead company had crossed the frontier. He himself crossed the border in the wake of Ehud's Pattons. But here, near a white United Nations outpost which had been vacated a fortnight ago, he waited.

The Pattons began to slow down. Drivers were ordered to follow in each other's tracks, thus keeping clear of mines, but the battalion was now in two columns. The lead company had entered the narrow streets of two small border villages where it was difficult for them to manoeuvre and where the way through was blocked. The other companies tried to bypass the villages, but found themselves in a ploughed-up area littered with numerous obstacles. The tanks began to crowd together. Egyptian artillery at Khan Yunis started raining shells on them and Colonel Shmuel's command group found itself blocked in a bottleneck.

"Shamir. This is Tirah," General Tal's voice called over the divisional radio from where he was with his command group on a high hill. "What's that smoke I see in your column? Over."

"Tirah. This is Shamir. Not a hit. Over," said Colonel Shmuel who had looked ahead and had been unable to see any smoke.

"Shamir. This is Tirah. Smoke is coming from your column. Over."

"Tirah. This is Shamir. Checking. Over."

Colonel Shmuel turned round. Sure enough, some twenty metres behind him, thick, grey smoke was rising upwards. The crew of his own Centurion came running up to him. The Egyptian barrage was thickening and getting nearer to its target. He could hardly believe the enemy had scored a hit right on the border and on his own tank.

"Sir," the sergeant said, "we wanted to catch up with you, and we reversed to get out of the jam and join you here. The Centurion piled up on the jeep behind it. The jeep's on fire."

"Where's the tank?" asked Colonel Shmuel coldly.

"Sir, the back of the tank piled up on the jeep and then its motor went dead. The tank's still on the jeep, Sir."

"Get back there on the double and take it off before it catches fire. Move."

"Whose jeep is it?" asked Yossi B.

"Don't know. Yossi run and see they put the fire out and get the tank off," said Colonel Shmuel.

"Yes, Sir."

Yossi jumped down from the half-track and raced back. The bombardment had intensified and the tank drivers were trying to get out of the bottleneck, and from what could well

123

become a death-trap should the shelling become more accurate. The tanks of S/10 Battalion drew away from the tracks of the Pattons and began to stream along a new course further south. Yossi ran between the tanks and reached the burning jeep. Tankers from brigade headquarters were trying to put out the blaze with fire extinguishers before the tank too caught fire.

"Squashed flat."

"First casualty, from an accident; it's a bad omen, damn it," said a tanker.

The driver of the Centurion managed to start the motor and roll it forward. The front part of the jeep was crushed and flattened like junk through an hydraulic press. Flames were merrily licking the back seats. The burning tyres gave off an acrid smell and black smoke was pouring from them so that it was difficult to breathe. Yossi could not identify the driver, who had been crushed to death at the wheel. The flames had consumed the canvas and the back part of the jeep was now exposed; it was then that Yossi saw the broken bottles of wine and the burst cans of beer. All his supplies, his clothing and possessions were at the mercy of the flames. He tried to get closer to what had been the driver's seat.

"You can't help him, friend," said a tanker who was directing a fire extinguisher at the burning jeep.

When Yossi returned to the half-track, the brigade commander's Centurion was next to it. Because of the intensified shelling Colonel Shmuel had decided to transfer to the tank, and Yossi was told to join him there. "Drive quickly," the Colonel instructed his tank driver.

"Tirah. This is Shamir," he called over the division's radio. "One jeep has been burnt out in an accident." But this communication was not heard. The tank's radio was no longer functioning and for the next hour Colonel Shmuel's contact with the division had to be via the brigade signals officer.

The command group was cast in gloom. To those going to war the first casualty is always a shock, reminding them of death, that aloof and cunning figure, who like a tipster gets its profit from both sides, winner and loser alike. Yossi spat out the butterscotch, which was soon covered in fine dust on the ground.

But in war first impressions fade quickly, returning only when the war is over to imprint themselves on the mind. Colonel Shmuel began to spur Ehud on. The break-through battle was nearing its peak.

CHAPTER SEVENTEEN

From the frontier to Khan Yunis is less than four miles and from there to the Rafa Junction a further ten. The way seemed short and open, but in fact it was defended by a large force. In Khan Yunis and its vicinity were several battalions of the Palestinian National Guard; one 25-pounder field artillery battalion; and a reduced battalion of tanks and anti-tank guns. Stationed in Rafa and its surroundings were five infantry battalions of the Palestinian National Guard and a battalion of field artillery and anti-tank guns. They were all Palestinian units under the command and within the organisation of the Egyptian Army. These forces comprised one defence locality. In the Rafa Junction–Sheikh Zuweid area was Egypt's 7th Division headquarters plus additional elements of Engineers. Two brigades were deployed there, one at the junction's defence locality, the other south of the junction. Five battalions of artillery, about ninety pieces in all, were arrayed to defend the fortified positions of the Rafa Opening. In their deployment area from Khan-Yunis to El-Arish the Egyptians had between one hundred and one hundred and fifty tanks, including thirty Stalin Mk 3s.

'S' Brigade leapt forward to execute its plan, their objective, the capture of the Rafa defence locality, their target, the Palestinian brigade positions, which formed an acute angle commanding the sites of the Rafa camps (built by the British Army during the second world war). The vertex of the angle was on the Um-el-Kalb crossing, with one line extending north-west towards the sandy beaches and the other due west to the Rafa railway station and the sea. After taking the Rafa locality, 'S' Brigade was to make contact with the enemy at Sheikh Zuweid and be prepared to attack, if needed, the sector assigned to 'Z' Brigade and the T/01 Patton Battalion under its command.

A party of the brigade reconnaissance company, at the head of S/14 Battalion, crossed the border first, two Patton tanks driving on the right, on the left the half-tracks with the party's commander, Lieutenant Yossi Algamis. Ehud wanted Major Ben-Zion Carmeli's tank company to be the first to take up its positions on the heights of Beni Souhila, a township east of the Gaza–Khan Yunis road (actually an eastern suburb of Khan Yunis), from where it would be able to give cover to the other companies attacking the military installations and the town of Khan Yunis. According to the plan these other companies were to reach Khan Yunis from the north-east, thus bypassing the minefields. The break-through at Khan Yunis was for out-flanking purposes only.

As S/14 Battalion crossed the border, they were met by an artillery barrage. But it was not this that delayed the Pattons. The main roads and paths, except for those which were covered by anti-tank guns and troops armed with anti-tank weapons, were heavily obstructed. Anti-tank ditches yawned half-way across these roads, from the left- and right-hand sides alternately, so that vehicles were obliged to move in low gear only, and to zigzag from side to side. Heavy vehicles such as tanks had to manoeuvre back and forth several times to get through, making an easy target. On either side were lined concrete pill-boxes with embrasures for machine guns and bazookas, and to these were added section and platoon defence positions with dug-outs and strongpoints. These defences stretched across the fields and farmlands on the outskirts of the towns and on empty plots and vacant areas in the towns, at the railway station and along the railroad track. Egyptian tanks lurked along tree-lined avenues and behind cactus bushes. The attacking Pattons, in trying to avoid the heavily defended routes, sought alternative bypaths, but here they ran into further difficulties. The paths led them into the narrow streets and alleys of villages and of Beni Souhila, Khan Yunis and later of Rafa. Where the alleys were blocked, the Pattons took to the cultivated fields, but these too were difficult to traverse because the small farmed patches were fenced in by stone walls and high soil ramps on top of which grew cactus bushes planted as a protection against erosion and wind; these sometimes proved worse obstacles than those created by the Egyptian Army.

The leading tanks caught glimpses of the farm workers still working in the fields and orchards and of the village streets and squares teeming with activity. But at the first signs and sounds of war – the exploding shells, the bursts of machine gun fire in the exchange with the forward defences, the terror-stricken flight of the Palestinian troops at the sight of the massed tanks – the fields and lanes emptied. Suddenly not a soul was in sight. Strict orders had been given not to shoot at civilians, but the villagers were not to know this. Accustomed for generations to hide during feuds, whether inter-tribal or between armies, the inhabitants of the Gaza Strip, women,

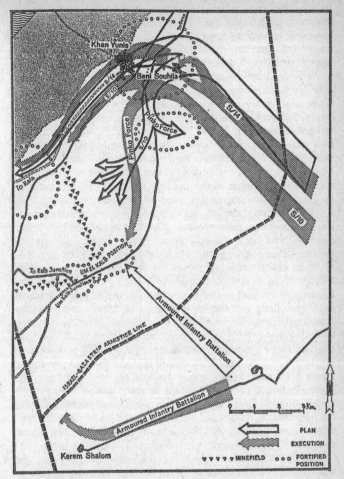

3 *'S' Brigade's break-through at Khan Yunis (1000 hours, 5 June).*

old people, men and children, vanished as though the ground had swallowed them up.

Quickly the tanks drove through the ghost town. Passing through an area usually inhabited and full of bustle but now silent and deserted was like travelling through a jungle in which the traveller can see not a single animal, though they watch him from every cave and tree-top. Thousands of pairs of frightened eyes watched from their hiding places as the tanks stormed into their miserable villages. In one almond orchard an old man with a deeply lined brown face and a mane of white hair suddenly materialised out of the ground. Black pantaloons were held up round his waist with a girdle and on his body he wore a white striped sleeveless and collarless shirt. Raising his long arms, his hands spread out, his fingers gnarled, for all the world like a traffic policeman on point duty, he ran backwards, facing the tanks, pointing to alternative paths and pleading to spare his almonds. So arresting was his strangeness and behaviour that the young tank drivers, for whom this was their first taste of war, involuntarily obeyed him. Tank drivers from agricultural settlements and kibbutzim were dismayed at the sight of the trampled almonds and tried their best to manoeuvre round them.

The two columns of the battalion were to rendezvous at the Khan Yunis railway station, but the closer the tanks drew to Beni Souhila, the fiercer grew Egyptian opposition and the more difficult it became to force a passage. Tanks lost their way in the narrow alleys on the outskirts of Beni Souhila. Yossi Algamis' tanks, as part of the brigade reconnaissance group, which had been moving forward on the right flank all the time, now got lost in one of the narrow streets and the lieutenant was forced to carry on without their protection. Finding a gap he began to lead the way through it, not from the north as the plan directed, but in a straight east–westerly direction. At the entrance to Beni Souhila the tanks were met with fierce rifle and machine gun fire and, for the first time, with anti-tank gunfire. Then the artillery liaison officer's half-track was hit by an anti-tank gun firing from a fortified position; crimson flames soon enveloped the half-track. Lieutenant Yossi Algamis was immediately notified of the whereabouts of the anti-tank gun position. He hurried towards it, standing upright in the half-track and clutching his 0.5 Browning machine gun, while on his left the medical orderly, who had only a few moments ago silenced an enemy position which had opened fire on them from one of the orange groves, manned the 0.3 Browning. But the way to the enemy emplacement was blocked; an anti-tank ditch had been dug across the road. Yossi gave the order to circumvent it, but the left wheel of the half-track slipped into the ditch, spun wildly, and dug an even deeper hole for itself. Facing the half-track, on top of a water tower, was a machine gun nest which now opened concentrated fire upon the vehicle and its occupants.

As Yossi raked the tower with bursts from his weapon a Palestinian soldier armed with a bazooka appeared on their left. Yossi signalled to the medical orderly on his left to deal with this new threat, but the enemy machine gun on top of the tower, besides hitting both aerials, had sent a burst into the 0.3's magazine, severing its cartridge belt. Yossi Algamis swung his 0.5 towards the bazooka-wielding soldier, but at that moment a bullet struck him in the head and he fell to the floor of the half-track. The medic hurried to attend to him. Yitzhak Koslov took over the 0.3 Browning, quickly repaired the cartridge belt and shot the Palestinian. Signals Sergeant Shmnuel Bayliss grabbed the 0.5 and sent burst after burst at the tower, silencing the machine gun inside it. He then ordered the driver of the half-track to withdraw. Eventually managing to extricate the left front wheel, the reconnaissance party took themselves back to a rear position to await the arrival of Yossi Algamis' second-in-command, who was commanding the jeep platoon from behind. A jeep rushed Yossi Algamis to the battalion aid post which had not yet crossed the border, but he died under the hands of the doctor.

Lacking guidance the tanks rumbled aimlessly into alleys and byways; the companies got mixed up one with the other. Not far from where Yossi Algamis had been hit, the column of tanks under Major Ben-Zion Carmeli had come to a halt. Manned anti-tank ditches had blocked their passage and in an attempt to outflank them two tanks had driven over mines. By staying where they were the Pattons were sitting targets for anti-tank guns hidden from their view – one tank had already been hit – and, in an attempt to circumvent the mine fields and anti-tank guns, they had wandered into alleys which were cul-de-sacs or were impassible for their tortuous bends and turns. Contact between the companies and brigade headquarters, and between the companies themselves, became spasmodic; the buildings formed a screen which disturbed communications.

The tank commander in Major Carmeli's tank radioed over the company network that the company commander had been wounded. The major's deputy, who was at the rear of the column, did not receive the message but the section commander, Lieutenant Berko, picked it up. He climbed down from his tank and ran under fire towards the major's tank, clambered into it and started to bandage the major's injuries. Major Carmeli had been wounded near the eye and his face was covered with blood. The tank withdrew slightly and

Lieutenant Berko climbed down, carrying the major in his arms towards the company command half-track. Laying the company commander on the floor of the vehicle he ordered the driver to get to the Khan Yunis railway station, the battalion rendezvous point.

The half-track set off. At one stage it even got on to a highway and, completely unprotected, drove for some distance without incident. Suddenly machine gun fire was directed at it from some camouflaged dug-in infantry positions to the right of the road. The half-track stopped. The driver was about to reverse when a burst hit him in the neck. The medical orderly and the rifleman pulled the driver from his seat and laid him down next to Major Carmeli. He was dead. The commander of the half-track then jumped into the driver's seat and tried to start the engine, but the vehicle would not move. The commander ordered his men to throw smoke grenades to create a smoke screen, and under this cover the four men crossed the road and took refuge behind a mound of earth, ready to open fire with their Uzzi machine guns if the enemy came out of their positions and approached the half-track. They lay there for some twenty minutes, until they saw three Centurion tanks and a half-track drawing near. At the sight of the tanks the enemy fled from their position. In the half-track was the deputy brigade commander, Lieutenant-Colonel Pinko. He quickly picked up the four men and hurried on, believing the half-track to be empty. Major Carmeli was left lying helplessly on the floor of the half-track, next to the dead soldier. Flames licked at the front part of the vehicle. The crews of the tanks which sped along in the wake of the deputy brigade commander's half-track also assumed that the burning vehicle had been abandoned.

The advance through Beni Souhila was rough going. More mines, more anti-tank ditches, more anti-tank guns, formidable artillery bombardments and a ceaseless rain of rifle and machine gun fire. But the main difficulties came from having been forced to enter Khan Yunis through its lanes and alleys.

"Number Two. This is Shamir. What are you waiting for?" Colonel Shmuel radioed.

"Shamir. This is Number Two. Narrow axis," replied Ehud.

"Number Two. This is Shamir. I'm behind you. Advance."

Colonel Shmuel, who had seen the hold-up, wanted to view the war from closer quarters. Khan Yunis was not an objective in itself but was on the route to the Rafa Junction defences. He ordered the driver of his tank to catch up with S/14.

130

The Centurions and half-tracks of brigade command group began to move forward as fast as possible through the disorganised area. After advancing about two miles, which took an hour in the tank, Colonel Shmuel returned to the half-track. He needed good and quick communications. "Number Two. This is Shamir. I'm near you. What's holding you up?"

"Shamir. This is Number Two. Stiff opposition. I've got a battle. I'm moving into the lead."

"Number Two. This is Shamir. Approved. Over."

Colonel Shmuel had already realised that there had been an error in the estimate of enemy strength in Khan Yunis. A brigade was stationed there, not a battalion as had been believed in the division. His original plan had not taken such a force into account and he decided to change it in mid-battle. Instead of the S/10 Centurion Battalion bypassing Khan Yunis from the south in order to make a long-range contact with the Rafa defences, it too would assault Khan Yunis. Colonel Shmuel prepared a brigade attack immediately.

"Numbers One and Two. This is Shamir. Change of assignment. Orders. Over."

"Shamir. This is Number One. Roger. Over."

"Shamir. This is Number Two. Roger. Over."

"Numbers One and Two. This is Shamir. Number One will attack on the left together with Number Two. Battalion's boundary: the town square. Confirm. Over."

"This is Number One. Roger. Over."

"This is Number Two. Roger. Over."

"This is Shamir. Good Luck. Out."

Meanwhile southern command H.Q. suggested to General Tal that he commit 'M' Armoured Brigade, the divisional reserve, to the offensive against Khan Yunis; General Tal, however, thought there was no need for it and turned the suggestion down.

"Shamir. This is Tirah. Calling Sunray. Over."

"Tirah. This is Shamir. Sunray speaking. Over."

"Where from?"

"From my half-track. I've gone back to the half-track."

"It is important to press home quickly and with dispatch on Khan Yunis. Commit your Number One to the battle in Khan Yunis," said General Tal.

"Already done. Number One is already committed. I am being shelled by the artillery behind Rafa."

"You will get counter-battery fire. In ten minutes time the Fougas will again bomb Egyptian artillery concentrations. I

131

want you to know that it is of the utmost importance to finish the Khan Yunis chapter quickly. Out."

Ehud decided to outflank Beni Souhila from the north, so as to get on to the Gaza–Khan Yunis highway and race along it to Khan Yunis. He started off in his tank and with the three Pattons of the battalion command group, pushed northwards, their commanders signalling with their flags to the battalion tanks to follow them. Through cactus bushes and stone fences Ehud began to swing the battalion round and lead it in an outflanking movement northwards to the main roads. The tanks which joined up with him were a mixture of various companies. Most of Kahalany's company had managed to keep with him and were now moving along behind him, but part of the battalion, and in particular a large part of Major Carmeli's company, whose deputy had now taken command, did not see the battalion commander nor did they hear his orders. However, the unit and tank commanders remembered the brigade briefings which had been passed all the way down to the tank crews and carried on with the struggle to break through into Khan Yunis via Beni Souhila; they also remembered the battalion meeting point – the railway, from there turning to the left.

The battalion commander's column drew away, attracting fierce volleys of rifle and machine gun fire. Ehud's command half-track was hit by an artillery shell and its occupants wounded.

"Come on. Move now. Out!" Ehud's voice was heard over the battalion's radio network. They could see him standing up in the commander's cupola, his red nose pointing into the wind as he raced along the main road to Khan Yunis. The speeding tanks of the battalion command group and the well-known and confident figure of the battalion commander riding at the head of the column infused his men with new courage and as though awe-struck they braced themselves and leapt forward.

Meanwhile the force which had made for Khan Yunis via Beni Souhila had overcome its obstacles and the two columns met at the Khan Yunis railway station. The entry into town had been at high speed. Simultaneously the Centurions of S/10 had begun to pass through the eastern sector of Khan Yunis as they made for their own meeting point in the town square. At the sight of the two battalions comprising many scores of tanks, the defenders fled from their dug-outs and fortified positions. As S/14 sped through the town, the streets were still filled with people waving white flags of surrender. Colonel Shmuel ordered Ehud to move quickly on to the two defended positions which, according to the plan, he was to attack. One lay between Khan Yunis and Rafa and the other north-west of the Rafa camps. Ehud moved his battalion forward along two axes of advance. The one under his command proceeded rapidly along the dirt-track which led from Khan Yunis to Rafa and entered the main street of the town. The second column moved parallel to the main Khan Yunis–Rafa highway, advancing more slowly because it had to overcome a fortified position containing anti-tank guns, as well as anti-tank obstacles and minefields. Four of its tanks touched off mines.

Ehud's column soon entered Rafa. Inside the town there was little opposition, rifle fire being the most serious hazard. Ehud left the armoured infantry company in the town to mop up enemy positions there, while he pushed on to attack the fortified positions north-west of the Rafa camps, on the edge of the sand dunes. The comander of the armoured infantry company later recounted that in one quarter of the town he had actually come across some Egyptian soldiers sitting in a café playing draughts. Incredible though it may seem, only after they had been fired upon did they seem to realise that the explosions they had heard meant that there was a war on, and they had jumped up and fled. Ehud had ordered his men not to shoot at surrendering troops, but at that stage there was no possibility of taking prisoners and they had to be allowed to go wherever their legs would carry them; in fact they returned and reorganised after the tanks had gone on.

Colonel Shmuel parted from S/14 in front of Rafa. He drove straight for the Rafa camps and parked his command group near the water tower on the main Rafa Junction highway.

That part of S/10 Battalion which had been committed to the attack on Khan Yunis now advanced upon the fortified positions south of the town, where it met stiff opposition. The battalion, led by the battalion commander, was obliged to enter an alley from which there was only one exit, and that was blocked by anti-tank guns, mines, concrete dragon teeth and iron crosses, and raked with machine gun, bazooka and artillery fire. Its battle in Khan Yunis continued even after the Pattons had left the town. The streets of Khan Yunis emptied. Blue, green and pink shutters barred the windows and iron shutters were lowered over shop fronts. When the

Centurions eventually began to pour into the square, the streets were almost deserted, but outside one house stood a woman with a baby in her arms, her breast bared to the suckling child. The door to her house stood wide open. This was the way she had chosen to indicate that her house was peace-loving and that there would be no shooting from its windows. The tanks whose machine guns were firing at buildings which were concealing snipers did not touch the house in front of which stood the mother and her baby.

When they reached the square, white flags were already flying from the windows. The square was deserted except for one old man who walked about, a red armband tied round his arm, clapping his hands in wild enthusiasm. Saliva dribbled from his gaping mouth which revealed two large, yellowing fangs.

CHAPTER EIGHTEEN

Pinko, the deputy brigade commander, was impatient. Colonel Shmuel had placed him in command of two companies of S/10 Battalion and had ordered him to comprise the brigade reserve force, which was to await orders on the road between Khan Yunis and Rafa. In other words, when S/14 broke through, and in its wake part of S/10, Pinko was to stand by for orders. He did so reluctantly, and to help pass the time assisted in relieving bottlenecks which had cropped up in the brigade's axes of advance into enemy territory. Then he waited near the supply echelons, got bored with the desultory bombardment directed at them and planned opportunities for intervening in the battle. First he moved forward with his command group half-tracks to catch up with S/10 and collect his two companies. When he saw that the battalion was held up at Beni Souhila he turned back with the two tank companies, picked up the crew of Major Carmeli's command half-track and began to look round for an alternative exit. With his half-track he crashed through a mud-brick wall and drove along what he thought was a parallel route. Maps he did not have; they had been left behind in his station-wagon. It was not long before his advance was again blocked by a mud-brick rampart. Again Pinko ordered his driver to "break through it", but this one was more solid than the first and the half-track got stuck halfway through. Pinko radioed to Company Commander Aharon to extricate it, which the captain did with the aid of a tank and tow-cable.

"Terrific!" said Pinko. Rifles and machine guns spluttered around him but he was not worried. He turned left and ordered the driver "full speed ahead". A wall of cement blocks barred the way. "At it!" he ordered. The half-track burst through the wall and continued its headlong journey, the tanks following. They entered an alley made narrower by a two-storey, mud-brick house. "At the house!" he yelled to the driver. The house collapsed and settled on the half-track, which they could not budge, neither backwards nor forwards.

"Nothing at all," said Pinko, covered from head to foot in dust and debris. "What are tanks for?" He signalled one of the tanks to draw near and it extricated the half-track from beneath the ruins of the house. "Move now! Full speed ahead!"

And so they raced along to the place where he had to wait for orders. There he sat, drearily listening to the brigade radio and hoping his orders would soon arrive. He heard Colonel Shmuel order Lieutenant-Colonel Gabriel to join Ehud in the attack on Khan Yunis and not to bypass the town from the south as had been called for in the original plan, and realised that there must be bitter fighting in Khan Yunis. Later the radio went dead. Screening prevented his receiving Colonel Shmuel, who was at that moment moving forward in his tank. Pinko radioed to the operations officer at brigade rear headquarters, who told him that to thwart a possible counterattack by Egyptian tanks against Kerem Shalom, General Tal had withdrawn the armoured infantry battalion from the brigade and had placed them under divisional command. The armoured infantry battalion had been ordered to defend Kerem Shalom.

Pinko knew a good opportunity to join the war when he saw one. With his two tank companies he would do what had been assigned to Lieutenant-Colonel Gabriel and part of the S/10 Battalion in the original plan, which had been to establish long-range contact with the fortified positions defending the Rafa army camp, and to open a breach for the armoured infantry battalion, approaching the army camps along the highway to avoid the minefields. Pinko informed the operations officer that without waiting for the brigade commander's orders he was committing the reserves into the battle in order to attain the objective assigned to S/10 under the original plan. The operations officer relayed Pinko's message to Colonel Shmuel, while Pinko ordered his eighteen Centurions to traverse their guns sideways and with their guns firing to race ahead on the main road towards the camps' defence positions at the vertex of the V, on the Um-el-Kalb junction. In their advance, the Centurions opened machine gun fire at infantry positions whose troops fled at the sight of the tanks. When Pinko reached the vicinity of the enemy positions he dispersed his Centurions, ordering them to find cover among the trees alongside the road and to hit the positions from the road.

Opposition from the enemy positions was weaker than he had anticipated and again he had nothing to do. Nor, when the battle ended, was Pinko quite sure where he was. Fortunately for him radio contact with the brigade commander was renewed. Pinko informed him that he had wiped out the defensive position at Um-el-Kalb and requested a recce party to guide him to a new assignment. However, lacking the patience to wait for the recce party, he advanced to the highway's level crossing; the railway gates were closed and behind them were dragon teeth, anti-tank obstructions. Shells from the Centurions' guns soon breached the barrier and they moved forward. Advancing parallel to the railway track, Pinko and his Centurions entered the Rafa railway station and silenced whatever opposition there was there.

"Shamir. This is Deputy-Shamir. I have taken the railway station. What do I do now? Over," said Pinko to Colonel Shmuel. Hearing this, the colonel and his command group broke away from the tail of S/14 and made rapidly for the water tower near the Rafa–Junction road.

The overall picture of the brigade offensive could now be summed up as follows: S/14 had moved in a single swing from Khan Yunis in two columns: the first column, commanded by the battalion second-in-command, Major Haim, had then approached a battalion defence zone located near the railway track in an area overlooking the town and the Rafa army camps, west of the town; the second column, commanded by Ehud, had advanced on to a battalion defence zone south-west of Rafa in an area overlooking Rafa and the camp. S/10 Battalion under Lieutenant-Colonel Gabriel had completed its assignment in Khan Yunis and was moving on to Rafa. Lieutenant-Colonel Pinko with the brigade reserve force had overcome the enemy positions at Um-el-Kalb and had reached the railway station.

Colonel Shmuel could now feel that the brigade was moving forward more smoothly and that 'S' had completed its primary mission in the Rafa area; it had gained its objective, the Rafa army camp. The camp itself was not the target, but the regions overlooking them. Only small-arms fire met them in the camp, and Shmuel did not want to be bothered with it; this was the job of the mopping-up and occupying units which would follow 'S' Brigade. He decided to push on to the next assignment, which was to establish contact with Sheikh Zuweid. Over his radio he asked the reconnaissance company commander, "Where are you?"

"Shamir. This is Number Five. I am behind you. Over."

"Number Five. This is Shamir. Report to me."

Captain Ori, tall, his black hair ruffled, jumped out of his command half-track and ran towards Colonel Shmuel. He was given two orders: one, a reconnaissance party under his command was to move along the road and establish contact with the junction so as to gauge the enemy strength there. If the junction had been abandoned, as Colonel Shmuel was inclined to believe, then the party was to proceed to Sheikh Zuweid, some eight miles from the junction. Ori was also instructed to send a recce party to Lieutenant-Colonel Pinko and to lead him to the junction's fortifications.

The reconnaissance party set out; two Pattons, three half-tracks and four jeeps. A hundred metres short of the junction they suddenly came under heavy fire. Captain Ori then noticed a defence position deployed along a fold in the ground, expertly entrenched and camouflaged; the position would have been completely missed by him but for the firing which revealed it. He immediately notified Colonel Shmuel that the position was manned and looked well defended. Contact with Captain Ori was then broken as he immediately had to fight for his company's life.

The first blast of fire from the enemy position scored a hit; an anti-tank shell struck the track of the engineers' half-track. Second-Lieutenant Yaacob Yarkoni, commander of the jeep platoon, who was riding behind the half-track, ordered his driver to draw closer to the damaged vehicle, and shouted to Lieutenant Shlomo Kenisbuch, commanding the engineers, if he could do with any help.

"Not a thing. We'll get out of this by ourselves. You carry on," replied Lieutenant Kenisbuch. Machine gun fire was raking the road, and as Yarkoni was running back to his jeep he was hit in the hand by a bullet. The jeeps drove round the disabled half-track and carried on behind the rest of the party towards the junction. Egyptian artillery now began an accurate shelling of the road.

At that moment Captain Ori saw two enemy tanks emerging from their dug-outs as though levered out of the ground. Zwicka, the commander of the first Patton, destroyed both with two quick shots at a range of two hundred metres. The shelling and machine gun fire intensified, nor could Captain Ori locate the exact position from which the firing was coming; in actual fact it was concealed by a fold in the ground. He realised that he had driven into a trap, and perhaps an ambush. To withdraw was impossible; while turning on the road – on both sides of which were minefields – he would be a fatally easy target. The only way to get out alive was to burst into the death trap and destroy it from within. Captain Ori was in the first half-track immediately behind the two Pattons.

"Right wheel! At the objective! Tanks first!" Captain Ori commanded.

The two Pattons turned off the road to the right; spread out behind them came the half-tracks and jeeps, firing all their machine guns. Seventy metres from the highway a single barbed wire indicated the beginning of the minefield. At first Ori thought of stopping, but in a flash he realised that if he stopped his men would at once become flaming torches. He was in a low-lying area, in the centre of a minefield, while the enemy was dug-in, superior in numbers and on higher ground. The minefield extended almost to the lip of the trenches to prevent the mines being quietly removed at night, and in order to assault the ditches themselves the party would have to negotiate the entire minefield. "Forward, into the minefield, and on to the objective!" he called over the radio to his men. The reconnaissance party burst into the field.

The first to touch off a mine was Gaby's jeep. It was thrown into the air and overturned; the four occupants were badly injured. Three jeeps were left. Sergeant Fenichel sprang out of his jeep and ran towards the overturned vehicle. Only after having seen to the evacuation of the wounded to the highway in the weapon carrier, did he return to his jeep. Then he was hit in the leg. Cursing roundly, he refused to join the wounded and went on fighting. The second to touch off a mine was a Patton. Its crew continued to fire its gun and machine guns.

Second-Lieutenant Yarkoni, whose hand had already been injured, still managed to operate the jeep's 0.3mm Browning machine gun and had actually reached to within twenty metres of the trench when his machine gun jammed. Without a word, Yarkoni jumped from the jeep and ran to the trench. Leaping in he began killing the men with his submachine gun.

138

He silenced that sector of the trench but as he was scrambling out a wounded Egyptian shot him in the back and Yarkoni collapsed at the edge of the trench. Lieutenant Amos, a member of the recce party, jumped down from his half-track, which had already silenced the sector of the trench in front of him, and ran towards the wounded second-lieutenant, at the same time calling to Yarkoni's driver, Mookie, to come to the trench's edge. There the two of them lifted Yarkoni on to the stretcher which was strapped to the side of the jeep and placed him in the back of the vehicle. Mookie began to drive in reverse gear, trying to follow his own tracks so as not to go over a mine.

The two remaining jeeps, the two half-tracks and the Patton continued the assault. The men in the half-tracks did as Yarkoni had done, jumped out of their vehicles and entered the trench, with the machine guns on the half-tracks covering them. With the battle still raging, Mookie and his jeep managed to reach the centre of the minefield when an anti-tank shell fell near him, the explosion lifting Yarkoni out of his stretcher and throwing him on to the bonnet of the vehicle. Mookie stopped the jeep and placed his officer back on the stretcher. He felt the wounded man's pulse and breathed a sigh of relief. It was still beating.

"Water," whispered Yarkoni.

Mookie looked around him. There was no water in the jeep, but he noticed a black water container on the ground about forty metres away which must have been thrown from Gaby's jeep when it had overturned. Mookie sprang from the jeep and crawled towards the jerry can. Bullets whined above his head, but just when he was within arm's reach, a burst of machine gun fire pierced the container and sent a spray of water into Mookie's face. Angrily he stood up and raced back to the jeep empty handed.

"There'll soon be water," he said to his commander.

Still driving in reverse, Mookie reached the road. There a wounded soldier from the tank which had struck a mine was loaded on board. The jeep then raced off in the direction of Rafa but soon had to stop again; out of the ditch at the side of the road came Shlomo Katz, one of the occupants of the engineers' half-track, terribly burnt. He stumbled towards them and collapsed near the jeep. Mookie picked him up, placed him on top of the radio equipment and drove on, only to stop once again. Another soldier, wounded and burnt, lay on the roadside; Mookie lifted him into the jeep too. He drove with his left hand and with his right held on to the injured men to keep them in. Eventually he succeeded in getting to the battalion aid post, but Second-Lieutenant Yarkoni died of his wounds.

The Egyptians were now beginning to flee from their trenches. The mopping-up of the position had been more or less completed and Captain Ori decided to get what was left of his unit back on to the road. However, on the way back his own half-track drove over a mine. Its occupants moved in to the only remaining half-track, while the wounded were placed in the weapon carrier which followed in the wake of the combat vehicles. Sergeant Haim Fenichel was persuaded to climb into the weapon carrier, but as progress through the minefield became increasingly hazardous, Fenichel clambered off the vehicle, and inching forward on one knee while dragging his injured leg behind him, prodded the ground before him with the cleaning rod of his machine gun, uncovering mines. He cleared a path of more than a hundred metres for the weapon carrier until it reached the highway. Then he climbed back into the vehicle and lay down on the floor among the other wounded. The weapon carrier was speeding to the battalion first aid post, when a mortar shell fell on it and killed Sergeant Haim Fenichel.

Now the Egyptians began shelling the defence position which had previously been in their hands. Captain Ori had to evacuate it quickly, but passage through the minefield was extremely slow and he was obliged to order his one remaining Patton to lead the way through the minefield, clearing a lane for the other vehicles. The Patton lumbered along, ploughing wide tracks which the other vehicles could follow, until near the highway it touched off two mines. At last the reconnaissance party reached the road and could begin to reorganise: Ori was left with a half-track, two jeeps and half his men. They also met up with what remained of the reconnaissance party which had been sent by Colonel Shmuel to lead Lieutenant-Colonel Pinko and his force to the junction fortifications. Ori's party began to struggle back to headquarters at the junction.

While the recce party's struggle for the defence position of the junction was at its height, Pinko with his two Centurion companies and the reconnaissance party arrived at Colonel Shmuel's command group near the water tower, some four kilometres from the battle scene. Shmuel could hear the noise from the battle and concluded that the party was in a tough spot. He ordered Pinko to get on to the dust track which led off the roadway into the desert at the point where it made a sharp left turn toward the junction. Pinko's force was assigned the task of attacking along the length of the dust track.

Aharon's company was the first to move off the road and on to the track. The party then turned left and moved forward, parallel now with the road towards the junction, but Aharon's Centurions had not advanced fifty metres when the whole desert zone, which till then had been dormant, erupted in vicious firing. From where he was, Colonel Shmuel could see the entire zone come to life, from the junction to the beaches. The first three Centurions got through the curtain of fire, but the fourth, Lieutenant David Peltz's, was hit by a shell from a T/34 tank. The Centurion caught fire and Peltz sprang from the turret, rolling over and over in the sand to extinguish his blazing clothes. Although he suffered burns, he immediately dashed back to the burning tank, which could any moment blow up, to see what had happened to the crew and whether they could be extricated. The signalman was dead; the driver and the gunner were badly injured. Inside the tank, which by this time was an inferno of smoke and flame, Lieutenant Peltz struggled against white hot steel to release the wounded gunner. With a great effort he managed to extricate him, and through bursts of machine gun fire dragged him to a safe refuge. Again he returned to the blazing tank to fetch the driver. A half-track came forward to collect the wounded, but hardly had they been carried on to it when a shell hit it and Lieutenant Peltz was killed.

Pinko could not stop to pick up the wounded. He had to attack in full force. But when only a part of his column had passed the enemy trench, Colonel Shmuel called Pinko to him. Pinko raced back in his half-track, passing the Centurions with their guns blazing away and under heavy bombardment from Egyptian artillery. The Centurions' skirting plates were riddled with marks, there were gashes in the turrets and several hulls carried holes from direct hits by armour-piercing shells. Shrapnel had scratched the faces of the tank commanders, and many had been more seriously wounded.

Colonel Shmuel's command group had moved closer to the junction. In a cutting, at a point where the road cut through a sheltering sand hill, about one and a half kilometres from the junction, Colonel Shmuel made his plan. He realised that a large force must be positioned at the junction.

Here the Egyptians had achieved perfect camouflage. The terrain was rolling, soft sand, covered with desert shrubs, cactus bushes, and ricinus plants. The Egyptians were dug-in below ground level and their tanks were hidden in large dug-outs over which camouflage netting had been spread to conceal the pits in which the tanks lurked. Anti-tank gun positions had been dug out behind the ricinus plants and camouflaged with nets. Colonel Shmuel had already noted that the anti-tank guns were firing in salvoes of five simultaneously, by doing so reducing the chance of missing and making it more difficult for them to be located. Colonel Shmuel was now at one of the most critical moments of the war. As was later ascertained, the junction defences were the Egyptians' strongest in Sinai. Whoever commanded the junction would be in a position to thrust into Sinai along several axes, and it was natural, therefore, that the Egyptians should defend it with a large force, but Colonel Shmuel had not imagined that it would be quite so heavily defended.

For the sake of clarity it is worth while to divide the junction defences into two sections: one extending from the El-Arish road to the north; and the other from the road to the south. (The second section was attacked by Colonel Raphoul, the two forces executing a divisional pincer movement.) The defended area in Colonel Shmuel's sector was spread out in length and depth, from the El-Arish road up to the beaches in the north. It consisted of continuous, zigzagging ditches which (again for the purpose of description) we will divide into four parts. Part A was the positions closest to the junction and bordering on it. One of these positions, the one actually closest to the junction, had already been attacked by the reconnaissance party commanded by Captain Ori, while a second position was now being assaulted by a recce party under Lieutenant Eli. Part B was a series of defended localities which Pinko had brushed against at their very extremity, just over a mile north of the junction. Part C was the anti-tank defence locality which was the northernmost of the three, some two and a half miles from the junction. Part D extended in depth through the junction's defence zone; a series of defence locations dug-in in linear dispositions running for several miles along the El-Arish road.

The column of Centurions was now dispersed over the whole area. Part of them, Shamai Kaplan's company, were very close to the road and actually inside the enemy's defence zone, where they had taken up positions and were exchanging fire with the Egyptian tanks and anti-tank guns. The Egyptian artillery had also renewed its bombardment. The Fouga jets had chased the Egyptian gunners away but their bombs had

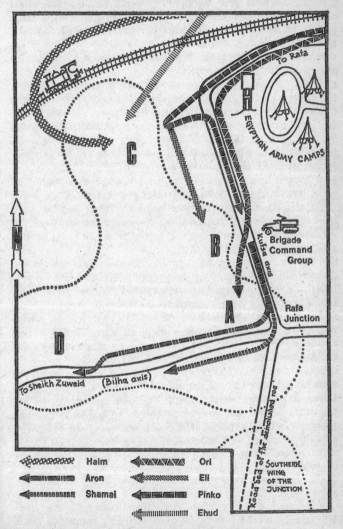

4 'S' Brigade's break-through at the northern wing of the Rafa Junction (1200 hours, 5 June).

not destroyed their guns, so that when the planes disappeared the gunners returned to their weapons. Colonel Shmuel could not hide his satisfaction at the fact that the Centurions had hardly suffered from the bombardment; the most the shells seemed to be able to do was to cut down the tanks' aerials. He actually saw a shell hit a Centurion's 105mm gun without leaving a scratch. "What a tank! What steel!" Pinko exclaimed. But he was not so happy when another shell hit the engine cover and stopped the motor.

"Sir," Pinko said, "we must attack the junction and make a dash for Sheikh Zuweid. The entire defence zone is coming alive. We mustn't stop for a minute Sir."

"No, Pinko. Look at the size of the zone and its depths. We must make a brigade-scale attack. Ehud will attack from the north in two columns and you will advance on 'K' axis and turn to 'B' axis only on my order...."

"Point where with your finger, Sir. I don't have any maps."

Colonel Shmuel pointed towards the Rafa–Junction road. "Don't pass the junction until ordered, which shall be when Ehud has attacked the northern defence location. Then you advance under his covering fire, turn right to the El-Arish road and make a dash for Sheikh Zuweid."

The colonel intended to exploit his success and penetrate at speed deep into enemy territory, even before the defence zone had been mopped up. The armoured infantry battalion, which had previously been assigned to do that job, was still under the division's command, deployed for defence at Kerem Shalom. Colonel Shmuel now requested General Tal to provide another air bombardment on the Egyptian artillery and a counter-barrage. The general consented willingly.

The time was 1100 hours. The sun was nearing its zenith. Pinko got back to his Centurions in his own half-track, somewhat regretting that the assault had been halted. But he had hardly reached the dust track before he began to hear the noise of Ehud's battle. He could see the Pattons moving swiftly forward in the dust and smoke, then, quite suddenly, two sheets of flame as two Pattons received direct hits.

CHAPTER NINETEEN

"Shamir, this is Number Two. I'm going to lead the attack."

"Number Two, this is Shamir. Approved."

In briefings before the war, Colonel Shmuel had forbidden battalion commanders to advance ahead of the leading company; at most they were allowed to follow immediately behind. This time he gave Ehud permission to lead the attack, as he had at Beni Souhila and Khan Yunis. His consent, like his decision to commit the entire brigade under his command into the battle, was a result of the divisional commander's directive – to carry out the first day's movements aggressively and at all cost, because this first day would decide the outcome of the war.

Ehud decided that he would lead the frontal attack while his second-in-command, Major Haim, with a larger force, would outflank the enemy position and storm it from the rear, from north-west to south-east. Major Haim was to take his force in a deep flanking movement to the edge of the sand dunes, and Ehud's plan was to concentrate all the enemy fire on himself, thus drawing attention away from Haim's outflanking movement.

Ehud now ordered the commanders of the units accompanying him to storm the enemy position, but radio communications were not working properly, and he had no way of knowing if his orders were being received. "Move, now, at full speed, follow me!" he called. His Patton raced to the top of the hill, where the enemy position was entrenched, but he was the only one. The company commanders had not heard his order, nor had they seen their objective, and were under the impression that the commander was making a solitary reconnaissance. The Pattons stood immobile at the unsatisfactory firing positions they had selected. The dug-in and camouflaged anti-tank guns upon the hill met the solitary Patton with a concentrated salvo. One shell sliced through the basket rack, setting fire to the folded camouflage net. A second shell struck the right track-guard, tearing it off. Shell splinters severed the microphone attached to Ehud's helmet, cutting his face and piercing the palm of his right hand which was resting on the commander's cupola ring. Other splinters injured Ehud's operations officer, Lieutenant Amiram Mizna, in the eye and shoulder. Both had been standing upright in the turret in order to get a better view of their objective.

Ehud asked for the reserve microphone and the signalman gave him a hand microphone which he immediately connected to the control box. "Driver, reverse!" he ordered, and the Patton drove in reverse to the bottom of the hill. The commanders of the other Patton tanks, who up to now had not moved, mistook Ehud's retreat for a temporary withdrawal and put their own tanks in reverse; Ehud immediately halted his tank, ordered the driver to climb the hill again, and over the microphone ordered the unit commanders to follow him and storm the enemy positions.

"Shamir, this is Number Two. I don't see my tanks following me."

"Number Two. This is Shamir. It's O.K. They're behind you. I can see them," said Colonel Shmuel from his position on the road.

This time the order had been heard. The Pattons surged forward to storm the objective. From his previous reconnaissance of this enemy position, Ehud knew he was climbing straight for the anti-tank gun locality. Now able to read the battle well, he allocated the various assignments against the anti-tank guns and T/34 tanks which were seen to be drawing near. At this moment, the anti-tank guns which were hidden behind the ricinus plants thundered in unison; three Pattons were hit and ground to a halt. A second later the battalion second-in-command, Major Haim, appeared with the bulk of the battalion's tanks at the back of the defence area. His tanks had come through the sand dunes from a direction which the Egyptians had not anticipated. Practically undisturbed they had calmly taken up firing positions behind the Egyptian tanks which were now bearing down upon Ehud and his tanks. Major Haim advanced to within a range of eight hundred metres before ordering "Fire!" Nine Egyptian tanks burst into flames simultaneously. The Pattons now turned their fire on to the anti-tank guns, the ammunition trucks and the field guns.

"Don't waste ammunition. Don't fire heavy ammunition at trucks!" Ehud's voice was heard calling over the battalion's radio. "On trucks, tankers and the like, use only machine guns." Major Haim's force advanced on the enemy defences like a hurricane. A Patton whose machine gun had jammed rode through the positions, crushing anti-tank gunners under its tracks.

In Major Haim's force there was a unit of new recruits,

commanded by Lieutenant Oved, who had been trained only in tank trades. At first, after Oved's crew had hit an enemy tank with their opening shot, his doubts had been dispelled. There you are, he said to himself. One can fight a war even with new recruits. But his complacency was short-lived. A brave Egyptian came out of a trench carrying a bazooka and crawled towards his tank, aiming his weapon.

"Crew, bazooka, Fire!" Oved commanded.

In vain. The recruits had not been through crew training. They simply did not know that on hearing this order they were to open fire with all machine guns and that the driver was to race towards the danger-spot and crush the bazooker-aimer under the tank's tracks. The crew did nothing, but sat in their narrow, dark compartment, blind to what was going on and to the danger threatening them. The bazooka rocket whined close above Lieutenant Oved's head. His hair all but stood on end when he saw the Egyptian taking fresh aim. "Men, blast that bloody bazooka with your machine guns, for God's sake!" he called to the recruits in the vernacular. This the gunner understood and he fired the machine gun, but his shots were very wide of the mark. Lieutenant Oved saw death staring at him through the black tube of the bazooka, but fortunately for him the section sergeant saw what was happening and raced towards the Egyptian, squashing him beneath the tracks of his tank.

The flight from the ditches was now in full swing. Gunners were abandoning their guns, the infantry fleeing from the trenches, truck and tank drivers abandoning their vehicles. The Patton crews stood in the open hatches firing their machine guns until the barrels almost melted with the heat. One Patton changed cartridge belts ten times. The fleeing Egyptians were leaving behind them tanks and personnel-carriers still emplaced in dug-outs beneath their nets.

While S/14 was attacking the northern sector of the junction's defence zone, Pinko's force attacked the southern sector, Captain Aharon's company on the right and Major Shamai Kaplan's on the left. The Egyptians in sectors A and D of the defence zone put up a fierce battle; Egyptian artillery shelled the two companies ceaselessly and powerful batteries of anti-tank guns fired almost incessant salvoes. Major Shamai's company fought deliberately and expertly. Shamai's orders were that the men were not to change their firing positions as long as the Egyptian artillery's shots were ranging, but that the moment the bombardment became accurate they were to move to new firing positions. To an onlooker the quick changes in position resembled the nimble footwork of a competent boxer. Shamai's voice was calm and clear. As the tanks were hidden from each other, Shamai served as the eyes of the company, and his remarks over the company's radio sounded very like the report of a sports commentator.

"Very nice. That was a fine shot, Dan. That makes Dan's third T/34 in this battle. From the left, 300, anti-tank battery, below the ricinus plant! A very nice shot there of Lieutenant Hanoch. Two guns were lifted, one after the other. Now change to new firing positions. They're beginning to find their targets."

Across the crest of the hill Captain Aharon's company pushed on to the junction. Not all the tanks managed to keep up the same speed, and soon Lieutenant Solomonov, leading the company, found himself a good hundred metres inside the objective, only to discover that he was isolated. Looking back he saw two of the company's tanks "sitting" back, apparently doing nothing, like spectators at a firing demonstration. Solomonov got so angry that he forgot all about the Egyptian shelling. He stood up in the cupola, with half his body exposed above it, and with his flags signalled to the two tanks to advance to firing positions; no reaction. Solomonov roundly cursed them over the radio. Still there was no reaction. Meanwhile he observed an Egyptian crew taking advantage of the delay to bring up a recoilless gun which they now aimed at the Centurion's left side. Solomonov ducked back into his cupola and traversed the turret. His gunner, Kramer, mowed down the Egyptians with a long burst, not a moment too soon.

"Thanks, Kramer," said Solomonov.

"Thanks for what, Sir?"

"For not having wasted heavy ammunition."

Lieutenant-Colonel Pinko drove his half-track through the shooting, in the wake of a T/34 so as not to touch off mines, and found himself a spot between the two companies from which both could see him. It was obvious that the El-Arish road was still well defended. Pinko ordered Major Shamai to advance over the crest of the hill and to place snipers there to destroy the tanks and anti-tank batteries blocking the passage. Shamai raised a flag to signify he had understood, but at that moment a shell fell near his Centurion and splinters injured both his hands. He began to bleed badly but carried on calmly issuing orders to his company. Surmounting the crest they began locating new targets and within two minutes of

Pinko having given the order, Shamai's company had set fire to two Egyptian tanks.

Pinko now requested Colonel Shmuel to lay down an artillery barrage for him. In a few moments the self-propelled guns of Lieutenant-Colonel Zvi were firing their first ranging shot. Too far, Pinko thought to himself. The second, too short. But the third time a perfect barrage was laid down. "And that's that," said Pinko and prayed for the brigade commander's orders to advance.

Colonel Shmuel's voice came over the radio: "Deputy Shamir, this is Shamir. Move now. Over." Pinko immediately radioed his force to pass through the junction and to race for Sheikh Zuweid. Three Centurions stormed through and were on their way, but the fourth, one of Shamai's company, was hit by anti-tank fire and burst into flames. In a second the crew had jumped out and were rolling themselves in the sand to smother their burning clothing. They then turned to their tank and tried to put out the fire with extinguishers, but to no avail; the tank was a mass of flames. Another Centurion from Shamai's company thrust forward, its commander, Lior, standing upright in the cupola, and almost drove into the burning Centurion. "Reverse!" Lior ordered the driver, meaning to bypass it, but at that moment a bullet struck him in the head. The driver, who had received no further orders, continued in reverse, and there was almost a collision, but the gunner took over command of the tank and ordered the driver forward.

The crew from the burning tank clambered aboard another tank, but the sight of the damaged and burning tanks near the junction, and the blackened and burned faces of the men, instilled a split second of uncertainty into the crews of the Centurions. Pinko could feel that the assault had reached a moment of crisis; if it was not renewed it might collapse. He moved forward in his half-track towards the junction, jumped up on top of the half-track, and sticking two fingers in his mouth blew an ear-piercing whistle to attract Shamai's attention, a whistle which could be heard even above the shriek of the bullets, so that several tank commanders turned to look at him as he waved his flag. Shamai looked across and understood his signal. He raised his flag with bloodstained, bandaged hands, and ordered his driver to move forward through the junction. The Centurion sprang forward, cut through the junction and climbed on to the road. "Follow me in a column. Move now! Over," Shamai commanded over the radio, without

149

looking back to see if his order was being obeyed. His plunge into the firing line and spurt along the road renewed the assault. His own company's Centurions and those of others which had reached the junction raced after him like goslings behind their mother. "Full speed, full fire power in all directions!" Pinko shouted into the microphone, placing himself fourth in the column of racing tanks.

Spitting fire on both flanks, Shamai's company crossed into section D of the defence zone; behind him came the whole of S/10 Battalion, for while the battle had been raging the companies which had been with Lieutenant-Colonel Gabriel, the battalion commander, had arrived at the junction and had fallen into positions behind him. Racing along, Shamai's gunners set four T/34s ablaze. S/10 battalion passed through the junction and mounted the road to El-Arish, at exactly 1136 hours.

At Colonel Shmuel's command 'S' Brigade now advanced in two parallel columns. S/14, with Ehud at its head, charged towards Sheikh Zuweid through the sand dunes along an axis parallel to the railway line; S/10 was advancing two kilometres to the south on an axis parallel to and on the El-Arish road. Except for an occasional Egyptian tank, anti-tank gun battery, armoured personnel-carrier, truck, tanker or other enemy vehicle crossing its path, which were destroyed, S/10 raced forward almost unchallenged. At Kafr Shan, however, the column was fired upon by dug-in T/34 tanks, an extremity of the junction's southern defence area where Colonel Raphoul was fighting. The Centurions hit seven T/34s and raced on. On their left the Centurions saw Colonel Raphoul's Pattons destroy the rest of the locality's tanks – some twenty of them – and race on in the opposite direction. This had in fact been the physical meeting of the two prongs of Tal division's pincer movement, effected at great speed.

To prevent one Israeli unit from opening fire on another, previously agreed identifying signs were used, denoting Ehud's Pattons, now racing westward to Sheikh Zuweid, Pinko's Centurions, thrusting forward in the same direction, and the Pattons led by Lieutenant-Colonel Uri which were now chasing back eastwards to the junction.

Pinko was hoping that his column would reach Sheikh Zuweid first, but Captain Aharon had actually passed through quite some time ago. His company had sliced straight through their sector of the defence area with hardly any delay and had reached the El-Arish road far ahead of the other companies. In fact Captain Aharon did not even realise that his was the lead company, knowing nothing of the others' delay in passing the junction. He did recall, however, that at the briefing they had talked of blocking the road to Sheikh Zuweid where the road and railway crossed; he also remembered what the battalion commander (who was quoting the brigade commander, who was quoting the divisional commander) had said, that in war nothing went according to plan, but that everyone had to bear in mind his main assignment. Captain Aharon therefore made for the level crossing, hoping to find the battalion's companies already there.

Behind him he could see only two Centurions, but over the radio his second-in-command, Lieutenant Solomonov, had informed him that there were another four Centurions with him. Unfortunately, Solomonov did not know where he was either, whether he was running behind Captain Aharon or racing ahead of him. He had heard Captain Aharon yell "Forward!" over the radio, and taking this as a command to catch up with the captain had ordered his four tanks to develop maximum speed. Still he could not see the captain's three Centurions. The road twisted and turned, rolling up and down with the terrain, and after a while Solomonov began to think that he was ahead and that Captain Aharon was trailing behind, spurring him on to even greater speed.

Lieutenant Solomonov was actually the last of Aharon's company to mount the El-Arish road. At that moment the Egyptians opened up an intensified machine gun barrage and a burst hit the tank's periscope, piercing Solomonov's steel helmet and sending splinters ricochetting off the base of the 0.5 Browning which penetrated his thumb and ear. When he caught up with the other three tanks of his company, he learnt that Lieutenant Abraham Munitz had been seriously injured in the eye; Munitz had not said a word to his crew, afraid that they would stop to evacuate him and that the assault would then grind to a halt. Blood was gushing from his eye, so that the gunner and signalman had screamed at the sight of him. Munitz had slapped one of them in the face; he realised they were suffering from shock but he was concerned lest their screams should reach the driver, who might get confused and lose control of the heavy, speeding vehicle.

"How do you feel, Munitz?" Solomonov asked, by radio.

"I'm all right. I can carry on."

"Can you speak?"

"With difficulty."

"Can you see?"

"With difficulty."

"Tell your driver to take his place at the rear of the column."

At that moment Lieutenant Shuali identified two T/34s waiting in ambush on the left side of the road at a range of five hundred metres. "Tanks on the left!" he called to the other Centurions. His own gunner fired immediately, the flash momentarily blinding Lieutenant Shuali. Lieutenant Solomonov opened his mouth to bark an order to Kramer, his gunner, but before he could utter a sound Kramer had fired an armour-piercing shell which hit the other T/34, setting it ablaze. A third T/34 appeared and Kramer sent his second shell on to it.

"Very nice, Kramer," said Solomonov.

But then Solomonov's blood froze. On the road, opposite, had appeared three Centurion tanks, their 105mm guns pointing directly at him. There was no time even to give the gunner orders. Lieutenant Munitz was blind in one eye and in bad pain. Sergeant Avital, in the third Centurion, was wounded in his back. For real fighting only two Centurions were left. Shauli's and his own, and Shuali's gun had jammed after destroying the T/34. He called "Gunner!" and began counting the split seconds he still had to live.

Captain Aharon, who was some few kilometres ahead of Solomonov, was beginning to wonder. He had tried repeatedly to make contact with his battalion commander, Lieutenant-Colonel Gabriel, in order to find out where the battalion was, but had received no response. Could they possibly have wandered so far from the battalion as to be out of radio range? He did not even know whether he was far behind or ahead of them. He searched the surrounding desert for some signs of war which would tell him whether the battalion had already passed this way. But everything seemed undisturbed. Here and there were Egyptian units, deeply dug-in in the sands; tanks, trucks, armoured personnel-carriers, tankers, radio cars, and a mobile workshop, perfectly lined up inside huge, camouflaged dug-outs. The sight of his three Centurions racing along the road caused shock and panic in the Egyptian soldiers; they could not have expected so quick a breakthrough. Near Sheikh Zuweid intense machine gun fire was directed at them. The Centurion behind him was hit on its skirting plates by two bazooka rockets. Captain Aharon yelled: "Move, Move now, Out," and at that moment felt a sharp blow on his steel helmet. The three Centurions sped past Sheikh Zuweid. Captain Aharon looked sideways into the prism of the commander's telescopic sight; blood was flowing from underneath his helmet. A bullet had pierced it at the front and had come out at the back. Aharon wanted to take his helmet off, but changed his mind. The inner support was pressing against his head and he believed it would staunch the flow of blood until it coagulated. He also decided not to tell his men he had been wounded. The battalion was in any case far away and could not come to his rescue. It was better that the men should think their commander was fit.

Now he was convinced he was ahead of the battalion and he toyed with the idea of carrying out the blocking of the road himself, but six kilometres past Sheikh Zuweid he still had not found the spot where the road and the railway lines intersected and he began to realise how dangerous it was to penetrate so deep into enemy territory with only three tanks. If the Egyptians were to counter-attack, his three Centurions would not stand a chance. He called a halt and ordered them to drive back, wanting now, more than anything else, to rejoin the battalion. A few minutes later his eyes almost popped out of his head. Four tanks were immediately ahead of him.

"Gun, A.P., On, four tanks in front!" cried Captain Aharon.

"Gun, A.P., On . . .", yelled Lieutenant Solomonov.

Then Solomonov recognised the face of his commander, who had stood up in his cupola, covered in blood, but unmistakeable nevertheless. Only Captain Aharon stood like that in the turret. He raised a flag. Captain Aharon had also recognised his second-in-command, and both thanked their lucky stars they had not had to taste each other's guns.

Once again Captain Aharon turned his tanks round, this time towards El-Arish to which he pointed with his flags. "Move now. Follow me. Out," he called to the seven tanks which remained of his company. The seven raced along, paying no attention to what went on around them. They passed the road-rail intersection and about two kilometres beyond it, ten kilometres west of Sheikh Zuweid, they halted, dispersed and took up hull-down positions, deploying themselves to block any Egyptian force which might come from the direction of the Jiradi. It was 1200 hours. In less than four hours from General Tal's first order to move, the vanguard of his division had reached the enemy's rear, behind its fortified lines, forty kilometres from the border of Israel. Between Captain Aharon and El-Arish, twenty kilometres apart, stood only the fortified Jiradi pass.

"Cut motors," ordered Captain Aharon, to save fuel, and there was suddenly deep silence. The tank crews were not used to it. The drivers, gunners and loaders had been close to vomiting from the gases of the ammunition and the motors, and after placing lookouts Captain Aharon permitted them to take a breath of fresh air. Together with his second-in-command he inspected the condition of the tanks. Every single tank had been hit, and the two officers were amazed at the strength of the steel. In some of the tanks it was actually possible to see straight through the holes made by Egyptian armour-piercing shells. But their chief concern was the tanks' fuel and ammunition supplies, for they had not the slightest idea when the battalion would join up with them or when they might be called upon to fight Egyptian reinforcements.

Captain Aharon could not contemplate the idea of taking off his bullet-riddled helmet. The blood had now congealed inside and he was afraid that if he took it off the insides of his head would fall out. "For better or for worse," he said to Solomonov, "what's keeping my head together is my helmet."

Solomonov went over to Munitz's tank. The lieutenant's left eye was a gash of congealing blood, and a wound in his cheek made talking difficult.

"How are things, Munitz?"

"We're alive," said Munitz.

Compared to Munitz's wounds, the injuries of the others seemed slight, and the men were ashamed to report them or complain. A strange feeling of peace descended on them; the fresh air practically intoxicated them, and they began to notice the scented desert air, carrying the whiff of the palm trees of El-Arish and the tang of salt from the deep, sandy dunes. It was Captain Aharon who brought everyone back to the realities of war. "Come on, lads. Back to your tanks and guns."

The seconds ticked away endlessly and Kramer was beginning to get bored next to his gun. But then to his joy an Egyptian convoy made its appearance, travelling unconcernedly to Sheikh Zuweid from El-Arish. It was a small supply convoy; tankers and trucks. It had not dawned on its commanders that Sheikh Zuweid had been captured.

"With one shell I can smash the whole convoy," Kramer said to Solomonov.

"No need. Pity to waste the ammunition. The 0.5 will do."

"Ah!"

Solomonov switched the 0.5 Browning to single-shot fire. One bullet set the tanker ablaze, which began to burn like an oil refinery.

"Waste of fuel, Sir," said Kramer.

"You'll see the dismay it will create, Kramer. They'll see that thick smoke and not a single Egyptian tank will come near us."

"And that'll be a pity," said Kramer, his hand stroking his gun.

Lieutenant Shuali, firing his 0.5 Browning on single-shot, set fire to two trucks in the convoy, which began to explode like fireworks.

"Ammunition," said Shuali.

And that was how Captain Aharon's company passed the time away. There was to be a further two hours before the battalion joined up with them.

Aharon's incredible speed along the road had surprised, alarmed and stunned Egypt's 7th divisional headquarters and the units attached to it. The sight of the seven racing tanks had thoroughly confused them, where apparently nothing was known of 'S' Brigade's attack. Thus when the companies of 'S' Brigade deployed for the attack on Sheikh Zuweid, they came upon a very incoherent scene. There were Egyptian units whose men, stunned and frightened, had crawled beneath dug-in tanks and armoured personnel-carriers and hid, the weapons in their hands remaining silent. Others had removed their shoes and taken to the dunes. There were also those who gave battle, and in one exchange S/10 set fire to ten T/34s.

After that final battle the companies began to pour into Sheikh Zuweid. It was here that the first prisoners-of-war were taken. Colonel Shmuel had ordered that Egyptian soldiers who raised their arms in surrender were not to be shot at, but at first the Egyptians were so confused that they raised their arms with their weapons still in their hands.

The tanks began the mopping-up operations. Colonel Shmuel saw a Centurion pass over a trench in which he had noticed three Egyptian soldiers hiding, filling it with sand, and gave orders that a group of prisoners be given shovels to dig them out. At first the prisoners refused, not understanding what the commander was getting at and fearful of some cruel punishment for them, but eventually the order was forced upon them, and they dug out the filled-in ditch. By a miracle the three Egyptians emerged unhurt from the trench; one of the prisoners who had been digging ran over to Colonel Shmuel and attempted to embrace him.

"My brother!" the man cried in Arabic.

"Is he calling me brother?" asked the astonished colonel.

"No, Sir, his brother was buried in the trench and rescued."

Around Colonel Shmuel's jeep the commanders of his units now gathered: Major Ehud Elad, Lieutenant-Colonel Gabriel, Captain Ori, Lieutenant-Colonel Zvi (commanding the artillery battalion), Lieutenant-Colonel Zwicka, and the second-in-command, Pinko. They were in high spirits. Ehud gave Colonel Shmuel a look of victory and pride. The colonel noticed that he was moving his arm with difficulty, that his left hand was bandaged and its fingers covered in congealed blood, that his upper lip was badly cut. His smile, however, was undaunted. The two men held each other in a lengthy embrace. Then Colonel Shmuel went back to directing the attack.

"What are your losses, Ehud?"

"Fourteen killed, Sir. Eight at Khan Yunis, five at the junction, one here. Twenty-three wounded; thirteen at Khan Yunis, seven at the junction, three here. I have not counted those who have not been evacuated."

"And you, Gabriel?"

"Ten killed, Sir. Seven at the junction, two at Khan Yunis, one here. Eight wounded, five at the junction. Those not evacuated are not included."

"And you, Ori?"

For a moment Ori could not speak. The reconnaissance company's losses had been heavy. "Ten killed, Sir. One at Khan Yunis and nine at the junction. Eleven wounded and evacuated. Nine at the junction."

He turned his head away. The count continued. 'S' had lost twenty-six men at the junction, eleven at Khan Yunis, one at the frontier crossing and one at Sheikh Zuweid; thirty-nine killed. Twenty men had been wounded at the junction, fifteen at Khan Yunis and one at the frontier crossing. Altogether seventy-seven fighting men were missing from its ranks.

"What about Carmeli?" Colonel Shmuel asked.

"The ordnance officer, who happens to be Carmeli's brother-in-law, recognised his half-track. He discovered Carmeli lying on the floor of the abandoned vehicle. It seems he

156

has lost an eye," said Pinko.

"How many tanks?" asked Shmuel and again the count began.

"Up till now everything has gone well. I am satisfied," said Colonel Shmuel. "We will now continue to Jiradi. S/10 will move in front, S/14 on the left flank; the reconnaissance company. . . . Is the recce company in a state to lead, Ori?"

"Yes, Sir. From the three parties we had we've formed two."

"The reconnaissance company leads. . . ."

"Sir, the divisional commander wishes to speak to you," said Major Israel, the brigade's signals officer. Shmuel returned to the command half-track.

"Tirah, this is Shamir, Sunray speaking."

"Shamir, this is Tirah. Sunray speaking. Send a sub-unit to help Raphoul, on the El-Arish axis in the direction of Rafa Junction. There is strong opposition at the junction. Over."

"Tirah, this is Shamir. Roger. Returning with S/14. S/10 goes on to Jiradi, makes contact. If it proves easy going they will proceed through Jiradi. Over."

"This is Tirah. Agreed. Over."

The time was 14.32.

Jiradi was not one of the assignments which 'S' was to carry out "whatever the cost". Its brief was to make contact with the enemy and to pass through Jiradi if it proved easy; but if not, the division had planned a night attack in which 'M' Armoured Brigade, moving in from Jiradi's rear, was to play an important role. Colonel Shmuel, however, was anxious to exploit the brigade's successes, and did not want to stop the momentum of its forward drive. This was why he had requested permission to continue with the brigade's plan even though he himself now had to return with one of his battalions to assist Colonel Raphoul. His armoured infantry brigade, augmented with tanks, would be under divisional command, fighting and mopping up the Rafa defences in the rear; the Patton battalion would be returning to the junction; and the Centurions would have to attempt what had been assigned to the entire brigade. Again Colonel Shmuel decided to form two command groups: while he returned to the junction, Pinko would command 'S' Brigade's advance party. "But, Pinko, you will advance through the Jiradi only if it is easy. Under no circumstances are you to get involved with heavy losses and grinding battles. Is that clear?"

"Yes, Sir," said Pinko.

The moment the two forces separated, a company of T/01

Pattons which had been fighting with Colonel Raphoul made their appearance. Lieutenant Ein-Gil, their commander, had made a miscalculation and arrived at Sheikh Zuweid instead of Kafr Shan. Pinko received the company with great enthusiasm and immediately began issuing orders as though its chance arrival had brought the unit under his command, but Lieutenant Ein-Gil informed him that he had received no orders to join up with another brigade.

"All right then," said Pinko, as though he had been snubbed, "if you don't want to fight, stay right here." He raised his flags and ordered his column of Centurions off towards Jiradi, joining up with Aharon's company on the way. Shamai's company was now leading the column.

As Colonel Shmuel was organising their return with the command group to the junction, he heard a noise. Near the locality where he had actually established his command group they found a large dug-out. The vehicles had been removed and the camouflage netting had fallen in and now lay sprawled out on the bottom of the dug-out. But now and then the netting moved. When they lifted it up they found dozens of terrified Egyptian soldiers cowering there, their weapons in their hands.

"Collect them," ordered Colonel Shmuel. In addition to all his other problems he must now leave a unit behind in Sheikh Zuweid to guard them. He was concerned about how dispersed and spread out his units were. It was for this reason that he had chosen the Pattons for himself; faster than the Centurions, he hoped they would soon be done with this new assignment and be able to return to the brigade. He wanted most of all to get back in time to attack Jiradi by daylight, so as not to require help from another brigade.

CHAPTER TWENTY

At 0855 hours Raphoul's force crossed the green line about six kilometres south of Kerem Shalom and then split into two columns. Israel Force – so called after its commander – turned south to act as a blocking force, while the main force, two paratroop battalions riding in half-tracks and T/01 Patton Battalion, turned towards the southern defence area of the Rafa Junction.

The northern defence area, against which 'S' had launched itself, was laid out on the Rafa–Junction road; the southern defence area on the old Rafa–Nizana road. At one time it had been an asphalt road, but when Zahal had vacated Sinai in 1957 it had torn up the roads. The Egyptian Army had re-turned and re-built most of them, but not Rafa–Nizana. Along the bed of the demolished road, south of the junction, the Egyptian Army had established a brigade defence zone of the linear disposition type: dug-outs, ditches, minefields, anti-tank and anti-personnel obstacles entrenched in and shielded by deep sand-dunes. It had many anti-tank guns and numer-ous tanks, among them the heaviest tank in the arena – the Stalin Mark 3 with its 122mm gun. At the rear of the defence zone were the positions of an Egyptian artillery brigade, sixty pieces in all.

To control the Rafa Junction it was necessary to rout the Egyptian brigade on the southern part of the junction, the more so since General Tal's plan called for 'M' Brigade to move on to El-Arish through the sands along an axis parallel to the El-Arish road. One of the tasks assigned to 'M' was to attack the Jiradi at night from the rear should the frontal attack fail; however, at this stage 'M' was still the divisional reserve.

In this sector armour and paratroopers met for the first time in a closely combined operation. At first General Tal and Colonel Raphoul had planned to transport the paratroopers to their battle sector in T/01's Patton tanks, as an elite ar-moured infantry force, and during the lengthy waiting period which preceded the war, the black berets and the red boots had become close friends, the tank crews teaching the para-troopers to drive tanks and load guns. It was finally decided, however, to transport the paratroops on half-tracks. These were to follow the Pattons in two columns, a northern one and a southern one. The plan was to roll up the enemy defence zones and artillery from the rear and from their southern flank to the north.

On the morning of 5 June, then, Colonel Raphoul waved a Red Sheet out of his caravan, and his forces set off, Israel Force turning southward to its blocking assignment, 'Z' and T/01 continuing westward towards the Egyptian defence zone. Fifteen minutes later the lead company of the main column was already under heavy anti-tank fire. The comman-der of the company, Captain Amnon Giladi, was killed in his cupola and his Patton set on fire by an anti-tank shell. Lieu-tenant-Colonel Uri immediately ordered Lieutenant Ein-Gil, whose company was the northern neighbour of the lead company, to go to its assistance; Ein-Gil wheeled round and in his eagerness to carry out the task assigned to him made a mistake. The plan required that the lead company explore and locate the Egyptian position so that the main strength could just brush against the defence zone along its least defended flank and outflank it without having to pay the heavy price of a frontal attack. Ein-Gil, however, went straight at the enemy position and cut through it laterally, managing to lose sight of the Z/1 Paratroop Battalion, riding in half-tracks, whom he was supposed to be guiding. Z/1 was to have attacked the defence zone from south to north along the bed of the demolished road, a part of the plan which had a great bearing on the pace of the southern part of the pincer movement against the Rafa Junction.

Ein-Gil had seen the lead company commander's Patton go up in flames, while behind him, doing nothing, the Pattons waited in line. The Egyptians' initial strike had sown a certain lack of confidence in the lead company, and they were waiting without knowing what to do, in an area which was being heavily bombarded with artillery and anti-tank gun fire.

On receiving Lieutenant-Colonel Uri's order Ein-Gil had sent a section of his company to take up firing positions to the left of Giladi's company, and with the rest of his unit had spread out and begun to exchange shots with the enemy defence position. But the rain did not permit him to adopt good firing positions, as the sand dunes rolled from west to east. The tanks were too close together and exposed to the Egyptian anti-tank guns.

"To hell with it," said Ein-Gil, "we'll cut them in two."

He raised his flag and indicated to his company to follow him. In a matter of minutes his company had drenched the objective with fire, wiped out the anti-tank guns and reached the other side of the enemy position. At that moment a jeep from the rear came racing up to Ein-Gil, and the officer in it told him to change his frequency band; Ein-Gil did so and heard: "Move, now, move. Out."

That was the sort of order Ein-Gil preferred. He and his company continued advancing north-west, while Z/1 Paratroop Battalion turned south to outflank the defence zone which Ein-Gil had already cut through; the two units drew further apart and were never to come together again, though

160

16. Colonel Shmuel with Major Elad a few days before the outbreak of hostilities.

17. Colonel Shmuel at the Jiradi, Monday, 5 June.

18. Major Ehud Elad reviews S/14 Battalion.

19. (*below left*) Lieutenant-Colonel Biro.

20. (*below*) Dr. (Major) Raphael Mokady.

21. (*above*) Colonel Bren
as a battalion commander
after the 1956 Sinai
Campaign.

22. (*above right*) Captain
Avigdor Kahalany in a
military hospital, six
months after the war.

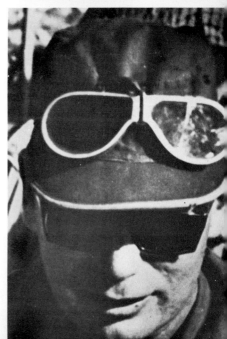

23. Colonel Albert, the
commander of 'A' Brigade.

24. Lieutenant-Colonel Pinko on his command half-track after the Jiradi break-through.

25. A young officer from 'S' Brigade giving water to an Egyptian prisoner.

according to the original plan, Ein-Gil was supposed to have moved ahead of Z/1 along the bed of the demolished road, and roll up, from south to north, the southern defence zone of the junction. Until today the mystery of who it was who told Ein-Gil to change his frequency band has not been solved, though there is a theory that the order was intended for Giladi's company, which had been left without a commanding officer, and that the person who had delivered the order had made a mistake and given it to Ein-Gil.

However that may be, Ein-Gil's company moved forward. He had nine Patton tanks with him, and leading the force were he and Sergeant Benny Inbar. The terrain was similar to that north of the El-Arish road, except that it was more undulating and sandier. It was very difficult to find the bed of the demolished road, but when they finally did mount it, Ein-Gil and Inbar felt a strong whoosh of air followed by a thunderous roar as a shell hurtled above them, to be swallowed up in the sand. They were being fired at.

Searching the terrain Ein-Gil identified two Egyptian tanks. He calculated that they were T/34s, at 1500 metres range, moving from north-west to south-east. His and Benny Inbar's Pattons were somewhat ahead of their company, which had not had time to reorganise properly after cutting through the Egyptian defence zone. The Egyptians managed to fire six shells at Ein-Gil and Inbar before they could improve their firing positions. Benny Inbar was injured by shell splinters in his neck, but continued to fight.

The two enemy tanks went down and out of Ein-Gil's sight. From reports he was receiving from his unit he realised that they were part of a larger force which was moving up to block the axis of the demolished road from the south. Thus they were in a position to be able to outflank him from the south. An idea occurred to Ein-Gil, an idea which appealed to him; he would outflank the outflankers. He ordered four of his Pattons to move south and to meet the Egyptian tanks head on; such a confrontation would give the Egyptians the feeling that they had the upper hand. Meanwhile Ein-Gil and the other five Pattons made for the rear of the Egyptian tanks, managing to reduce the range to 1000 metres. Driving up for an observation, he discovered six enemy tanks, some of which were facing away from him while others stood in profile. He prayed that his other four Pattons would quickly reach the Egyptians, but their progress, so it seemed to him, took ages. Ein-Gil began to doubt the wisdom of his strategy.

At last, after five long minutes had passed, the four Pattons appeared, apparently causing great joy to the Egyptian tank commanders, who reckoned that they were in a superior position both in terrain and numbers. There were more than six of them; Ein-Gil had not seen the full complement. The Eygptian tanks opened fire on the four Pattons, and at the same moment Ein-Gil and Benny Inbar, with the three Pattons behind them, surged up to firing positions, their first shots setting two Egyptian tanks ablaze. Only later were they identified as Stalin 3s, the most heavily armoured tanks ever built.

The Stalin crews were taken completely by surprise. They now tried to alter their positions, but inevitably this placed them at a disadvantage vis-à-vis the four Pattons facing them from the front. The movements of the Egyptian tanks were slow, like the men who manned them, and before they had altered their positions, traversed, loaded and eventually fired, Ein-Gil and Benny Inbar had set another three Stalins on fire. All in all, ten enemy tanks were now engulfed in flames. The battle was over. The Stalins rested in a variety of positions, as though after an earthquake; some in battle positions, others half-turned or in reverse. Soon their ammunition began to catch fire; two turrets shot into the air, one landing back on to its own turret ring, its gun upside down.

By now Ein-Gil had completely lost contact with Z/1. He tried to resume contact with his battalion commander, Lieutenant-Colonel Uri, but in vain. He decided to continue attacking, and went over in his mind the briefings. The enemy's anti-tank locality was situated at Kafr Shan, south of the El-Arish road. He turned in this direction, but miscalculated and instead of reaching Kafr Shan arrived at Sheikh Zuweid further west and part of "S" Brigade's sector. Here it was that Pinko tried to talk him into joining up with him in his drive to Jiradi. However at 1300 hours radio contact between Ein-Gil and Lieutenant-Colonel Uri was renewed. Uri ordered the lieutenant to stay where he was and to await orders.

Captain Amos, whose Patton company had been assigned the task of protecting Colonel Raphoul's southern flank, then to disperse on the west side of the demolished road's bed and destroy the Egyptian artillery positions, completed his part of the plan and arrived with the Paratroop Battalion to attack the anti-tank locality of Kafr Shan. From there he was to attack the enemy positions south of the Rafa Junction from the rear. His company had lost one tank, which had touched off a mine and another, the captain's, whose hydraulic system had failed. Captain Amos changed tanks. On the way to Kafr Shan the company came up against a two-company defence area in which were many anti-tank guns. In a fierce battle they destroyed it, then dispersed and began to fire on Kafr Shan. At this stage Captain Amos had eleven Pattons.

The Pattons entered Kafr Shan with the paratroopers. Captain Giora Eytan, Colonel Raphoul's nephew, drove in his half-track next to Captain Amos' Patton along the main dirt road of the village, in whose alleys lurked Egyptian forces and tanks. East of the village were a further twenty-two T/34s, part of the anti-tank locality of the Egyptian defence dispositions.

Captain Giora Eytan's and Amos' Patton led the column. Captain Amos was the first to spot an Egyptian T/34 hiding in an alley to the left of Giora's half-track; it was taking aim at the paratroop company commander's half-track. Amos fired a perfect shot and the T/34 went up in flames. At that same moment Giora pointed to the right, towards a second T/34 hiding at a range of some sixty metres behind a cactus hedge, but he spotted it a moment too late. The T/34 fired and hit Giora's half-track, which caught fire and exploded and Captain Giora Eytan was killed. Quickly Amos traversed his gun in the direction of the T/34. The two tanks fired simultaneously and both scored direct hits. Amos and his men jumped out of the burning tank and rolled on the ground to extinguish their burning clothing. When Amos got up he was wearing a sleeveless shirt and short trousers.

Meanwhile the rest of his company was engaged in destroying part of the Egyptian tanks which were east of the village. Captain Amos boarded another Patton and went on fighting until Kafr Shan had been taken and mopped up.

Captain Danny's company also completed its first part of the plan. It had first had to protect the southern flank of the task force and had then assaulted the enemy artillery positions assigned to it. Captain Danny had then been ordered by the battalion commander, Lieutenant-Colonel Uri, to get on to the bed of the demolished road and to advance along it northwards, an order necessitated by the fact that Ein-Gil had lost Z/1. Uri was in fact detailing Captain Danny to take over Ein-Gil's original job and to lead the Z/1 Paratroop Battalion to its assignment. But the fortunes of war decided otherwise, and Captain Danny was also to lose Z/1.

At first everything went well. Danny's company advanced northwards along the road bed with the paratroopers following in their half-tracks. The Egyptian brigade defence zone was teeming with infantry, armoured personnel carriers, truck-drawn guns and anti-tank guns. The first two platoons made their initial strike against the anti-tank guns, and some thirty of them were blown into the air with the first shots. The Pattons then began to attack the objective from its narrow side and to roll it up, while the Egyptian soldiers took to flight. When Danny considered that the objective had been thoroughly destroyed, he turned sharply to the left in the direction he thought was the Rafa Junction. In this manoeuvre, however, he lost sight of the road bed, which was most difficult to find again in the sea of sand and deep depressions, and while searching he managed to lose Z/1 which was by now far behind, the half-tracks labouring slowly through the deep sands. As had already happened several times before, the Egyptians recovered from the initial shock of the tank attack, and after Danny's Pattons had passed through them, returned to their positions, ready to receive the Z/1 paratroopers. Thus Z/1 wasted the advantage given them by the Pattons. Also, the Egyptians had an able and brave major in command, the brigade operations officer; he had taken over from the brigade commander who had fled. Thus Z/1 could expect some hard fighting, without tanks and cut off from the rest of Colonel Raphoul's force, which had gone off in a westerly direction.

Captain Danny's company, consisting of nine Pattons, proceeded in a north-westerly direction. Danny climbed a hill for observation purposes, but could see nothing in the undulating terrain, which looked like a raging sea of sand. He raised a flag to renew the advance, and his tank drove forward, down to more or less level ground. Suddenly, at a range of eight hundred to a thousand metres, he saw two T/34s, an SU/100 tank and two anti-tank guns whose crews were traversing in his direction. In a matter of seconds Captain Danny had hit a T/34 and his section commander Sela had hit the SU/100. With another shell Danny got the two anti-tank guns, some of whose crews were killed, while the others fled. Part of his company was already moving on to do battle with another enemy force sighted ahead, consisting of armoured personnel-carriers, anti-tank guns and another SU/100. At that moment his motor went dead.

"Driver, start up!" said Captain Danny to his driver.

"It won't start, Sir."

There was a fiery flash above his head, coming from behind. The shell fell and exploded in front of him. Danny gritted his teeth. Still the engine would not start. In his earphones Danny could hear the commander of the reconnaissance section of his paratroopers, who had managed to stay with him, call out: "Danny, Danny, heavy-heavies are shooting at you from behind! I repeat, Danny, heavy-heavies are shooting from behind!"

Danny turned his head round and saw two tanks burning; one tank commander was lying on the turret. A third tank seemed to be out of action though not burning, and in that one too he could see the tank commander lying on the turret. The three tanks were no more than 150 metres away from him, and he was already thinking: "Not bad! Another three gone!" when it dawned upon him that they were three of his Pattons. The tank commander lying on the tank that was out of action was Second Lieutenant Ami Goren, the one on the burning tank Yossi Millo. He could not see any of the crew from the third tank.

Danny was annoyed with himself for having betrayed his agitation to the driver. This time he spoke in a calm and controlled tone: "Driver, start the auxiliary generator."

To his relief he heard it cough.

"Start the main engine."

The noise of the fuel exploding in the combustion chamber could be heard, at first irregularly and then with a steady beat. Captain Danny ordered his company back, out of the level and exposed area.

"Driver, now quickly in reverse."

Firing ahead of them, the Pattons drove back in reverse; several anti-tank guns were now very active in front. It was a T/34 which had fired at them from its hiding place in their rear, but even that became known to Captain Danny only after the battle. At that stage he could not see the enemy, which had him surrounded. He withdrew his six Pattons into a small valley, about two hundred metres by two hundred, where they took up firing positions against the invisible enemy from behind and at the anti-tank guns whose location was known. Danny turned his own Patton round again and climbed up to an observation position, from where he sighted five Egyptian tanks in firing positions along the ridge of a sand hill, aiming in his direction.

Danny placed two Pattons in firing positions to the front, in the direction of the anti-tank guns, and four Pattons facing the rear. The range in front was between 900 to 1200 metres and in the rear from 1200 to 1500 metres. His four Pattons facing the rear had already located five Stalins. Rapidity and accuracy in firing was here decisive. Danny himself hit the far right Stalin, which was exposed; it burst into flames, emitting thick yellow-coloured smoke so that for a moment Danny thought the Stalin's commander had thrown a yellow smoke grenade. Within a few minutes five Stalins were blazing. However, more Stalins were racing forward so as to surround the six Pattons besieged in the valley. They had soon taken up positions, further away and better than those of their predecessors. To make matters worse an Egyptian position now began to shell the Pattons with heavy mortars. The Pattons were fighting a pitched battle in the course of which they were obliged to change their firing positions several times so as to prevent the Stalins from outflanking the company. The battle continued, with the fire exchange getting more measured and discriminating as each side manoeuvred to attain better firing positions. But the strength of Danny's company was beginning to wane.

Sergeant Gershon now arrived on foot from one of the three Pattons which had been the first to be hit. He climbed on to the deck of Danny's tank and reported that two of the Pattons had exploded with their ammunition, and that the third had been hit in its turret so that its entire firing mechanism had been demolished; Platoon Commander Ami Goren had been killed in his cupola.

"How many killed altogether?"

"Four, Sir."

"Wounded?"

"Three, Sir."

"What about the motor of the Patton whose turret was hit?"

"Working, Sir."

"Get Ami, cover him with a blanket, tie him to a stretcher, put him inside the tank and bring it here with the injured and the rest of the crew." Danny noted with relief that the five survivors from the three tanks were waiting calmly, their weapons in their hands.

The platoon sergeant's Patton, which was on the company's right flank, now reported to Danny that it had no traverse and that it could not sight the gun on to the target, then that the gun's elevation system would not work.

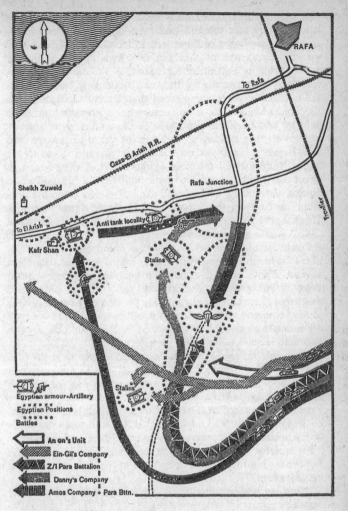

5 *Colonel Raphoul's tactical manoeuvres at the southern
wing of the Rafa Junction*

"Leave the tank with your crew and see what you can do
for the wounded," Danny said. The casualties were thus given
first aid.

But the company had now only five tanks left. After

considerable effort spent in locating the battalion commander by radio, Danny succeeded in making contact with him and reported to him his dire situation. Uri had left his command half-track and was at that moment in a Patton taking an active part in the battle near Kafr Shan.

"I'll try to get to you with Amos's company," Lieutenant-Colonel Uri said. It was agreed that Danny would indicate his whereabouts with a coloured smoke grenade. But time went by and he did not turn up. The Egyptians were anxious to exploit their numerical and topographical advantage and now began to close in on their prey, advancing slowly as though they had all the time in the world. Danny began to direct each tank, so that he could both defend his flanks and destroy the enemy. "Number Two, move left. There's something moving on the ridge. Two thousand from our left. Check and open fire." The Patton's crew checked, perfected their sights, fired and set a Stalin ablaze.

Danny again reviewed his situation, coming to the conclusion that his most dangerous enemy might well be a shortage of fuel. The Egyptians would be able to keep him pinned down in his present position until his fuel ran out, when they would move in for the kill. He decided on fuel economy; at his command each Patton shut off its motor until he gave the order to restart. However, when he gave the order to one Patton to re-start, a fire broke out in it.

"Cut motor at once!" Danny commanded over his radio.

The crew cut the motor and jumped down from the tank to put out the blaze with their extinguishers and sand which they threw on with a shovel, then climbed back into the Patton to await orders. Danny thought a fault had developed in the ignition system and was afraid it would catch fire again when re-started. He ordered fire extinguishers to be collected from nearby tanks and placed in readiness. Soon, as the Egyptians improved their positions, it became essential to move it again.

"Start-up and move quickly in reverse," Captain Danny ordered.

The driver switched on and again fire broke out, this time catching the camouflage netting. The crew fought the flames with the extinguishers, but to no avail. Danny ordered the two nearest Pattons to their aid and the crews worked hard to smother the fire by shovelling sand on to it, but the flames had already spread to the rubber of the tracks, the motor and transmission, and could not be extinguished.

"Abandon tank!" the captain ordered. But the crew went back into the turret of the burning vehicle and retrieved their weapons, maps, optical instruments and other equipment. Finally they withdrew and the tank was soon consumed in a mass of flames. (Only later was it learned that the fire had not been caused by a fault in the ignition system; an Egyptian hollow charge shell had struck the rear under-belly of the tank, near the fuel pipe. Sparks from the ignition had set fire to the leaking fuel and set the tank on fire.)

Now only four serviceable tanks remained to the company. But a short while later Danny heard Captain Amos over the radio inform him that he was moving in the direction of the junction; he requested him to identify himself with a smoke grenade. Danny discharged several coloured smoke grenades, but the smoke stayed close to the ground and would not rise. He fired a rocket and waited for Amos. Meanwhile the mortar barrage directed at him thickened, and his fuel supply was getting lower and lower.

CHAPTER TWENTY-ONE

At General Tal's command group the picture of the breakthrough battle at the Rafa Junction was darkening. The Egyptians on the left flank of the junction had displayed initiative in throwing a battalion of Stalin tanks into the fray, forcing the Patton companies to do battle with them and cutting them off from the Z/1 Paratroop Battalion – first Ein-Gil's company and then that of Danny.

Until midday the situation did not seem dangerous; indeed Z/1 was still managing to hold on at the edge of the brigade defence zone, even after having lost several half-tracks in the deep sands. The paratroopers were fighting without tanks against a dug-in Egyptian force equipped with tanks and quantities of anti-tank weapons; the paratroopers' half-tracks were easily hit by anti-tank guns, and their losses were heavy. Nevertheless they attacked, and in a hand-to-hand fight overcame their opponents. As the afternoon progressed it seemed to them that they had captured the whole of the battalion defence zone; they had begun to assemble their wounded near an isolated building when they were menaced by a Stalin Mark 3 which advanced upon them, undisturbed by the rockets fired by Paratrooper Avi's bazooka, which had no effect upon it even at a range of 150 metres. It was threaten-

169

ing to crush the battalion first aid post under its tracks, but when its driver opened his hatch to get a better view of the terrain Paratrooper Dooby was given a golden opportunity. Till then he had been an anguished onlooker as he watched two of Avi's bazooka rockets leave the Stalin unscathed. Now he aimed his grenade rifle at the opened hatch and when the range had closed to within forty metres, fired. The grenade shot through the opening and exploded, reducing the driver's compartment to a mass of flames and catching its ammunition. Two of the Egyptian tank's crew were killed inside and two more leaped out enveloped in flames. After that it became comparatively quiet and the paratroopers began to attend to their wounded, most of whom were suffering from burns received when their half-tracks had been hit by Egyptian anti-tank guns.

Just after midday it had seemed to Colonel Raphoul that his forces were on the verge of completing their assignment. At 1236 hours he radioed General Tal: "Tirah. This is Zebra. I've got a present for the division. One damaged Stalin and one practically untouched. Ten enemy tanks are on fire."

This was the first news Tal had received of what was happening in that area; he had reason to feel extremely satisfied.

At 1257 hours General Tal ordered Colonel Men to advance with 'M' along his axis, which ran parallel with the El-Arish road. He was to get to the rear of El-Arish and there prepare himself to attack the Jiradi pass by night, if this proved necessary. By 1307 hours it appeared to divisional headquarters that Colonel Raphoul was on the verge of completing his assignment, and the division's war room cabled southern command: "Two enemy brigades in Colonel Raphoul's operational area are about to be finished off."

Only three minutes later the divisional headquarters learned of the fierce battle Captain Amos was fighting at Kafr Shan, in his encounter with the T/34s, and General Tal ordered Colonel Shmuel, who had by this time reached Sheikh Zuweid, to move to his assistance. However within a few minutes Lieutenant-Colonel Uri and Captain Amos had decided the battle at Kafr Shan and joined forces; General Tal cancelled his order to Colonel Shmuel, but released the armoured infantry battalion of 'S' Brigade, which had been positioned to defend Kerem Shalom, and dispatched it to mop up the enemy positions at Rafa. The armoured infantry battalion moved from Kerem Shalom towards the Rafa Junction, taking with it heavy engineering equipment to clear the extensive minefields around the junction.

170

By 1330 hours divisional headquarters deemed the situation satisfactory, and General Tal drew the boundaries between 'S' and 'Z', ordering 'S' not to go south of the El-Arish road. Even so the general still felt somewhat uneasy about the outcome of the battle on the Rafa Junction; it seemed to him that there was still strong opposition on its southern flank, and he considered the possibility of committing 'M' to the attack there, but Colonel Raphoul, who was driving and pushing forward his forces like quicksilver, announced that he was concentrating all his strength for a final assault which would smash the Egyptian opposition at the junction's southern flank.

At 1351 hours Z/1 radioed that the brigade defence zone was in its hands and that it was now reorganising. But then the picture began to change rapidly. Twenty-five minutes later Colonel Raphoul radioed General Tal: "Tirah. This is Zebra. I have come up against strong enemy force. I and my command group are engaged in fierce battle. I need assistance."

And indeed, over his radio General Tal could hear the noise of the battle raging around Raphoul's command group. In fact the colonel was actually holding the speaker with one hand while with the other he was firing his Uzzi submachine gun. His voice was cool and matter of fact, but even without the sounds of battle in the background his carefully worded message was very disquieting for Tal knew that a daring and experienced fighter like Raphoul would not describe a battle as "fierce", and would not ask for assistance, unless he and the forces at his disposal were very near to the end of their tether. Certainly, the battle for the junction had not been decided yet. It appeared to the general that the Egyptians were gathering their forces in an attempt to turn his break-through to their advantage; if the southern flank of the Rafa Junction was in their hands, then they would be in a position to dominate the entire junction.

According to the original plan, Colonel Raphoul was supposed to have advanced with Ein-Gil's company, which was to have served as his brigade reserve after it had lead Z/1 to its assignment. Raphoul was now carrying out the plan in full even though Ein-Gil was no longer with him. Tal's concern for Raphoul and his men was enhanced by his feeling that the fortunes of the day's campaigns were now in the balance. He immediately ordered three battalions to race for the junction: 'S' Brigade's armoured infantry battalion, one of Colonel Shmuel's battalions (from Sheikh Zuweid) and 'M'

Brigade's armoured infantry battalion. Tal informed Raphoul of each step he was taking, while the colonel fought with the Uzzi in his hand, threw grenades into the enemy trenches and directed his units, whether near or far, with unruffled composure.

At 1440 hours the T/01 commander, Lieutenant-Colonel Uri, completed his armour versus armour encounter near Kafr Shan and announced he was returning towards the junction with Captain Amos' company. At 1442 hours the divisional operations officer Kalman reported this to General Tal, who immediately informed Colonel Raphoul that Uri was moving in the direction of the junction with his Pattons. At 1446 hours Uri informed Raphoul that he was approaching but could not identify Raphoul's command group. Uri was at the moment one kilometre east of Kafr Shan and about six hundred metres south of the El-Arish road. Raphoul guided the Pattons to his position, some two kilometres south of the junction.

(Before Colonel Raphoul and Lieutenant-Colonel Uri joined forces, Amos' company had rushed to the aid of Danny's beleaguered company. Amos had spotted Danny's rocket and in a moment Danny saw the nine Pattons racing to his aid. He had already warned Amos that on his right flank, at a range of fifteen hundred metres, were enemy tanks which he, Danny, was unable to destroy as they were in dead ground, hidden from him. Amos had swung right, surprised the Egyptian tanks on the flank, and destroyed seven of them, including two Stalins. This had completed the destruction of the battalion of Stalin/3 tanks on the southern flank of the Rafa Junction. The mortar bombardment from the south upon Danny's company had intensified at virtually the same moment as his five still mobile Pattons had moved off in a column to the left of Captain Amos' nine Pattons.)

At 1536 hours Colonel Raphoul started his attack with Lieutenant-Colonel Uri, Captain Danny and Captain Amos, a total of fifteen Pattons taking part, together with the half-tracks of Colonel Raphoul's command group. They went for the junction itself; sweeping from west to south then back again, destroying the enemy fortifications in numerous fierce encounters, they finally assured the outcome of the struggle at the junction.

By 1915 hours the Egyptian position was silenced. Colonel Raphoul's sweep was seen as marking the completion of the campaign on the southern flank. The evacuation of the wounded by air now started. A helicopter landed, guided by flares, and the injured men, who had been waiting patiently and silently since the morning hours, were flown to hospitals in Israel. When the officers took a check roll-call it was found that Lieutenant-Colonel Uri had lost fourteen men killed and Colonel Raphoul thirty. 'Z' Brigade had over forty wounded. The Egyptian commander of the southern defence zone, the brigade operations officer who had assumed command when his brigade commander had fled, had been taken prisoner.

Meanwhile, 'S' Brigade's armoured infantry battalion had reached the junction and it now started to mop up the last pockets of resistance in the defence zone. It became possible to move the supply echelons forward to Colonel Raphoul's and 'S' Brigade's forces, the first of whose Centurions had arrived at El-Arish at 1600 hours.

At 1545 hours Colonel Herzl had transmitted General Tal's orders to Colonel Shmuel that 'Z' Brigade no longer required his assistance and that he was to return to his forces. By 1600 hours Lieutenant-Colonel Pinko with S/10 Battalion had reached the outskirts of El-Arish.

'S' was now dispersed over an area of forty kilometres, stretching from the Rafa Junction to the outskirts of El-Arish; its tanks at the El-Arish outskirts were by now almost out of fuel and ammunition, and the concentration of enemy forces for a counter-attack at El-Arish spelt disaster for S/10 if the other units of the brigade and its supply echelons were not rushed to it. Colonel Shmuel, fully aware of S/10's vulnerable position, ordered Ehud to cross the Jiradi at full speed and to join up with S/10 at El-Arish. He also busied himself with rushing the supply echelons through the junction towards his units at Sheikh Zuweid. He himself rushed in his jeep to his forward units; he caught up with S/14's tanks, headed by Ehud, and at Sheikh Zuweid met up with Ein-Gil's Pattons, still awaiting orders.

"Do you want to fight?"

"Yes, Sir."

"Then come on; join up with the S/14 Pattons."

"Without the battalion commander's permission, Sir?"

Radio contact with T/01 was not operating properly, but Ein-Gil followed his instincts and joined up with 'S', taking his place in Ehud's column of Pattons racing to the Jiradi.

The Jiradi locality is a narrow pass between sandhills which are not negotiable to vehicles. The road winds for fourteen kilometres until it reaches the outskirts of El-Arish. The Egyptians had set up powerful fortifications at three places, in defiles among the sandy dunes, the last of them six kilometres before El-Arish. The narrow pass had been named the Jiradi by the Israelis, after a railway stop there; in 1956 General Haim Bar-Lev's armoured brigade had passed through it, at such cost that the name now inspired fear. Since then the Egyptians had improved and further fortified the narrow pass with concrete ditches, trenches, bunkers, machine gun nests, anti-tank gun dug-outs with overhead covers, and tanks. So great was the Israeli's respect for the Jiradi that when Pinko notified divisional headquarters that he had passed the Jiradi and reached El-Arish, they thought he was either joking or that he had made a mistake in reading his map and had meant Sheikh Zuweid. But Pinko could not have misread his map — he did not have a map.

Pinko, with only seventeen Centurions and two Pattons, had driven as rapidly as possible through the Jiradi, all the time bearing in mind Colonel Shmuel's order not to get involved in heavy fighting and losses. Major Shamai Kaplan, with both his hands bandaged and his face pale from loss of blood, led the fast moving column. Behind Shamai's company, among which was also Pinko's command group in half-tracks, came Lieutenant Eli's reconnaissance party together with two Patton tanks, and then Captain Aharon's company. With them was Lieutenant Munitz, who was now blind in one eye.

As they had approached the Jiradi, Pinko ordered his force to open fire. Major Shamai, at the head of the column, could see the Egyptian tanks in heavy concentrations on both sides of the roadway, in dug-out emplacements, their guns aimed at the narrow entrance to the pass. There were also batteries of anti-tank guns camouflaged under nets; mortars, with the range pre-set on the road, positioned in hidden locations in the hills; machine gun positions and rifle pits spread out in the hills and fortified heights and invisible from the road; and mines laid along both sides of the road for the entire length of the fortified pass. The Egyptians were taken so completely by surprise in this fortress of a defence zone that they did not even open fire on the first tanks when they stormed in upon them. The range between the assaulting tanks and the dug-in Egyptian tanks was no more than fifty metres, and it seems that in their panic the Egyptians had hid under their camouflage nets, so that the vanguard of the Israeli force believed the Jiradi had been abandoned. So sure were they of this that Pinko did not even bother to destroy the tanks; he presumed they were unmanned and wished to take them, equipped and undamaged, as booty for Zahal. In retrospect this was a tragic mistake, a mistake prompted by Zahal's constant lack of supplies.

When the head of the column reached the end of the pass, the men in Pinko's half-track were actually listening in to the news from Radio Cairo; the Egyptian announcer was reporting the capture of Beersheba by the Egyptian Army and the capture of Afula by the Jerusalem forces. One of the men who knew Arabic translated for the benefit of the others, and the news caused great amusement to the vanguard of Division Tal as they approached the outskirts of El-Arish, the capital of Sinai. However, by the time the reconnaissance party, halfway down the column, had reached the top of the slope, the situation had changed. The Egyptians were beginning to creep back to their posts and to man the anti-tank guns, and as the reconnaissance party's Patton took the crest of the hill it was hit by an anti-tank shell. The Patton withdrew immediately to get out of the field of fire, but as one of the reconnaissance party's jeeps drew up to enquire if help was needed, a second shell, intended for the Patton which had now begun to reverse, hit the jeep, killing its occupants and setting it on fire. Another shell hit Sergeant Shuval's half-track, which was behind the jeep. The sergeant yelled to his men to grab their weapons and jump clear of the half-track. A moment later another shell struck the half-track and blew it up. Sergeant Shuval led his men in a crouching run to a spot behind a fold in the sands and began to return the fire.

Captain Aharon's company at the end of the column managed to continue its forward drive, but an armour-piercing shell struck Aharon's Centurion, which was leading the company, drilling a hole straight through it and decapitating the signalman; it also broke off radio contact in the tank itself and with the company and the battalion. A second shell hit the top of the turret, striking the hinge of the signalman's hatch and blowing it off. Fire broke out in the turret and the 0.5 Browning ammunition began to explode; in no time the turret was filled with smoke and flying shrapnel. The captain was hit in his hand and back; he found that he could not move his left hand.

"Crew, fire in the turret. Crew, action!" Aharon shouted into the microphone. But the intercom was not working. The fire was getting livelier by the minute, but inside his compartment the driver was oblivious to what was going on; the two shells which had pierced the tank had left his compartment unscathed. Aharon ordered the gunner to stop the driver and the gunner climbed out of his hatch, crawled along the lurching tank from the turret to the driver's hatch, and placed both his hands over the periscope. This, the gunner thought, would make him stop. But the driver thought an Egyptian soldier had jumped on to the tank to block his view and picked up his submachine gun. The gunner then pressed his face against the periscope. At last the driver recognised him and brought the tank to a halt.

Captain Aharon and two of his crew put out the fire with their extinguishers. The other Centurions in his company pulled up to him, but the captain ordered them to bypass him and get out of the field of fire. Lieutenants Solomonov and Shuali, however, decided to remain for a while and destroy the enemy emplacement which had already done so much damage. A few minutes later, the fire extinguished, Aharon's crew climbed back into their Centurion. They placed the signalman's body in the ammunition store, then the driver resumed his race for El-Arish. Lieutenants Shuali and Solomonov followed immediately behind him.

The column of Centurions vanished, and the six members of the reconnaissance party were left alone. Sergeant Shuval took command. They had to hide for about two hours in the sandy area, while machine gun and mortar fire rained about them, but by sheer good luck no one was wounded. Observing carefully, Sergeant Shuval noticed considerable preparations going on in the defence fortifications. It seemed that the Egyptian soldiers had been given definite orders; they began moving tanks and ranging guns. Later it was indeed learned from prisoners-of-war that the Egyptian Army in the Jiradi had been ordered to defend the position and fight to the last man.

CHAPTER TWENTY-TWO

The solitary Zahal jeep, its tall aerial quivering above it, raced towards the top of the rise. If it crested the hill it would enter a death-trap several kilometres long. Sergeant Shuval left his hiding place and made a suicidal dash for the highway. Machine gun fire sprayed the ground around his feet. He reached the road and waved his arms in agitation. The jeep braked, its tyres burning the asphalt road; it came to a halt only two metres from the top of the hill, then reversed and drove up to the sergeant. In the front seat was the brigade commander, Colonel Shmuel, his submachine gun across his knees.

"Sir, no further, Sir. It's a death trap," Sergeant Shuval said. He told the colonel how the S/10 column had got through the Jiradi, and how the Egyptians had organised themselves in time to fire at its tail. On all the evidence the pass was now sealed and Shmuel decided it would need at least two brigades to break through.

If 'S' proved unable to break through the Jiradi, then eighteen Centurions, one Patton and several half-tracks and jeeps would be cut off from the main force, without fuel or ammunition, and before long the Egyptians would be able to bring a superior force to wipe out Division Tal's vanguard. This was the most critical moment of the war for Colonel Shmuel, and for General Tal when the colonel told him of the situation.

Fully conscious of the enormity of the decisions he was taking, General Tal ordered 'S' Brigade, which was then moving through the sands parallel with the El-Arish road, to continue with one battalion to its original destination – that of blocking the Bir Lahfan–El-Arish road south of El-Arish – and to turn two battalions northwards, to attack the Jiradi from the south. In the original plan 'S' Brigade had been assigned the job of making contact with the enemy at the Jiradi, when if the break-through there had proved difficult it would have combined with 'M' in a night attack. The general wished to implement this plan now, but the 'M' battalions were stuck in the sand dunes. Their progress was slow and time was precious; 'S' therefore would have to break through the Jiradi on its own.

Twenty minutes later the vanguard of S/14 Battalion appeared. The lead tank stopped close to Colonel Shmuel, who climbed out of his jeep and walked along the road without his steel helmet on, as though tempting death. The brigade commander's unprotected head and the sight of him at the front line instilled great confidence in his men. The column of Pattons was headed by Lieutenant Avigdor Kahalany's company, and his brilliant smile telegraphed a greeting to Colonel Shmuel. In one of the first tanks was Major Ehud Elad. Shmuel informed him of the position; that the Jiradi was blocked, with anti-tank guns, mortars and tanks along the ridges to the right. He instructed Ehud to attack the fortified position simultaneously from the road, frontally, and through the sands, outflanking it from the south. For this S/14 would have to turn left off the road and pass through the sands, at the end of which, in all probability, were minefields. The orders were given for the flanking movement. Kahalany's Patton moved first, followed by his company. He turned left, drove off the road into the sands, and began climbing up the slope. The sands became deeper and deeper, and soon it was necessary to put the Patton into low gear. A heavy and pre-ranged barrage was immediately laid down on the area; anti-tank guns, tanks, field-guns and mortars, and the air was thick with lead. The shells fell into the white sands with an angry hissing noise, ugly whitish circles forming round them.

At last Kahalany's Patton reached to within a hundred and fifty metres of the road. He ordered the driver to halt and got ready to observe and locate the enemy's fire, particularly the tanks and the anti-tank gun batteries. But he did not have time. A direct hit from an anti-tank gun set his Patton ablaze. In no time the tank was a mass of flames. The rest of the crew managed to scramble out of the furnace but Kahalany, petrified with shock, found himself unable to move. At last, making a supreme effort of will, he raised himself up with his hands, pushing his body upwards until he was half out of the commander's cupola, and projected himself towards the red hot hull. From there he rolled on to the ground, his clothes a mass of flames. Gathering up all his strength, he dug his hands into the soft sand and scooped it over his clothes until the blaze was subdued. The barrage was getting heavier and the Pattons had now taken up positions and were beginning to fight. With his burnt arms he signalled to them not to stop and become easy targets for the enemy. He got up and stumbled towards the Pattons which had not yet been exposed to enemy fire, strips of burnt flesh which were hanging from his arms and legs swaying as he ran. As he scrambled into Lieutenant Ilan's Patton, the fire burst out again on his belt and shirt. Ilan sat Kahalany down in the fighting compartment, told the loader to smother the flames on Kahalany's clothes, closed the hatch of the compartment and ordered the driver to go back to the road at full speed. The driver drove zigzagging in reverse, coming to a stop next to the brigade commander's half-track. Kahalany was still on fire; Lieutenant Ilan tore his clothing off him, leaving him completely naked except for his boots, then helped Kahalany climb into

178

one of the reconnaissance party's jeeps, which had come with S/14 and was evacuating the wounded. Nobody believed Kahalany could live; all were shocked when he managed to give them his dazzling smile, the one thing the flames had not stripped him of.

The driver of the Patton behind Kahalany's had seen his company commander's tank burst into flames. He charged on, bypassing the burning vehicle on the right, but then a direct hit got him too. Two Pattons were now burning in the sands to the left of the road. On the right two Pattons attempted to storm through, but touched off mines and were brought to a halt. One of the crews went on fighting from the minefield with the tank commander, Sergeant Dov Yam, locating anti-tank guns which his gunner destroyed, but soon an anti-tank shell hit his tank too and Dov Yam's hand was severed at the wrist. Without a hand, he leaped from the Patton and ran to the brigade commander's half-track. His face was frighteningly white and the shock had temporarily unhinged his mind, but as they placed him on to a stretcher he whispered, "I think I did everything I could."

Four Pattons had now been hit at the Jiradi Pass. The third tank in Kahalany's column was Ehud's. His Patton was heavily scarred, as indeed were the two officers who stood in the turret; Ehud could move his hand only with difficulty, a large gash cut across his face, and there were shell splinters in his back. Next to him stood Lieutenant Amiram, the battalion operations officer, his injured eye covered with sticking-plaster, his wounded hand bandaged, and with splinters in his shoulder. At Sheikh Zuweid, Ehud had said to Colonel Shmuel and Major Haim: "We're living on luck."

Now Ehud's Patton was in the lead again. He radioed the battalion to disperse to the left, still hoping to get through the sands. His Patton was firing unceasingly, but the loading of the gun was not being done correctly. Five men were in the compartment and it was very congested. Ehud had taken a radio technician with him, to make sure his communications equipment worked well. The technician had been taught to load the gun, but in this he was not too successful, as he lacked training and practice, and every now and then Lieutenant Amiram Mizna would have to give him a helping hand. Now, as Ehud thrust forward into the raging fire of the Egyptian defence zone, there was again a hold up. The Patton was already two hundred and fifty metres from the road. Once again Amiram bent down to help the technician load the gun. In the

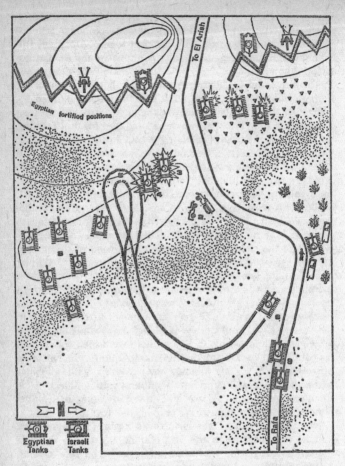

6 *S/14 Battalion breaks through the Jiradi.*

1. Colonel Shmuel and his command group. 2. The recce company's half-track and jeep hit while S/10 passed; from here Sergeant Shuval ran to alert Colonel Shmuel. 3. The Patton which bypassed Lieutenant Kahalany's Patton and was hit. 4. Lieutenant Kahalany's Patton, leading the attack. 5. Major Elad, commander of S/14 was killed here. 6. Major Elad's Patton, under the command of Lieutenant Mizna (Amiram) drives back to Colonel Shmuel,

pause, Ehud straightened up in his cupola, the binoculars to his eyes searching for the locations of the enemy's guns and looking for a possible way through for his battalion. All around him the ground was exploding violently, and the flashes of fire were blinding, but the vital thing was to keep the assault on the move, not to let it break, not to falter for a moment. "Driver, faster!" Ehud called through the intercom.

They were the last words he spoke. Amiram heard a thump, and Ehud's body tumbled into the compartment, headless. Amiram wanted to scream with anguish, to cry out, Ehud is dead! A sharp pain stabbed through his brain. But he pulled himself together, stood up in the cupola and looked around for the second-in-command, Major Haim. He spotted his Patton struggling through the deep sands, and radioed to him to take over command, but the major did not acknowledge the message. He signalled again, with flags this time, but Major Haim was too preoccupied with the battle. Then Amiram spotted Colonel Shmuel on the road and told the driver to return to the highway. Bending down, he spread a map of Sinai over Ehud, for he did not want anyone to see their commander's headless body. Driving up to Colonel Shmuel's jeep, Amiram gave him the thumb's down sign to indicate what had happened. Colonel Shmuel, glancing up at the empty cupola, understood his meaning immediately. He shouted to Amiram to bring his tank close up to him, and told him not to report Ehud's death to the battalion, but to carry on transmitting orders as though he were still alive, still fighting; Colonel Shmuel would give the orders. At that moment he saw the personnel officer, Lieutenant Ilan, who had picked up Kahalany and taken him out of the battle.

"What are you doing here? Why isn't your tank fighting?"

"The gun doesn't work, Sir."

"Since when?"

"Since the junction, Sir."

"Drive quickly and tell Major Haim to take over command of the battalion. Do not tell anyone that the commander has

---

Major Elad's body in its turret. 7. The three Pattons which entered the minefield on the right of the road. 8. The major part of S/14 (many more than 5 Pattons) striving hard in the deep dunes. About 16 Pattons were stuck here when they were left with no fuel. 9. Lieutenant Ein-Gil's company, which broke through the Jiradi and led S/14 to El-Arish.

181

been killed. Tell all tank commanders to come back on to the road, to get out of the sands. We will attack from the road."

"Yes, Sir."

"And . . . one moment. Take over command of Kahalany's company."

"Yes, Sir."

"Move."

Colonel Shmuel's voice was already hoarse. "Bring the heavy mortars here. Lieutenant Yossi will give corrections from the Patton," he said to Amiram, and Amiram passed on the orders as if they were coming from Ehud. The colonel continued sending a stream of orders to the battalion as it struggled and battled in the sands and it occurred to nobody that the battalion commander was dead.

Lieutenant Ilan drove from tank to tank, signalling with his flags that they must return to the road. Finally he found Major Haim. He climbed down from his tank and went over to him. Major Haim was still struggling to find a way through the sands, still executing Ehud's last order.

"Ehud has been killed," Ilan said softly, as though afraid his voice might carry above the din and crash of the artillery bombardment.

"What?" shouted Haim.

"Ehud has been killed," Ilan said again. "The brigade commander has ordered you to take command."

Major Haim immediately ordered his driver to get back to the road. He was deeply perturbed about their situation; the commander killed, three company commanders out of action, their operations officer, Lieutenant Amiram, also wounded. There was not a single tank in the battalion unscathed, and the battalion was now throwing itself against a solid wall of fire, floundering through sand with minefields on all sides. The only ray of light in this otherwise frighteningly gloomy scene was that Ein-Gil and his company had now joined the battalion.

With stubborn efforts the Pattons which were still able to move pulled out of the sands and back on to the road. Apart from those which had received direct hits, eighteen had no fuel left and were obliged to stay where they were until the supply echelons arrived with fuel – which would be after midnight.

Ein-Gil's company, which had been the last in the column when S/14 reached the blocked pass, had not moved far from the road. Ein-Gil picked up the order to return, that an attempt would be made to break through the defence zone from the road. These were the sort of orders he liked.

"Move now, follow me!" he called to his company. They charged along the road into the defence zone, with the battalion, except for Kahalany's company, behind him, their guns and machine guns firing in all directions.

The time was 1800 hours.

The forward tanks were driving at a speed of 45 k.p.h., and the distances between each tank was growing, for not all could maintain the same pace. Major Haim was worried that the Egyptians would be able to pick off each vehicle one after the other. About two kilometres down the road, close to the enemy's artillery positions, he turned left off the road with part of the force and began shooting at the enemy artillery, tanks and anti-tank guns, which were now to his rear. He ordered the rest of the force, which brought up the rear of the column, to carry on towards El-Arish. Again they were in the enemy's rear, as at Rafa Junction. Anti-tank guns were sent flying and dug-in enemy tanks reduced to flames. When he had a moment Major Haim reported to Colonel Shmuel on the situation and of his intention to destroy the defence zone from the rear.

"Leave everything, get to El-Arish," Colonel Shmuel ordered. He was extremely concerned about the Centurions which had got through with no fuel or ammunition.

S/14 resumed its race. Again the distances between the tanks lengthened, with each tank driving through its own stretch of hell and the gunners working like men possessed as their tanks sped along. The Egyptians were again recovering from the shock; one of their gunners took aim at Benny Inbar's Patton. Benny had already been injured but had refused to be evacuated. The first anti-tank shell hit the loader's compartment, and the second, which followed immediately, hit the hull, severing the rod of the fuel pedal. The Patton stopped, its engine dead. The crew jumped out and ran for cover, the loader, Joseph Freyenta, badly burnt on both hands. A Patton passed by the crew, two of whom left their cover, jumped on board and were saved. The other two were mowed down by a burst of machine gun fire. One of them was Benny Inbar.

Two shells struck another Patton, in its air filter and its driving sprocket. The crew did not abandon it and continued driving the tank, crippled and disabled and lurching from side to side, until it reached the outskirts of El-Arish. On the Patton which Joseph Freyenta had joined, the commander had been wounded. He collapsed on the floor, and the crew's loader assumed command of the tank, Freyenta taking over as loader. With his burnt hands he loaded the gun until they reached El-Arish. Then he fainted.

As the sun was setting the Pattons struggled into El-Arish, mutilated, bedraggled, their aerials severed, their hatches missings, begrimed and sooty. In Ein-Gil's company only seven Pattons remained. At the level crossing the barriers were demolished. Near the windlass lay the scorched body of an Egyptian soldier, crouching on all fours, its head between its hands, its bare, burnt buttocks raised to heaven.

When the time came for Colonel Shmuel to pass through the Jiradi with the half-tracks and jeeps of his command group in the wake of the speeding S/14 Battalion, he found it blocked once again. Heavy fire poured down on the column of soft-skinned vehicles and on the brigade commander in his jeep, far too heavy for the supply echelons to get through to service the two battalions at El-Arish. The command group withdrew to its previous location just before the entrance to the pass, from where Colonel Shmuel reported to General Tal on his situation and requested the return of his armoured infantry battalion, which was still under divisional command, mopping up the Rafa area. Shmuel wanted to attack the Jiradi a third time, this time at night, and to hold it open. Meanwhile he radioed the Centurion company, which he had ordered to remain in Sheikh Zuweid as brigade reserve and to give protection to the first supply echelons which had reached there, and ordered it to move towards the Jiradi. When at last it arrived he ordered its commander, Captain Amir, to enter the Jiradi at nightfall, straight up the road, and gain a foothold, thus cutting the enemy defences into two and making it impossible for the Egyptians to move freely or to send reinforcements from one side of the road to the other.

Radio communication between Colonel Shmuel in the Jiradi and General Tal at the Rafa Junction was poor, and the station at 'S' Brigade's main headquarters, which at that stage was at Sheikh Zuweid, had to be used as an intermediary. Because of this, General Tal was not aware of the important fact that S/14 had successfully broken through the Jiradi and had linked up with S/10 in El-Arish. Influencing the decisions he took was still the thought that S/10 was completely cut off.

184

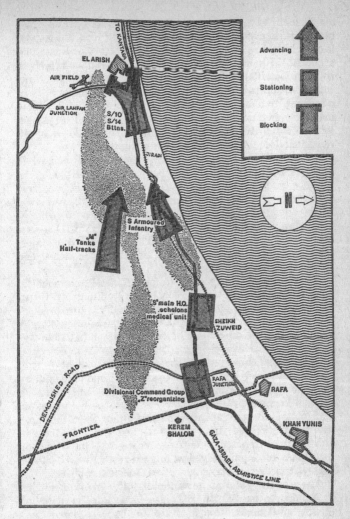

ADVANCING

STATIONING

BLOCKING

TO KANTARA

EL ARISH

AIR FIELD

BIR LAHFAN JUNCTION

S/10 S/14 Bttns.

JIRADI

S Armoured Infantry

"M" Tanks Half-tracks

S main H.Q. echelons medical unit

SHEIKH ZUWEID

DEMOLISHED ROAD

Divisional Command Group "Z" reorganizing

RAFA JUNCTION

RAFA

FRONTIER

KEREM SHALOM

GAZA-ISRAEL ARMISTICE LINE

KHAN YUNIS

7 *Division Tal: 2400 hours, Monday, 5 June.*

Colonel Shmuel's request for the armoured infantry battalion was a grave one. The Rafa Opening still teemed with Egyptian soldiers, who might be able to reorganise if mopping-up operations were called off too soon. At 1200 hours General Tal had advanced 'M' Brigade along its axis parallel to the El-

185

Arish road, to a point south of Sheikh Zuweid, to be in reserve for the assault on Sheikh Zuweid. As it turned out, 'M's' intervention had not been needed at Sheikh Zuweid. Later, General Tal had ordered Colonel Men to send his armoured infantry battalion to the assistance of Colonel Raphoul and his paratroopers in their bitter struggle on the southern flank of the junction, but as this battle too had been decided without 'M's' intervention, at 1550 hours Tal had ordered 'M' to advance westwards towards the defence zone south-east of El-Arish, between the El-Arish airport and the town.

'M' had moved forward secretly, ready at any moment to intervene in any of the division's battles, but all the time pressing forward towards its objective. The darker it became, however, the more difficult had become its progress; the route was not clearly defined and the sandy dunes were hard to negotiate. But when darkness fell, the track was lost and the negotiable places became impossible to find. The supply echelons moving behind 'M' sank deep into the sands, and soon it was running short of fuel.

When General Tal received Colonel Shmuel's communication, he first of all ordered Colonel Men to dispatch two battalions, a battalion of AMX/13 tanks and an armoured infantry battalion, to attack the Jiradi from the south and break through it for the third time, while the Sherman battalion was to continue its advance westwards towards 'M's' objective. At 1930 hours, however, Colonel Men informed the general that both the AMX/13 battalion and the armoured infantry battalion were stuck in the sands, out of fuel and without a hope of the supply echelons getting to them before dawn. Both battalions were already near the Jiradi when the tanks and half-tracks had run out of fuel, and Colonel Men had ordered the armoured infantry to proceed to the Jiradi on foot, but after a painfully slow and exhausting march of one kilometre through the sand dunes had ordered them back.

It was when Tal was informed of 'M's' predicament that he decided to use 'S' Brigade's armoured infantry battalion for the third break-through at the Jiradi. He ordered Lieutenant-Colonel Maxie to break off contact with the enemy at the Rafa Opening and concentrate the battalion at the Rafa Junction. This was a bold decision, for to break off contact at night is difficult and complicated even under normal conditions; the more so here, where the mopping-up was being carried out in trenches and defence positions which were spread over a wide area. It was a bold decision too because it stripped the division's rear echelons, and in particular its medical units, of adequate protection should the Egyptians be able to re-group and renew the fight.

At the sight of Maxie with his entire battalion in orderly columns at the Rafa Junction, General Tal could not contain his feelings and kissed him. Maxie had proved how well trained and efficient his battalion was. Tal ordered him to get to the Jiradi at full speed, to link up with Colonel Shmuel and to effect another break-through there under the command of Colonel Shmuel. Artillery support with illuminating shells would be provided. The general also ordered him not to ad-vance to El-Arish but to stay at Jiradi and mop it up, thus securing the division's axis of supply and evacuation.

At 2100 hours the situation in the area was as follows: two tank battalions of 'S' Brigade, S/10 and S/14 were at El-Arish, beyond the blocked Jiradi. 'S's' armoured infantry battalion was on its way to the Jiradi. 'Z' required twelve hours to re-organise and at that stage could not assist the division's opera-tions. 'M' Brigade was stuck in the sands without fuel. The T/01 battalion of Pattons was completely split up; part of it, under Lieutenant Ein-Gil, had joined up with 'S', part had been sent to assist the 'Z' Brigade paratroopers and part had been left as a divisional reserve force with the divisional com-mand group and was attending to refuelling and other ordnance chores.

The road from Rafa to El-Arish was strewn with casual-ties. Reconnaissance parties and other units attended to their evacuation to first aid posts which had been set up as near as possible to the battle fronts. In the Rafa railway station, where an aid post had been set up, the surgeons and medical order-lies had to split up, the surgeons attending to the wounded while the orderlies defended the post from enemy attacks. Both doctors and orderlies were saving a man's life one minute, and the next shooting another dead. The Medical Corps' ambulances were obliged to pass through areas which had not been cleared, many arriving at the aid posts riddled with bullets. When the ground fire was heavy and the heli-copters were unable to land, the wounded were treated on the road. Blood transfusions were given and fractures set by the light of ambulance headlights. At one roadside spot Dr. Segal performed a heart operation, and at Sheikh Zuweid a single

Egyptian tank, an SU/100, menaced the field hospital, being destroyed only at the last minute by a Patton which had been delayed by a breakdown and was trying to catch up with its unit.

Meanwhile the brigade and battalion supply echelons were moving up, and the narrow road to El-Arish was blocked with massive bottlenecks at the Rafa Junction and Sheikh Zuweid. Most of the supply companies were mobilised vehicles, civilian transport without front-wheel drives, and their elderly drivers tended to stick too close behind the vehicle in front. The road was an obstacle course of war debris; burnt out half-tracks and tanks, both the enemy's and Zahal's, and deep pits dug by shells, heavy mortars and aerial bombardments. Adding to the tumult and confusion were rear-echelon headquarters, engineering units, medical units, recovery units, damaged and burnt-out vehicles, and civilian lorries with ammunition and fuel. The truck drivers were afraid to move off the shoulders of the road, knowing for sure that their vehicles would get stuck in the soft sands.

'S' Brigade's armoured infantry battalion had no sooner set off for the Jiradi when it came up against a massive traffic jam near the junction. The situation on the road seemed desperate, completely blocked by burnt-out tanks and half-tracks, and by the civilian lorries and vehicles of service units, which were jammed between the narrow spaces between the damaged fighting vehicles. Genera Tal assigned his chief-of-staff, Colonel Herzl, the job of getting the armoured infantry battalion to its objective as fast as possible. "I can see what's happening on the road, it doesn't interest me," the general said. "Clear a passage, I don't care how you do it." Herzl and Maxie began clearing the way for the battalion, cajoling, shouting and ordering their tanks to push the vehicles, burnt out or roadworthy, off the road. They were even obliged to threaten one or two of the drivers with their revolvers when they refused to move their lorries to the sides of the road for fear of mines. The battalion degenerated into a long, disorderly and jumbled column, and eventually Lieutenant-Colonel Maxie had to order his units to turn off the road to bypass the other traffic. At Sheikh Zuweid the battalion was formed up again into an orderly convoy and from there proceeded to the Jiradi.

It was midnight before the armoured infantry battalion reached their destination. Maxie immediately reported to Colonel Shmuel for his orders. Captain Amir's Centurions had already gained a foothold in the Jiradi and were now fighting from their positions. The armoured infantry battalion moved straight into action, the tanks moving first, the half-tracks carrying the infantry following. The infantry poured from their half-tracks, which remained parked on the road, and by the light of illuminating shells fell upon the trenches and dug-outs of the Jiradi. After four hours of bitter fighting the Jiradi trenches were cleared; this time, however, the conquering force did not move on but stayed where it was to continue mopping-up and to hold the locality – once again under the command of the division.

Colonel Shmuel's command group reached El-Arish on Tuesday, 6 June, at 0200 hours. The two tank battalions in El-Arish had passed a night of vigil, for a large Egyptian force was stationed close by, and Lieutenant-Colonel Pinko feared a counter-attack which would find his forces without fuel and almost without ammunition. The first thing he had done was to station tanks to guard the entrances to the city, and with a company of tanks rake the highway to Kantara. Taking up their positions, the company fired shots in all directions. Pinko had also placed a company of armoured infantry together with a platoon of tanks on the El-Arish–Bir Lahfan road, thus blocking all the approaches to El-Arish. He had then decided that it was necessary to patrol the areas between his forces, and this he did in half-tracks. While patrolling in the lead half-track, Pinko had discovered his station-wagon and in it his driver, dead. Egyptian soldiers had crept up to the vehicle and killed the driver, who must have fallen asleep from exhaustion. Pinko had not stopped the patrol but decided to have the car towed away after finishing his rounds. The patrol had been fired on from all sides and the half-track's machine guns crackled incessantly. In the exchange the Egyptian fuel storage tanks and ammunition dumps in the El-Arish railway station had been hit and set on fire, and huge flames rose high into the sky, brilliantly illuminating the area. So fierce had been the conflagration that Pinko had given orders to move back the battalion's tanks in case their ammunition caught fire in the tremendous heat.

Major Shamai Kaplan deployed his company for the night. He had lost a lot of blood. Hanoch, Dan and others gathered round him to cheer him up. They knew how concerned he was for Nava and wanted to know if she had given birth. They also knew how much he wanted a second son, a brother for

Itai. And so they pulled his leg, saying it was a certainty Nava would have a girl.

"Nonsense," said Shamai, "it will be a boy. I already have a name for him."

"And we say, Sir," Hanoch said, "that it will be a girl. We even have a name for her – Adelaide."

"No thanks!" said Shamai who could hardly stop his hands shaking. "I tell you it is going to be a boy."

"Some men in the company, Sir, object to Adelaide. As it's going to be a girl, they want you to consider their suggestion – Havazelet," said Dan.

"All right, lads. I'll be happy if it's a girl, but leave the name to me. I can't rely on your talents!"

"Sir, are we permitted to suggest more names?"

"As many as you like."

Quarrelling over names dispelled the weariness.

When Colonel Shmuel reached El-Arish he decided to continue his forward sweep. As soon as the supply echelons arrived he ordered a special force to be refuelled, then to set out at once to capture the El-Arish airfield, nine kilometres south of the town, on the El-Arish–Bir Lahfan road. 'M' Brigade was still on its overnight route and there was no possibility of its making contact with the Egyptian dispositions south-east of El-Arish before dawn. The supply echelons arrived at 0400 hours, and two hours later Major Haim, who had set out for the airfield with Ein-Gil's seven Pattons, was able to report that "the airfield is in my hands". It had been captured after a battle against Egyptian tanks and anti-aircraft tanks with twin 57mm guns.

In less than twenty-four hours 'S' Brigade had battled its way through seventy kilometres of enemy territory.

At 0420 hours General Tal's command group had reached the Memorial Stone at the entrance to El-Arish. Colonel Shmuel ran over and jumped on to the general's command half-track. The two embraced.

"I want you to know it has been a heroic battle, Shmulik," said General Tal. "In the whole history of armoured warfare there are few examples of break-throughs and sweeps such as yours."

"Ehud is dead," said Colonel Shmuel. His face was black and grimy and the bristles stood out through the dirt. He took his glasses off, revealing two white circles.

For a moment there was a silence.

The general recalled his first meeting with Ehud. It had

been at the battle of Tauwfik in 1960. Ehud had been the company second-in-command, and he had directed the fire for the tank platoon. General Tal himself had been a colonel in command of 'S' Brigade. He remembered Ehud and his work in the Armoured Corps, and more recently as an expert on Pattons. He was a man who had sought perfection and thoroughness in everything.

"Ehud was a tiger," said Colonel Shmuel.

The roll-call of the dead and wounded brought on a mood of depression. 'S' had suffered heavy losses in its assaults and break-throughs. Its tanks were damaged and the technical details had to work ceaselessly to make them serviceable again. At that moment two Egyptian jet bombers, Sukhoy/7s, appeared overhead and began a bombing run towards the fuelling centre, where dozens of tanks were being refuelled. General Tal was about to give an order and Colonel Shmuel had already one leg outside the half-track, when above the Sukhoy/7s appeared two Mirages. Within a split second the two Egyptian jets had vanished, leaving trails of fire and smoke which were carried away on the winds.

The war "for Israel's surival" – as the general had described it in his last orders group – continued. The Egyptian defence zone at Bir Lahfan had originally been assigned to 'M' Brigade or 'Z' Brigade, to enable 'S' to rest its forces, but in the morning 'Z' was taken out of the division's command and transferred to the war in the Gaza Strip, and 'M' had not yet made contact with the Egyptian defences south-east of El-Arish, which was its objective; thus this enemy position still remained to threaten the division's left flank. General Tal now ordered Colonel Shmuel to take Bir Lahfan, and instructed Colonel Men to continue on to his objective. When Colonel Shmuel received his instructions, his chest welled with pride; once again the tough assignments had been entrusted to 'S', his brigade.

"But," General Tal told the colonel, "the decisive battle against the 7th Egyptian Division has been won. From now on we must direct things more cautiously, commit only one battalion, and for the first stage of the battle use long-range firing and no assault. I do not want another battle of attrition. A second battalion is to be committed only with my authority. If another battle of attrition becomes necessary, we shall coordinate it with 'M' later on." From now on the order was to spare lives.

Colonel Shmuel assembled his two tank battalions. The men were tired. All night they had been occupied with blocking the axes against counter-attacks, guard duties, attending to the wounded and evacuating them by the helicopters. And El-Arish itself had not yet been mopped up; this would have to be dealt with later. But when Colonel Shmuel gave the command, everyone woke up and immediately the units began to form a column. Major Shamai Kaplan's Centurion was the first to start moving, but suddenly it stopped in the middle of the road. The driver was not receiving any orders from his commander. Shamai had lost a lot of blood, and all night he had been busy with road blocking duties and organising supplies of ammunition and fuel for his company. He had not shut his eyes for a minute, although his men had asked him to rest when they saw how pale he was, and he had refused to be evacuated with the wounded. The wound in his left hand had begun to bleed again and it had taken some time for the medical orderly to stop the flow. A platoon commander who approached Shamai's tank could see him standing in his cupola, but when he climbed up to him and gently tapped him on the shoulder there was no reaction. He tapped a little harder and Shamai opened his eyes. He did not know where he was.

"What happened? Did I fall asleep?"

"Worse, Sir. I think you fainted."

"I never faint. I may have drowsed."

"Sir, perhaps you'll lie down in the command half-track and rest, and I'll take over command."

"No. I'm all right. Our assignment is...."

"Blocking the Kantara axis, Sir."

"That's it. Driver, straight ahead."

Major Shamai Kaplan's company set out to block the El-Arish – Kantara road against an Egyptian attack along the northern axis. It took up positions eight kilometres west of El-Arish, while the town was still teeming with Egyptian units.

Within a short while the Pattons and Centurions were ready to continue their forward sweep to the Bir Lahfan road, south of El-Arish. On Colonel Shmuel's command the battalion of Pattons and the battalion of Centurions surged forward.

CHAPTER TWENTY-THREE

The main tactical moves made by Zahal and the Egyptian Army during the first two days of the war can be summarised as follows: The first was the Israel air strike which gave Israel superiority in the air. While this was still under way, General Tal's division broke through the Egyptian defences at the Rafa Opening and in a rapid drive penetrated the enemy defences, in less than eight hours capturing El-Arish, the Sinai capital. The Egyptian Army's response to this break-through was an attempt to stabilise its first line of defence by means of two armour brigades which were sent to reinforce the defence zone at Bir-Lahfan, also included in Division Tal's area of operations. Its estimate that the main Zahal effort in Sinai would be made by Tal's division was correct. It was during the course of the first day that the orders were given to dispatch these two Egyptian brigades from Jebel Libni to Bir Lahfan. However, during that night these two brigades came up against 'K' Brigade, Division Yaffe, which had silently penetrated through the desert to the rear of Bir Lahfan Battle was joined and the Egyptian reinforcements were prevented from linking up at Bir Lahfan.

Next morning, Tuesday, 6 June, Division Sharon broke through the Egyptian defences at Abu Agheila, and the Egyptian Army now found itself in an untenable situation. The two main dispositions of their first line defences, at Rafa and Abu Agheila, had both fallen, their operational reinforcements had been thrown back by Division Yaffe, and Bir Lahfan had been captured by Division Tal. In short, Egypt had lost its front line and was forced to withdraw to its second line of defence. This the Egyptians then tried to do, as will be seen later, but Zahal was too quick for them and did not let them stabilise their second line.

The Israel Air Force wiped out the Egyptian Air Force within two hours and fifty minutes, and the air forces of Jordan and Syria within one hour. Most of the planes were destroyed on the ground; out of the four hundred and fifty-one enemy planes destroyed, only about sixty were knocked out in air combats. This air strike so stunned the Egyptian government that it claimed that fifteen hundred planes had participated in the missions, though nobody has ever estimated the total strength of Israel's Air Force – including fighters, bombers, transport planes and helicopters – at more than three hundred and fifty planes. Hence Abdul Nasser's claim that Israel was aided in her air strike by the air forces of foreign countries (a sorry excuse which did not prevent the dismissal of the Egyptian Air Force chief).

The Israel Air Force was greatly assisted by its air intelligence. It had precise information concerning the methods, qualities and shortcomings of the enemy air forces; it was because of this detailed knowledge, foreign sources say, that the air strike was planned for the thirty minutes between 0815 and 0845 hours Egyptian time (which is one hour ahead of Israel time), when most of the Egyptian officers were on the move, either between home and office or barracks and headquarters. Above all, however, it was the air force's technical ability in dispatching every single plane it had on a large number of sorties, and the fighting spirit of the men, which made their fantastic achievement possible.

Confirmation of Israel's successful strike was received by General Tal only at 1100 hours. During the first day's fighting the air force did not attack Egyptian tanks in Sinai, which were destroyed by the army, though air superiority enabled the Armoured Corps to develop to the maximum its forward momentum from the second day of the war.

'K' Brigade then, under the command of Colonel Iska, was to take up its positions on the Bir Lahfan intersection and block all enemy movements and reinforcements; it was not assigned any break-throughs. Under cover of Division Tal's first break-throughs in the north, and Division Sharon's in the south, 'K' stole across the frontier and through the desert along Wadi Haridin, from Nizana to the Bir Lahfan intersection. Probably only Zahal's staff would dare to send such a force, the size and strength of an entire armoured brigade, to penetrate enemy territory in virtually trackless desert.

'K' Brigade's Centurions moved over the sandy ridges for fifty kilometres, most of the time in low gear. At the frontier they had encountered Egyptian border forces in wireless vehicles; part were destroyed and the rest fled. At 1400 hours the lead battalion, K/113, commanded by Lieutenant-Colonel Abraham, had reached the Haridin defence position which was held by a company. A short fight ensued and the Egyptians fled. K/113s casualties were four Centurions which got stuck in the sands and had to wait to be extricated. At 1600 hours, when the 'S' Brigade Centurions were arriving at El-Arish, 'K' Brigade's Centurions arrived at the rear of Bir Lahfan and began their attack on the Radar position, manned by an infantry company and anti-aircraft guns. At 1845 hours, under heavy artillery bombardment from Bir-Lahfan, K/113 succeeded in blocking the Bir Lahfan junction, thus preventing reinforcements from Jebel Libni reaching El-Arish and throwing 'S' back in a counter-attack.

'K' Brigade's penetration to the Bir Lahfan junction through Wadi Haridin was one of the neatest and most elegant moves of the war. K/113 managed to block the junction with only twenty-four Centurions. Lieutenant Ilan Yakuel's company led the battalion, which in the late afternoon dispersed to block the intersection. Night fell, and the battalion was still subjected to artillery bombardment from Bir Lahfan, but to Ilan's satisfaction the Egyptian shelling caused no damage to the Centurions. From the beginning he had had great faith in the tank, and now once again it was proving how resistant its steel was.

At 2200 hours Colonel Bren turned up at Iska's command group, to take a battalion from him. From the moment war with Egypt had seemed a possibility Bren had been eager to capture Abu Agheila for the third time. The first had been in 1948, when he was a company commander in the Palmach's 7th battalion whose commander was Iska, the second in 1956, when he had been commander of the battalion which took Abu Agheila. But the allotment of assignments between the divisions had placed Abu Agheila in General Sharon's sector, and Bren, who was the second-in-command in General Yaffe's division, had already settled down to sleep in Wadi Haridin when Lieutenant-Colonel Natke's tank battalion was moving off towards Abu Aghelia by order of General Sharon. Bren's aspirations had at that moment seemed very far from fulfilment and he had already resigned himself to renouncing the idea of a hat-trick. But just before he fell asleep, division's main headquarters had contacted him with a request that he assist Natke. "What do you think of the idea that after linking up with Natke, 'K' and Natke capture Abu Agheila together?" To Colonel Bren's surprise the idea appealed to the general officer southern command. The answer was positive. The colonel was at once wide awake as he had never been in his life. He was about to complete his hat-trick. Immediately he requested Iska to prepare the battalion for movement orders, informing him that he himself would give instructions to the battalion.

"Why so suddenly, and why one of my battalions?" the surprised Iska asked.

"You can use Abraham's battalion for road-blocking here, and we can send Fedele's battalion to capture Abu Agheila with Natke's battalion from Sharon's division," said Bren.

"But why with a battalion from my brigade?"

"We will be coming from the rear, see?"

"True enough! But look, Bren, I'm here road-blocking. Any minute now there might be terrific pressure on me. I'm being attacked by artillery from Bir Lahfan and. . . ."

"Listen, Iska. The minute I'm finished with the battalion I'll return it to you. First thing in the morning," Bren promised.

"But I need my battalion here," Iska said.

"Honestly, Iska. It won't take a moment. It'll be a very short fight. Immediately we've captured Abu Agheila you'll get your battalion back."

"Right. An order's an order, and you're the second. But first thing in the morning, please."

"The very first thing. Oh, yes, and. . . ."

Iska had already turned away to hurry back to his brigade but he went back to Colonel Bren.

"Anything else?" he asked suspiciously.

"Well, yes. I have a message for you from the divisional commander. Two Egyptian brigades are moving in your direction to make a counter-attack, both from the direction of Jebel Libni. One is armoured, the other we're not so sure about – it's either infantry or armour. Good luck, Iska."

"Wait a minute!" Iska cried. "Just one minute! So what are you taking my battalion away for and leaving me with only one tank battalion?"

"Iska, you surprise me. They're only Arabs. There's nothing to worry about."

Colonel Bren's driver pressed his foot down and his jeep was swallowed up in the darkness. Iska grabbed his reconnaissance platoon and hurried with it to Lieutenant-Colonel Abraham, instructing him to send one company of Centurions forward so as to be able to fight at least a delaying action during the night; in the morning, if Bren kept his word, the second Centurion battalion would be back.

At 2300 hours the Centurion battalion commanded by Lieutenant-Colonel Fedele left for its joint assignment with Lieutenant-Colonel Natke: the capture of Abu Agheila under the command of Colonel Bren. Several minutes later Iska spotted a long snaking line of lights as the Egyptian convoy approached. The forward units of K/113 reported "An endless convoy. Its head is already here."

The column which was coming from Jebel Libni on its way to El-Arish to help repulse 'S', was moving quickly and was already drawing near to Lieutenant Ilan Yakuel's company. Lieutenant-Colonel Abraham ordered company commanders to take up firing positions and to open fire immediately. With the first shot the Egyptian tanks' lights were switched off and in a few moments the fire was being returned. The first shots from Ilan's company hit three enemy tanks and set them on fire, their flames revealing fuel and ammunition trucks travelling in the column, which Ilan's company also set ablaze. By the light of the burning tanks and trucks it was easy to pick out the enemy tanks, and the Centurions aimed their guns at them. They were T/55s equipped with infra-red lights. But soon, the Egyptian tanks had dispersed, keeping well away from the conflagration, and were swallowed up in the darkness. Yakuel's company was on the flank. Ilan lit his projector, and the strong beam of light sliced through the dark, silhouetting the Egyptian tanks so that they stood out like illuminated statues in a park. But the projector soon became a target for the Egyptian gunners and Ilan's Centurion received a direct hit. The projector was immediately extinguished and Ilan Yakuel was wounded by splinters. A reconnaissance jeep was rushed forward to remove him to the rear, but he was dead.

"Do not light projectors," ordered Lieutenant-Colonel Abraham.

K/113's first barrage hit the forward tanks. Most of the column was dispersed on the rear slope, beyond the Centurions' field of vision, some even outside the normal combat range. A pitched battle now developed between the forward Egyptian tanks and the Centurions, the exchange going on all night without either side attempting to force a decision. This suited Iska's plans; towards morning he contacted the divisional commander, General Yaffe, requesting aerial support and demanding the return of his Centurion battalion.

Meanwhile Bren was advancing with Fedele's Centurions towards the rear of Abu Agheila. He was trying to make radio contact with Lieutenant-Colonel Natke in order to coordinate their attack, but Natke was not to be found. Colonel Bren had already worked out how he was going to set about capturing Abu Agheila from the rear with one tank battalion, as he had done in 1956, and he urged the Centurions on even more.

197

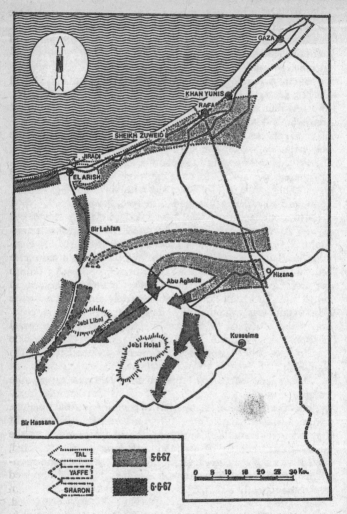

GAZA

KHAN YUNIS

RAFA

SHEIKH ZUWEID

JIRADI

EL ARISH

Bir Lahfan

Abu Aghella

Nizana

Jebi Libni

Jebi Holal

Kusseima

Bir Hassana

TAL

YAFFE

SHARON

5·6·67

6·6·67

0 5 10 15 20 25 30 Km.

8   *The movements of Zahal's three divisions in Sinai in the first two days of the war.*

But as much as Lieutenant-Colonel Fedele was looking forward to the battle, he could not move his battalion any faster; on his right flank K/113 was exchanging fire with the Egyptian armoured brigades, and on his left Egyptian service units were already fleeing in panic before General Sharon's division. Apart from the general confusion the road had been ploughed up in several places and was badly pitted. Perforce, the Centurions moved slowly.

When radio contact was at last made between Fedele and Natke, Natke's Centurion battalion was at the Ruaffa Dam, Abu Agheila's main defence location. Bren informed him that Fedele's battalion would attack Abu Agheila from the direction of Bir Lahfan. At the last moment, however, when the battalion was within two and a half kilometres of Abu Agheila, it was called back to the assistance of K/113 on the Bir Lahfan junction. General Abraham Yaffe had given the order on receiving Colonel Iska's communication.

It was exasperating. Bren's fingers were almost touching Abu Agheila, he only had to stretch out his hand and it would be his for the third time; but there was nothing he could do about it. General Yaffe's order was paramount, and the Centurions returned to the junction at Bir Lahfan, to do battle with the Egyptian armoured brigades. Abu Agheila fell to Natke's Centurions, and Natke himself was badly injured in both legs. By the time Fedele's Centurions got back to the junction it was already dawn.

As the first light crept over the desert Lieutenant-Colonel Abraham dispersed K/113 to its daylight positions, while with the commander of the forward company he went up to make an observation. The company commander reported that in the valley he had counted sixty-five Egyptian tanks, nine of them burning, as well as trucks and soft-skinned transports, some of them at a range of 3000 and even 4000 metres. Abraham now gave orders to fire at the Egyptian tanks, at the same time requesting aerial support. With daylight the bombardment of K/113 from Bir Lahfan was also renewed, but it was not accurate and it quickly halted when the attention of the Bir Lahfan defence zone became fully occupied by 'S' Brigade's Pattons and Centurions which had begun their attack. At 0600 hours the Super-Mystères appeared. The enemy defended itself well with its anti-aircraft guns, managing to shoot down one Super-Mystère (whose pilot managed to make radio contact with Abraham and was picked up on the ground), but by 1000 hours the Egyptian armour was defeated, and was in full retreat towards Jebel Libni from where it had come. 'K' wanted to pursue it, but first they had to refuel.

"What are our losses?" Iska asked.

"One killed," said Lieutenant-Colonel Abraham. "A company commander."

"Which one?"

"Ilan Yakuel."

"Don't know him," said Iska.

"He was once adjutant to General Tal," someone said.

But Iska was already absorbed in refuelling and supplying his brigade, so that as soon as possible he could set off in pursuit, which, towards evening, brought him to Jebel Libni.

The fortified positions at Abu Agheila were broken through by Division Sharon with a plan which from the outset was termed classic. Tanks smashed through the outer defences and captured them on the first day; the infantry overran the ditches in a night attack, paratroopers who had been landed by helicopters in the rear at night silenced the artillery, and then the tanks moved in again, penetrating in depth and destroying whatever was there.

The Abu Agheila defence zone was held by the Egyptian 2nd Division, a reinforced infantry brigade with about six battalions of artillery and eighty-eight tanks, T/43s and SU/100s. In accordance with normal linear disposition defence principles, the fortified zone hinged upon two natural barriers: very deep sands to the north and Jebel Delfa to the south. Between them, on the undulating heights, stretched concealed concrete ditches and bunkers, alongside which were minefields which forced the attacker along certain routes. To reach the defended zone, the tightly packed minefields had to be broken through, but in front of them were the outer defences, manned by mobile forces, tanks and armoured personnel carriers. These outer defences were also dug-in and enclosed in minefields, while covering them was the artillery at the rear of the defence zone.

The plan devised by General Sharon required that Colonel Motke's armoured brigade take the outer positions on the first day, while Natke's battalion reached the rear of Abu Agheila. The infantry attack on the trenches was planned for the night, as was the paratroopers' assault on the artillery. This meant, however, that the tanks would be exposed to the Egyptian artillery while it was still light, and to prevent this General Sharon took a daring step. He assembled all the artillery he could lay hands on and moved it up behind one of Colonel Motke's armoured battalions. The Israeli artillery was dispersed at a distance of three to four kilometres from the Egyptian lines. This placed it in considerable danger, but enabled it to enfilade the enemy zone. This bold step paid off, and the tank battalions suffered only minor losses from the Egyptian artillery. Their main problem, and particularly that of Lieutenant-Colonel Natke's Centurion battalion, came from the minefields.

The tank attack on the outer defences started on the morning of Monday, 5 June. It was only at 2200 hours that Division Sharon's infantry brigade began its assault on the trenches. When the infantry had captured the first three and had penetrated as far as the roadway, General Sharon moved his engineering units forward to clear the minefields and committed his tanks to battle inside the defence position. The paratroopers who had been landed by helicopters in the rear silenced the artillery and by 0100 hours of Tuesday, 6 June, Colonel Motke's tanks were already in the rear defence fortifications of Abu Agheila and advancing upon the anti-tank locality. The tanks engaged in fierce battle which lasted until midday.

Division Sharon's axis of advance was the Abu-Agheila–Nakhl route; it was the southern flank of the forces moving into Sinai, with Division Yaffe in the centre advancing along the Mitla–Suez axis and Division Tal on the northern flank advancing along two axes, El-Arish–Kantara and Jebel Libni-Bir Gafgafa–Ismailia.

The Israeli break-through into Sinai, therefore, was achieved by a massing of its armour in the northern part of Sinai. Along a front line of about 210 kilometres, Zahal concentrated most of its forces in the northern sector, between Abu-Agheila–Rafa, along a front line of fifty kilometres; the three divisions hammered hard at this narrow sector, burst through and immediately split into several columns along the length of the Sinai Peninsula.

Each of the three divisions adopted its own way of fighting. Tal's division assaulted the fortified objectives by ouflanking them and breaking through with armoured forces; Yaffe's division reached its objective in a silent penetration which required no break-through; Sharon's division chose to assault with infantry and armour in night attacks.

From the moment the divisions broke into Sinai they did not halt their headlong thrust until the campaign was over, when they reached the Suez Canal early on the fifth day of the war.

Thus while the break-through battle at Abu Agheila was still raging, and in the rear of Bir Lahfan 'K' Brigade was fighting its armour-versus-armour battle against the Egyptian forces who were trying to reinforce the Bir Lahfan defences, Division Tal was engaged in its fifth break-through action. But the one at Bir Lahfan was not made with the same swing and dash as those at Khan Yunis, the Rafa Opening, Sheikh Zuweid and the Jiradi. While 'M' Brigade attacked the defence zone south-east of El-Arish, 'S' began its attack on Bir Lahfan.

"Take it easy, Haim," Colonel Shmuel said to Major Haim, who was now battalion commander in place of Ehud.

"Yes, Sir."

"First commit only one company, then report to me."

"Long-range, Sir."

"Commit the other companies only with my authority. And I want an exemplary battle, no casualties."

"Like a demonstration, Sir."

Ein-Gil's was the first company to make contact with the enemy at Bir Lahfan – a brigade defence zone, well dug-in and containing tanks, anti-tank guns and infantry. The company took up firing positions to the left of the road and began to exchange fire at long range. Major Haim asked for an artillery barrage to be laid down on the enemy artillery positions in the rear of Bir Lahfan; he then reported to Colonel Shmuel that results from the long-range contact were very good, and the colonel gave him permission to commit more companies to the battle. He ordered Major Haim to outflank the objectives from the left, through the sand dunes, and two companies, under covering fire from Ein-Gil's company, penetrated through to the left flank of Bir Lahfan and there took up firing positions, where the Egyptians least expected them to be. Inside the defence zone fourteen Egyptian tanks were destroyed one after the other and several anti-tank guns were sent flying. The companies advanced unhurriedly, one sector after another, the gunners taking good advantage of the leisure given them and aiming with care and precision. When General Tal was satisfied that the action was developing as anticipated, he consented to Colonel Shmuel's request, permitting him to commit the second, the Centurion battalion into the battle. S/10 charged down the road and sliced through the defence zone like a hot knife through butter. The Egyptians began to flee in droves, only to discover that in the rear, on the Bir Lahfan–Jebel Libni–Abu Agheila junction, 'K's' Centurions

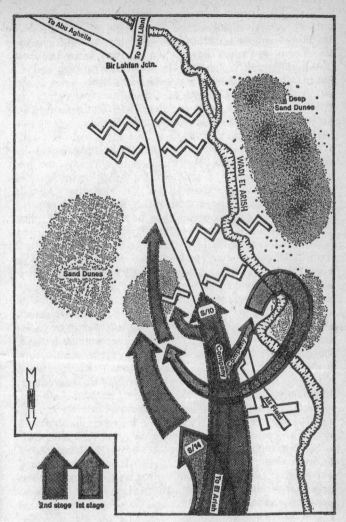

Map labels: To Abu Agheila, To Jebl Libni, Bir Lahfan Jctn., Deep Sand Dunes, WADI EL ARISH, Sand Dunes, S/10, Company, Air Field, S/14, To El Arish, 2nd stage, 1st stage

9 *'S' Brigade's break-through at Bir Lahfan (6 June).*

were waiting to mow them down. Some of the fleeing Egyptians made for the sands, only to get bogged down, others no
longer relied upon their vehicles to take them to safety, but

took off their boots, stripped off their uniforms, and hastily donned the white smock of the Beduin which they had brought with them. Thus attired they slipped away into the desert sand as though they had never served in the Egyptian Army. Nonetheless, to avoid the enemy reorganising and interfering with the division's advance, as had happened at the Jiradi, General Tal threw in 'M' Brigade's armoured infantry battalion behind the tanks of 'S' Brigade, to mop it up. So far Tal's division had destroyed six enemy brigades.

By midday the break-through at Bir Lahfan had been completed without casualties and 'S' and 'K' had linked up at the junction of Bir Lahfan–Jebel Libni–Abu Agheila. At the first divisional orders group since the beginning of the war, held at the El-Arish airfield, General Tal allocated the division's future assignments. The officers sat on a large stone which had been placed over the opening to a smelly cess-pit, and they were inundated with swarms of flies. The Sinai Desert is cursed with a vast number of flies, and at the El-Arish airfield they were swarming around like low-flying clouds. When a large map was spread out on the ground they seemed to regard it as an invitation to land and completely obscured its outlines.

The officers were by now so exhausted that they felt neither the burning sun nor the buzzing insects swarming over them. General Tal ordered Israel Force, which was later to be joined by Colonel Raphoul with 'Z' when it had completed its action in Gaza, to advance along the northern axis towards Kantara, while the rest of the division was to advance along the main Sinai axis to Ismailia. Lieutenant-Colonel Maxie, commander of 'S' Brigade's armoured infantry battalion, which was still under the direct command of the division, was told to retain a force at the Jiradi to secure the division's supply and evacuation lines and to take the rest of his battalion to mop-up El-Arish. The other units of the division were to move along the main Sinai road to Ismailia. But General Tal could not help noticing how tired his men were; he was particularly concerned about 'S' Brigade, who had been fighting non-stop for thirty-six hours, and decided to order Colonel Shmuel to rest.

"We don't need rest, Sir."

"It's an order. The whole of 'S' is to rest."

Colonel Shmuel returned to his brigade and ordered everyone to get some sleep. The brigade was formed up into sections, then the tank crews fell on to the soft sand and slept. But not for long.

At Sheikh Zuweid 'S' had collected its first prisoners-of-war, including a lieutenant-colonel. He was asked to sit on the ground, at a distance from the other prisoners, who were also asked to sit. Nobody knew what to do with them or how to hold on to them. The tanks were constantly on the move forward, and the officers had no time to think about prisoners; nor did the soldiers have the time to attend to them. Everyone wanted to pass the problem on to the next man. The unit which had captured them had surrounded them with a concertina of barbed wire, and as the lieutenant-colonel was sitting by himself, separated from the rest, he was given a concertina of barbed wire all to himself. The colonel was a source of curiosity, and in the little time there was between movements the men spoke to him in English. He was dressed in a well-ironed, light khaki uniform, with boots of soft black kid leather. He was wearing rings on his fingers. The skin of his cheeks was soft and tender, and when he sat on the ground, his stomach bulged. He did not give the impression of being a fighting man.

And indeed he immediately answered any questions gladly, quite chattily, saying that he was not in favour of war, that he had always been a man of peace. His duties in the Engineering Corps did not require him to fight, they were purely engineering jobs, service jobs, nothing else. He repeatedly pointed out to the 'S' tank crews standing near that there was no greater lover of peace in the world than he.

"How long have you been in Sinai?" a sergeant asked him.

"Twenty days, Sir. I came here from the Yemen war. Orders. Believe me, Sir, without an order nothing would have induced me to come here – except perhaps for the fishing which was an attraction, I must admit. I might even have disobeyed the order, but I'm an ardent fisherman. By nature, you see, I am not a fighting man. No, without that order I would never have come here, I can assure you of that. But I do enjoy fishing very much."

There were genuine undertones of sorrow in his voice.

A thin, moustached junior officer in the nearby enclosure shouted in Arabic to the lieutenant-colonel: "Shut up!", and the lieutenant-colonel gently rebuked him for his rudeness, at which a richly gesticulated dialogue developed between the two.

When the order was given to push on to El-Arish, one of the crew members placed his water flask on the ground next to the lieutenant-colonel, then the unit vanished from sight on its way to the Jiradi, and the prisoners remained unguarded except for a tank unit in the distance which was carrying out maintenancc and repair jobs. The prisoners remained sitting in their enclosures, the colonel all by himself on one side, and the rest, about thirty of them, on the other. There they sat, patiently waiting. Later, another tank unit stopped near them on their way to the Jiradi, and the men stared wonderingly at them in their enclosures. One of the tank commanders was furious. How could one leave prisoners without a guard? (though he personally had no men to spare.) What angered the tank commander most was the water flask lying next to the lieutenant-colonel. On it was a large Z, proving it to be Zahal property. The tank commander had just seen his best friend killed, and he snatched the flask away. The unit was then ordered to drive on and it vanished from sight. Then an armoured infantry unit arrived. One of the lieutenants was shocked at the sight of the prisoners; this was not the way to treat human beings. He gave them drinking water from a jerrycan, but then he too had to move on, and again the prisoners were left alone, unguarded, free to do as they pleased, and with plenty of water, until the next unit turned up.

At El-Arish, Division Tal had taken a large number of prisoners, including two generals: the artillery commander who had replaced the commander of the 7th Division, who had been wounded; and the commander of an artillery brigade. The acting commander of the 7th Egyptian Division had been brought to General Tal a short while before 'S' Brigade attacked Bir Lahfan. Tal asked the Egyptian to persuade his soldiers at Bir Lahfan to surrender, to avoid bloodshed, as in any case their fate was sealed.

"I love my soldiers as I love my son," replied the Egyptian general, "and I do not want their blood spilled. But I am a soldier and you cannot expect me to comply with your request." Instead he offered to talk to the gunners at the coastal batteries. "You do not know it," he told General Tal, "but those batteries can be turned 360 degrees, and could well endanger your rear. I can ask them to surrender, as in any case El-Arish has fallen." Units of Israel Forces drove him towards the coastal batteries, but when they got there the gunners had already fled, after sabotaging their coastal guns. A helicopter came and took the two generals to Israel for interrogation.

By the second day of the war, however, the number of prisoners taken had not been large. Most of the Egyptian soldiers had fled to villages and encampments beyond the first lines of defence, or into the distant sandy wastes; they surrendered only when lack of food and water forced them to, a few days later.

At El-Arish airfield the division had their first sight of the results of the Israel Air Force attacks. The airfield was like a ghost town. Everything was intact, nothing was missing, except that the aeroplanes were in ashes and the runways were pitted and destroyed. In the food supply stores and canteens there were masses of cigarettes, biscuits and tinned meat, not of the best quality, but at first taste it seemed a delicacy to the soldiers and they gorged themselves. Even the non-smokers were persuaded to try an Egyptian cigarette.

Ruby, Colonel Shmuel's radio technician, noticed that the brigade commander was eating nothing, only drinking black coffee which was prepared for him when the brigade came to an occasional and brief halt. He offered the commander a meat sandwich, which the colonel, still tense from the brigade's battles and under orders from General Tal to rest, refused. But when he realised that the food offered him was taken from Egyptian army stores, he was furious. From his half-track he saw two soldiers from one of the reserve units searching an abandoned enemy vehicle, looking for booty. He clenched his fists and was about to jump down from his seat and take the law into his own hands, but he controlled his anger and ordered Ruby to bring the two men to him. The one who had already taken booty was placed under arrest.

The arrested soldier felt wronged and began shouting: "If the Egyptians got to Tel Aviv, nothing would remain of it. And you arrest me for taking a souvenir!" Ruby was afraid Colonel Shmuel would tear the man to pieces, so he hushed him quickly.

A radio message from southern command now announced the imminent arrival of General Yeshayahu Gavish, general officer southern command, on a visit to the division. A coloured smoke grenade was released to guide the helicopter, and at 1820 hours General Gavish vaulted lightly from the helicopter. He had news. It had been learnt from prisoners-of-war that the Egyptian Army had been ordered to withdraw to their second line of defence; acting on this information the three divisions would continue their advance and pursuit. The two generals conferred, and it was decided that Division Tal would advance on the Bir Lahfan–Jebel Libni–Bir Gafgafa–Ismailia axis, with a second column along the El-Arish–Kantara axis.

The chase began, then, on the second day of the war and did not end until the last day of the war.

General Gavish flew off in his helicopter to the other divisions, and General Tal picked Colonel Shmuel to lead the division once again, as 'M' Brigade had not yet reorganised and had to be properly refuelled after its rough journey through the sands. Not only was the promised brief rest denied them, then, but they would again be acting as the vanguard of the division, a fact which caused Colonel Shmuel no regrets. At once he was wide awake, as though he had completely forgotten his several sleepless nights. At 1930 hours 'S' Brigade thrust into the silent desert. The skies were clear and dotted with stars.

General Tal sat on his elevated seat in his half-track and spread his map in front of him. His aides, Operations, Signals and Intelligence, clustered round him. Then Pinie, the assistant signals officer, approached to inform him that General Yaffe wished to speak to him.

"Tirah. This is Sunray Ayala. Over."

"Ayala. This is Sunray Tirah."

"Tirah. This is Ayala. We must coordinate plans. Over."

"Ayala. This is Tirah. Gladly. Suggest we meet at Jebel Libni airfield. Over."

"Tirah. This is Ayala. Agreed. Over."

The two command groups, those of General Tal and General Yaffe, approached each other. The meeting was also attended by Colonel Iska, who while recounting the battles and adventures of his unit, added: "Oh, yes, I've just remembered. Ilan Yaku . . . Yakutiel or something. The one who was your adjutant, I'm told. Killed."

"Ilan? Killed?" the general's voice faltered. "How?"

"In the battle against the 'President's Guard' Brigade. The only killed we had in that battle. Good man, too, I believe."

General Tal's voice regained its usual timbre of command. There were pressing matters on hand. General Yaffe anticipated stiff opposition in his advance southward, along the Bir Hasana axis, and now requested Division Tal to reduce the expected pressure on his division by attacking the airfields at Alhamma and Bir Hamma. They agreed on divisional zone boundaries between the two forces.

General Tal hastened back to his division and sent for

26. 'S' Brigade Centurions outflanking Bir Lahfan through the deep sand dunes.

27. The flash caused at the moment of impact when an armour-piercing shell from one of the outflanking Centurions on the road to Ismailia strikes an Egyptian T/55.

28. Egyptian T/54s and T/55s immobilised by 'S' Brigade on the road to Ismailia.

29. (*left*) Bir Gafgafa: abandoned Egyptian vehicles scattered along the road to Ismailia.

30. (*below far left*) An Israeli (M/100 Battalion) AMX/13 knocked out by an Egyptian T/55.

31. (*below left*) Two Israeli Shermans destroyed by Syrian anti-tank guns at the approach to Kala'a.

32. (*below*) Supplies being parachuted to Tal's division near Bir Rod Salim.

33. The three Israeli Shermans knocked out by the Syrians at the approach to Kala'a.

34. The entrance to the Mitla Pass: Egyptian armour destroyed by K/113 Battalion.

Colonel Shmuel and Colonel Men, informing them that the division would attack the airfields of Alhamma and Bir Hamma at dawn, with the support of the divisional artillery. 'S' was to attack, 'M' would be held in reserve and would enter the battle, if necessary, when ordered. While the commanders were conferring, an Egyptian unit crossed the movement axis of General Tal's forward command group. The two columns almost touched, and at first the Egyptians were sure that the command group was one of their tank columns and seemed to want to form up with it, for both sides were now hurrying in the same direction. But the command group recognised them as Egyptians and opened fire.

When the Egyptian unit had been wiped out, General Tal thought it essential to give his men, and himself, a little rest. He gave the order for two hours sleep. As for himself, he was desperately tired. A jeep was brought for him in which the gap between two seats had been filled so that he could spread out on the front seat. Except for the guards, everyone slept wherever they were; near tanks, underneath half-tracks, at the wheels of their jeeps, resting on the butts of Uzzi submachine guns, shell cases or fuel jerrycans. They had not even the strength to make tea or coffee for themselves, but just fell down and slept like so many Sleeping Beauties. The transmitter's generator emitted a final hoot, like an owl, before closing down, and the silence was complete. The night was cold and dry. A wind of sorts blew across the endless expanse; there were no bushes in its path to rustle, nor even blades of grass, but a few grains of sand and grit bowled along before it. There were no jackals wailing, no screeching night birds, even the flies had stopped buzzing. There was dead silence in the desert, uniting the living with the dead.

Suddenly a whistle broke the silence. The generator sprang to life, and the radio equipment began to hum. The general's A.D.C. was called to the radio operator, and then ran to awaken General Tal who was stretched out on the front seat of his jeep. A message: At southern command they did not agree with the plan coordinated between General Tal and General Yaffe.

General Tal went back to his seat in the half-track. He slipped the earphones on his head and received his orders; a change of assignment. Division Yaffe was to move south and Tal's division was to form the southern command reserve. Had the men heard they would certainly have been delighted, for it meant they would get more rest. But the dialogue was in code. It was between 800 and 1600. 800 (General Tal) did not agree with 1600, and 1600 did not agree with 800. Tal then asked his signals officer to connect him with a higher authority, with 2700. 2700 was not available. But General Tal did not give up. He told his signals officer to contact him, even if he had to bring down the archangels from heaven. The distances between the commands stretched across the desert, and Pinie, the signals officer, had to try several ways before finally he made contact with 2700 via an intermediary station.

Thus while everyone was asleep and all around was quiet, the voice of General Tal sped across the wide expanse of the cold desert. His voice is deep and the delivery cautious and deliberate, giving the impression that he speaks too slowly. He was determined to convince 2700 that 2700's plan to pursue the enemy, make contact and destroy it, was not as good a plan as his and General Yaffe's, which was to attack at dawn in a combined operation. The usual code was inadequate, and the conversation grew thick with improvised innuendos. A small flashlight lit up the map from which General Tal read off names and movement axes in code. It sounded as if the two were discussing the occupation of the moon.

Tal: Look here, 2700. I want to advance along the Cassiopaia axis to 34, when my Yeshiva-boy, you know the Gaon of Vilna, outflanks Stalingrad and advances to the Ocean of Storms. . . .

2700: Listen to me, 800. Leave the Ocean of Storms to Baal-Shem-Tov, and stay in reserve on the Worms axis. At the very most you may advance to Mexico City. . . .

Tal: Mexico City? Perhaps Pumbadita?

2700: Mexico City, and leave your Talmudists in reserve.

Tal: That's a bad mistake, 2700. I would have left the preacher of Mazrych where he was and would have attacked Porto Allegro with Baal-Shem-Tov and the Gaon of Vilna and advanced to Pumbadita.

The two hours General Tal had allocated for sleep had soon gone, but the radio conversation ended with Tal convincing 2700 that his and General Yaffe's original plan was more effective. Even when the discussion was finished General Tal remained on his elevated seat and did not go back to the jeep to take whatever was left of his rest period. Engrossed, he rubbed a finger round the splinter embedded in his cheek and studied the maps in front of him. One by one, his assistants gathered round his elevated seat; they had woken up while Tal was talking to 2700 and had immediately realised that important decisions were being taken. The command half-track took on the appearance of a Yeshiva classroom, with General Tal the head of the Yeshiva, sitting and learning with his disciples, searching for the answer to a Talmudic problem. Actually he was making mental calculations of mileage, fuel and ammunition; the problem was whether after two days of non-stop break-throughs and battles, 'S' was capable of leading the division and then bearing the brunt of the divisional attack on the third day. Tal enquired whether the arrangements had been made to parachute supplies and received a positive reply.

"Get ready to move," the general ordered.

The division sprang to life. The silence was shattered by the explosions of the engines starting up in the tanks and by abrupt commands. Then the division moved off, leaving behind the strong odour of burnt fuel in the columns of dust it churned up.

'S' raced past the Jebel Libni junction from the north, in order to deploy for the attack on Bir Hamma. The day before, 'K' had fought a pitched battle at that same place, and when they had met Colonel Iska had warned Colonel Shmuel to watch out for the flank where there were Egyptian Su/100 and T/54 tanks. 'K' had been sniped at and had suffered casualties from them. Colonel Shmuel now decided to deal with this problem thoroughly. What he needed was a quick, nimble commander, able to move his forces rapidly through the sands and take up good firing positions from where he would be able to destroy this troublesome Egyptian flank. He selected Major Shamai Kaplan. And indeed at the start of the attack those same Egyptian tanks fired from their advantageous positions on the flank, doing a clever and accurate job of tank sniping, until Shamai's company, fulfilling all of Colonel Shmuel's expectations, silenced them.

The sky slowly suffused with grey. 'M', too, joined them in the fighting line. 'S' operated from north of the Bir Gafgafa road, 'M' south of it. Then an uncertainty arose regarding the situation of the division's forces; it was feared that 'M' and 'S' might find themselves fighting one another and General Tal warned his commanders of the danger. Colonel Shmuel thereupon ordered S/10, who were in the lead, not to open fire without his explicit order, and as a result S/10 charged straight through the Egyptian armoured infantry defence area without firing a shot. It was only when they reached the rear of the area and all doubts as to the identity of the defenders were dispelled, that Colonel Shmuel ordered an about-turn to mop up enemy positions. By noon 'S' had taken Alhamma.

On a hilltop, near the forward command group, Egyptian defence positions, mostly armed bunkers, were discovered. Tanks and half-tracks climbed the hill and wiped out the Egyptian unit. At that moment Centurions with their guns pointing straight at the command group were seen rapidly approaching. They were shiny black (Zahal's colour is khaki) and looked so pretty in the brilliant sun that for a moment the men paused to admire them.

"Sir," said one of General Tal's aids, "we'd better get them before they draw too near."

"I'm not sure they're enemy tanks," said General Tal, looking through his binoculars.

His staff took a good look at the Centurions through their field-glasses.

"Perhaps they're Centurions from Kuwait?"

"Perhaps they belong to some special Egyptian unit."

"Those Centurions are ours," said General Tal.

"Sir, you are mistaken. If we don't get in first, they'll wipe us out."

At first there were some who supported General Tal's opinion that the Centurions belonged to the division, but one by one they moved to the other camp who maintained they were enemy tanks. For certainly Zahal did not have any black Centurions.

"How beautiful they are in black!" General Tal exclaimed. "Hold fire!" In the end he was the only one to insist that the Centurions were not enemy tanks. What surprised the others was that the Centurions did not open fire as they drew nearer. At last they were close enough to be identified. They were S/10 tanks which had hit an ammunition dump during the battle for Bir Hamma; storming through the dump, black soot had settled over them.

CHAPTER TWENTY-FOUR

The third day of the War, Wednesday, 7 June 1967, was racing day in Sinai. Zahal's three divisions competed with the enemy, especially with its 4th Division. Zahal pursuing, the enemy fleeing. The finishing line for that day's races was the desert outlets to the last line of retreat – the Suez Canal.

There were three passages through which the Egyptian

Army could hope for an orderly retreat and at the same time block Zahal's advance: through the sandy areas behind Bir Gafgafa, on the Ismailia axis; and through the Mitla and Jidi Passes on the road to Suez. For these the Egyptians made, with Zahal's divisions pounding after them. They carried out a wheel sweep, with General Yaffe's division racing with all its might to reach and block the Mitla and Jidi Passes before the retreating enemy got there, and General Tal's division racing to Bir Gafgafa to block the axis which the enemy was endeavouring to get upon from Thamad to the Ismailia road (a lateral axis which connects the Suez axis with that of Ismailia and joins the Ismailia axis west of the principal military airfield at Bir Gafgafa).

In the headlong pursuit of that third day the Israel Air Force also participated. The few roads there are in Sinai are as straight as rulers for most of their length, stretching like narrow asphalt rivers through the deep sands, and the fleeing Egyptian vehicles were easy targets. In some places the appearance of an Israeli plane halted an entire convoy, when the driver of first vehicle stopped and quickly ran to throw himself flat on to the sands, the other vehicles piling up one on the other and forming a train of trucks, tankers, armoured personnel-carriers and engineering vehicles, which were all set on fire by one napalm bomb. However, as much as the operations of the air force hindered the Egyptians in their flight towards the Suez Canal, it also hindered Zahal's divisions in their attempts to catch up with them, because the racing tanks were obliged to manoeuvre between the skeletons of burnt out vehicles.

Along the Suez axis the chase towards the Mitla and Jidi passes was at its wildest. At Bir Hassana, 'K' was inundated with vehicles, tanks and armoured personnel-carriers, streaming in a flood towards the Mitla and Jidi. The Egyptian retreat was now at its zenith, and the rounding-up of prisoners delayed 'K' in its pursuit. In its dash for the two passes 'K' Brigade's Centurion battalions had to twist and turn as though through the narrow alleys of some oriental town. K/113 had to race to the Mitla, reach it before the enemy, fight against a retreating enemy force whose fighting spirit had not deserted it completely, and at the same time act according to the rules of the Geneva Convention on prisoners-of-war towards enemy units whose spirit had been broken and who wished to surrender and be taken prisoner. To complicate matters even further, throughout the long race to the Mitla the commander of K/113 and the brigade commander,

Colonel Iska, were constantly concerned about the fuel supply.

This was what annoyed Colonel Bren. He received permission from the divisional commander to advance ahead of the divisional command group and entered Bir Hassana a few minutes after K/113 had passed through it. He rode in a jeep escorted by a reconnaissance jeep. Chasing after K/113 he could hear over the radio the complaints of the battalion commander that he had "No fuel! No fuel!" But at the same time K/113 had seen the dust clouds of Egyptian armoured fighting vehicles trying to get to Suez via the Mitla and had started to do battle with them. Colonel Bren was of the emphatic opinion that the fleeing Egyptian column was a defeated and scattered enemy whose fighting spirit was broken, not an active enemy at all. He felt that instead of wasting fuel on battle manoeuvres against a retreating enemy, it was more important to combine the effort and the fuel in an all-out push to the Mitla Pass, to block it. In short, Colonel Bren thought General Yaffe's division was not advancing fast enough. He ventured to express this opinion to Colonel Iska, who was deeply hurt by it. "What's the matter, Bren? You don't think we've done good work?"

"You've done very good work, Iska, but you take the Egyptians too seriously. There's no need to busy yourselves with fights like this, which only consume fuel. You've got to rush to the Mitla and block it."

Colonel Bren controlled his anger. But when he heard over his radio the commander of K/113 reporting that he had only thirty minutes fuel left and would not be able to reach the Mitla, he could not contain himself. He ordered his driver to race ahead and catch up with the battalion commander, but so urged his driver on that he suddenly found himself ahead of all the battalion units and at the outskirts of the Egyptian army camps at Bir Thamada. The 'K' brigade reconnaissance company drew up to Colonel Bren, and Bren sent a jeep back to collect the battalion commander. While waiting for the jeep to return, the colonel said to the recce company: "It's not nice standing here in front of these camps, doing nothing." Which is why the recce company captured the Bir Thamada camps all by itself, a fact which confirmed Colonel Ben in his opinion that the Egyptian Army was not a hard nut to crack. He then ordered the reconnaissance company to look for fuel in the camps with which to supply K/113.

Lieutenant-Colonel Abraham, K/113's commander, arrived at Bir Thamada and came over to Bren.

"Abraham," said the colonel, "stop this horse play with the Egyptians, and stop wasting fuel on unimportant fights with defeated forces. Advance quickly to the Mitla. The recce company will go with you."

"O.K., Sir," said Abraham.

"And don't use ammunition on abandoned tanks. It hurts to see those lovely T/55s burnt or damaged."

K/113 and Colonel Bren raced towards the Mitla. But ten kilometres beyond Thamada a message from the divisional commander ordered Colonel Bren to return to the command group. With a broken heart he took his leave of Abraham. "I've been ordered back. And you, carry on as quickly as possible to the Mitla."

The rear echelons of the division had not yet left Bir Hassana, and General Yaffe assigned to Colonel Bren the task of ensuring that the 'C' Tank Brigade carried out its assignment properly.

"Yes, Sir," said Colonel Bren, though he would much have preferred to be in the spearhead of the division than in its rear.

K/113 drove on in its attempt to forestall the retreating Egyptians at the Mitla Pass. Despite Colonel Bren's instructions the battalion (which due to fuel shortage and breakdowns now numbered only twenty-eight Centurions) had been obliged to fight against Egyptian tanks in the scurrying, confused, retreating columns of trucks, armoured personnel-carriers, command vehicles and tanks. By the time Abraham reached the Mitla he had only nine tanks left and of these two were being towed. The others had foundered in the race for lack of fuel.

With these nine tanks he reached to within two kilometres of the junction of the roads forking out from the Mitla, to Nakhl and Bir Hassana. While deploying for their blocking action, three other Centurions had run out of fuel. These were towed into defensive formation. In addition to the tanks there were two platoons of armoured infantry and three half-tracks armed with 120 mm mortars, two of which also lacked fuel.

It was 1830 hours, and the enemy, retreating in its numerous hurrying and disorganised columns, arrived at the Mitla opening at the same time as K/113. At the sight of the Centurions, some of the Egyptians jumped down from their vehicles and fled on foot, but a lengthy column managed to bypass the road-blocking Centurions and enter the Mitla Pass. Abraham immediately realised that he would have to set up his road-block elsewhere. Meanwhile the retreating columns crowded into the Mitla Pass. At that moment two Israeli Vautour bombers appeared overhead in the waning daylight and dropped their bombs upon the congested column moving along the narrow mountainous defile, causing a traffic jam and greatly impeding the retreat.

Abraham now gave the order to tow two Egyptian trucks into the road, several metres apart, to overturn them and set fire to them. Any Egyptian vehicle now trying to enter the Mitla was obliged to decelerate before negotiating this passage, becoming an easy target for the Centurions' guns. They were nine against an enemy many times that number, but being organised and under orders they were able to play havoc with the cowed and crumbling enemy. During the night self-propelled artillery units which had joined K/113 brought eleven barrels of fuel which they had found in the Egyptian army camps. They had no funnels and had to improvise by using empty biscuit tins. While they were busy re-fuelling, an Egyptian tank unit attempted to force the blockade and enter the Mitla Pass. The first T/54 succeeded in getting through; one of the trucks which had been set on fire was loaded with ammunition which now began to explode with blinding flashes, screening the movements of the Egyptian tank. When the T/54 was spotted again after penetrating the blockade, Sluczer, a Centurion commander, was misled into thinking his unit was advancing into the Mitla. He immediately followed the T/54 but soon became aware of his error and fired an armour-piercing shell into the rear of the T/54, which stopped in its tracks. Another three Egyptian tanks managed to get through the blockade, but a fourth was hit and burst into flames. Sluczer came out of the pass and took up a position from which he could hit the back of any tank which succeeded in penetrating the blockade.

At dawn, on Thursday, 8 June, the tanks were again without fuel, and this time almost without ammunition. Only in Captain Guy Jacobson's company were there any mobile Centurions – four of them. And along came a large column of retreating enemy forces, including twenty-eight T/54 tanks. Abraham quickly called for air support and until the air force came the four mobile Centurions fought against the Egyptian tanks. At last two Super-Mystères arrived to bomb the enemy column and set it ablaze, its occupants taking to their heels and running into the sands and mountains of the Mitla. When the blaze died down, the burnt-out vehicles looked like skeletons. From then on the air force destroyed the retreating convoys on the way to the Mitla. The quantities of Egyptian vehicles destroyed on the Mitla battlefield were the largest of the war; the burnt-out chassis were spread over an area of four kilometres.

Along the Ismailia axis the pursuit took a different form. Large elements of the 4th Egyptian Armoured Division tried to get away in an orderly, combatant withdrawal not through the Mitla or the Jidi, but along the Ismailia axis, which they were about to break on to along its lateral axis. Division Tal raced to block it.

After Bir Rod Saliem, General Tal's division changed its order of advance. 'M' Brigade now took the lead, its objective being the capture of Bir Gafgafa. 'S' Brigade was given a breathing space, mopping up in the rear of the division and combing out Egyptian defence zones on its way. On one occasion an Egyptian tank which had been in hiding mistook the 'S' Centurions and Pattons for Egyptian units and got into line behind Major Haim's Patton. It drove close behind him, aping his every movement. Major Haim did not at first notice that his faithful escort was not a friend, but after a while one of the 'S' tank commanders pointed out to him that a T/55 with tightly closed hatches was following him like a shadow.

What was Haim to do? Point out to the Egyptian tank's crew that it was a case of mistaken identity, that the one they believed to be their combat leader was really the enemy and that they had best stop their T/55 and surrender? First, how was he to convey the message to the Egyptian crew sitting imprisoned in their tank, oblivious to the world? Secondly, if he was to stop, climb down from his tank, bang on the T/55's hatches and identify himself, he would be risking his life. It was more than likely that the love and devotion the Egyptian crew had shown while under the impression he was one of them would change dramatically to hatred and shooting the moment they recognised him.

Haim had no other option but to act as one must in war, in which the only form of expression is killing. He had to get in first and destroy the T/55 before it realised its mistake. He increased the speed of his Patton and took a sharp swing to the left, so that the T/55 shot past him. Then he could hardly believe his eyes; the Egyptian crew was aiming its gun at two of his Pattons only a few dozen metres away. Haim closed in to within five metres of the T/55 and fired an armour-piercing shell. It penetrated perfectly, boring a clean hole in the T/55's steel armour no larger in diameter than the shell itself. So precise and clean was the circle that it seemed the T/55 had not been hit at all and that the hole in its rear was functional, perhaps a gas vent or the end of an air-conditioning tube. Even General Tal stopped his command half-track to have a close look at the perforated T/55 (he was actually photographed next to it).

"Haikma, bring me a sound and serviceable T/55. Can you?"

"Certainly, Sir."

'S' was reorganising, and Major Haim set out to find a T/55 in good condition for the division's commander. General Tal wanted to study the T/55 in action, in anticipation of future battles against that type of tank.

'M' advanced upon Bir Gafgafa with only minor encounters on the way. Its tanks were Shermans equipped with new engines and guns, and the original AMX/13s. At 1530 hours 'M' reached the complex of military installations at Bir Gafgafa and encountered the enemy. From south of the road an Egyptian force was approaching from the Bir Gafgafa airfield, and from the north, near a hill on which was a Radar installation, heavy firing from T/55 tanks was directed at them. General Tal ordered Colonel Men to hold on to the two junctions on the Bir Gafgafa road, each with one battalion, while the battalion of AMX/13 tanks was to advance westwards. During this battle against the Egyptians, who were trying to keep the Gafgafa axis open for their own forces, Egyptian MIG'S appeared overhead and also attacked 'M'. Super-Mystères hurried to assist 'M', but one of them was shot down. 'M' suffered several casualties from the Egyptian tanks.

General Tal's command group was at Jebel Khutumia at that time, observing the area, when they spotted thick dust from moving vehicles coming from the Ml'ez, a narrow fissure between a chain of mountains which forms a lateral junction between the Sinai's southern axes and the Ismailia road. As the directives at that stage were to surround all the enemy's armoured forces with the three Israeli divisions and destroy them, General Tal decided to obstruct and block the exit from the Ml'ez with 'M' Brigade in the region which lay between the AMX/13 Battalion under Lieutenant-Colonel Zeev — positioned some twenty kilometres from the brigade's two other tank battalions – and the junction of the Bir Gafgafa airfield road and the road to Ismailia, while using 'S' Brigade to strike in a wide flanking movement from Jebel Khutumia, from south to north, along the length of the axis connecting the southern Sinai axes with the road joining the Bir Gafgafa airfield road to the Ismailia road. As the Centurions of 'S' Brigade were busy re-fuelling, Tal added the divisional reserve, the T/01 Patton Battalion, to 'S' Brigade. Colonel Shmuel, at the head of twenty Pattons and with Lieutenant-Colonel Uri, raced to do battle. Again he and his men had been deprived of their rest.

"Where's Haim?" Shmuel asked.

"Looking around for a T/55," was the reply.

"Move now," the colonel ordered, deciding not to wait for Major Haim, the commander of the Patton battalion.

"Here he is!" Lieutenant Yossi B. called out.

Major Haim came into view driving a T/55, his head exposed, smiling broadly, looking like a white hunter in Africa who has trapped a white elephant.

"Haim, get off that T/55 and into your own tank at once. We're moving," Colonel Shmuel called to him.

Major Haim leapt from the T/55 and into his command Patton in a flash, and the force went in search of the enemy. At last Colonel Herzl, who was observing from another ridge, spotted the enemy and directed Colonel Shmuel towards them.

At 1700 hours Colonel Shmuel took an observation, then ordered Major Haim to advance slowly with his Pattons so as not to raise tell-tale clouds of dust. Then the Pattons thrust forward in two columns against the enemy column close to the Ismailia road along which it had been hoping to make its escape to Egypt. It was a force of brigade strength. The Pattons destroyed about a dozen tanks, and a similar number of armoured troop-carriers. The troops scattered in all directions.

Night fell, and Colonel Shmuel began taking his Pattons back from the battlefield. The return journey was slow. They had suffered no casualties, but two Pattons had broken down and had to be towed; the Armoured Corps had strict instructions never to abandon tanks.

Meanwhile Egyptian pressure on 'M' from the direction of the Suez Canal had considerably increased, and General Tal needed Shmuel and the tanks he had with him. It was known that Egyptian commandos were operating in the area, and orders went out to all units of the division to be prepared for night-raids; General Tal's command group found themselves a secure haven with S/10. Here General Tal met Major Shamai Kaplan for the first time since the beginning of the war. He did not recognise him at first, as the major was clean-shaven. The general shook hands warmly; but immediately realised that he had hurt Shamai, both of whose hands were bandaged. Since the death of Major Eli Globus, Shamai had also been the battalion's 2iC, and as he had not wanted to part from his company, he was serving in both capacities.

"What news, Shamai?" the general asked.

"Everything seems fine, Sir," Shamai replied.

"Will you put me up for the night?"

"Half of what I have is yours, Sir," Shamai said.

"And who gets the other half?"

"The company, Sir."

"Won't you settle for the one job of Battalion 2iC?"

"What will the men say, Sir? That I deserted them in the middle of the war?"

"How is Nava?"

"She should give birth any day. Perhaps she already has."

Tal asked to be connected with Colonel Shmuel, still on his way back from the Ml'ez. He was worried that the division might find itself in the centre of enemy pressure, coming from the direction of Egypt and from southern Sinai, wanting to force its way out of the divisional trap which was closing in on it.

"Shamir. This is Tirah. What's the delay? Over."

"Tirah. This is Shamir. I have two Pattons broken down and am towing them. Over."

"Shamir. This is Tirah. When will you reach S/10? Over."

"Tirah. This is Shamir. Not before 0600 hours."

This was too late. He did not want Colonel Shmuel and his Pattons, which had little fuel left, to remain in an area teeming with the enemy, and he also wanted to dispatch the colonel to relieve the pressure on 'M'. He immediately issued orders to prepare a convoy of half-tracks loaded with fuel for Shmuel's Pattons, but according to his calculations even the fuel would not assure his earlier arrival. There was nothing else for it but to order him to abandon the crippled Pattons.

"Shamir. This is Tirah. Leave the two Pattons behind and get here as quickly as you can. Over."

"Tirah. This is Shamir. I'll try and get to you quickly, with the Pattons. Over."

"Shamir. This is Tirah. Leave the two Pattons behind and get here quickly. Over."

"Tirah. This is Shamir. I'll get to you quickly. Over."

"Shamir. This is Tirah. That is an order. Leave the tanks where they are. Over."

Suddenly the general understood the reason for the colonel's obstinacy. According to Field Orders of the Armoured Corps, no tank is to be abandoned without its crew to guard it, and Colonel Shmuel was under the impression that General Tal was ordering him to leave behind the two Pattons with their crews in an area teeming with enemy forces, including commando units. The colonel considered this tantamount to sacrificing his men who would be murdered in their sleep, for he knew how exhausted they were, having had no rest for four days.

"Shamir. This is Tirah. Without the crews. Without the crews. Over."

Colonel Shmuel's sigh of relief could be heard over the radio.

"Tirah. This is Shamir. O.K. That's fine. Over."

"Shamir. This is Tirah. Are you crazy? Did you think I would order you to leave the tanks with their crews? Over."

For a moment there was no reply; the only sound was the murmur of the radio equipment, as though it was filling in for Colonel Shmuel, saying: "Sir, in war anything is possible. Everything is crazy." But then Shmuel's voice came over the radio saying: "Tirah. This is Shamir. I'm leaving the tanks behind. Roger. Over."

"Shamir. This is Tirah. Get here quickly now. Roger. Out."

Colonel Shmuel abandoned the tanks and raced to 'S' headquarters, arriving at 0200 hours. He and his men were tired and starving, but when they got to the field kitchen, they found that the men already there had hungrily eaten part of the food intended for the Ml'ez detachment. When Colonel Shmuel saw that there was not enough hot soup to go round he flew into a rage and kicked the cauldron over, spilling the soup. "If there is not enough for everybody, there is none for anybody," he ground out between his teeth at the officer in charge. With empty and growling stomachs his men went back to work, to attend to their tanks and weapons, in preparation for their next assignment.

CHAPTER TWENTY-FIVE

When Colonel Shmuel arrived at the 'S' leaguer, M/100, 'M' Brigade's AMX/13 battalion, was in the throes of an Egyptian attack. In fact M/100 Battalion experienced the only all-out Egyptian assault of the Six Days War. The only other unit to be subjected to a similar attack was Israel Force on the Kantara axis.

M/100 had halted where it was on the Ismailia road after General Tal had radioed it not to proceed westward because of the large enemy forces there. The general estimated the strength of the enemy's forces west of M/100 to be about a hundred T/55s. He ordered Lieutenant-Colonel Zeev to set up a defensive position along the Ismailia road and to secure the division's flank against what would certainly be desperate enemy attempts to break through. At that stage Zeev was nearer to the Suez Canal than any other Zahal unit, except for Israel Force on the Kantara axis.

Zeev had to contend not only with enemy forces from the west, but from the east as well. Large Egyptian forces, infantry, soft-skinned vehicles, tanks and armoured personnel-carriers had burst through the tiny gaps in the division in their attempt to mount the road to Ismailia. Some had succeeded but had then come up against the M/100 position. Zeev had to be prepared not only for a frontal tank offensive from the Ismailia side but an attack from his rear on the Bir Gafgafa side too. Besides these dangers, he also had to defend himself against a possible infantry attack which might approach in vehicles, dismount and attack from all sides. Lieutenant-Colonel Zeev wanted to be prepared for all eventualities. In spite of his men's utter exhaustion, he ordered them to attend to their tanks, for the AMX/13 can suffer from numerous obstructions if not properly maintained. The men cleaned their guns' breech-blocks and their machine guns and worked on their tanks until 2300 hours.

As the night was very dark and there was the danger of infantry attacks, Zeev arranged his position very compactly. One column stayed on the road and two columns, one on the right and the other on the left, parked off the road with tanks positioned in front and behind each column. The men of the armoured infantry company were dispersed on the ground with machine guns to guard against enemy infantry attack, and when a reconnaissance company turned up and was given permission to stay, an additional column was added, further to the right.

By midnight on Thursday, 8 June, most of the men in the position were sound asleep. Some time later Zeev received a warning from brigade headquarters that retreating enemy tanks were likely to reach his rear and at about 0300 hours he received advice that two Egyptian tanks had passed the brigade lines and in all probability would soon be appearing on his rear. However, friendly units might also make their appearance from the same direction, so Zeev ordered his men on watch to hold their fire and to shoot only when given the order, at the last moment.

"Fire!" Zeev ordered when the silhouettes of two vehicles approached without identifying themselves. The guard posts spat fire. Both vehicles burst into flames, and it was then seen that they were two trucks loaded with Egyptian infantry. At the same time the noise of tanks was heard, approaching from the direction of Ismailia.

Zeev reckoned that he was either coming under a counterattack from Egyptian armour or that the vanguard of the Egyptian relief force was arriving. He alerted his positions and ordered the 120mm half-track destroyer to shell the Egyptian tanks, which were moving with their small lights on and could be seen, eight to ten of them, rapidly advancing from the west. He then ordered the 81mm mortars to fire illuminating flares. The AMX/13s had already started to disperse, and the soft-skinned vehicles were ordered to spread out at the back of the columns. Before he could do more the Egyptian tanks were upon him.

The first Egyptian tank fired and scored a direct hit on the heavy mortar half-track, setting its ammunition ablaze, and catching the crew with their first shell in their hands. Three Egyptian shells, one after the other, struck the engineer's half-track, which was laden with explosives; another Egyptian tank hit the air-support liaison officer's half-track and then the reconnaissance company's. Within two minutes M/100 Battalion had suffered sixteen men killed and twenty badly wounded. The position was a mass of smoke and flames. The ammunition began to explode in the burning half-tracks, and the men near them fled into the sands. In Lieutenant Hagei's AMX/13 the gunner panicked, jumped out of the tank and ran into the sands, leaving Hagei to carry out three jobs: platoon commander, tank commander and gunner.

According to information received, the enemy was concentrating large numbers of tanks west of Zeev on the Ismailia road. He now discovered that the tanks were in fact T/55s, against which he would have to fight with AMX/13s. The T/55, a Russian tank, is an improvement on the T/54. In all respects it is a modern tank, equivalent to the new type of Patton (M/60), and in comparison the AMX/13 is an old, light French tank. It entered service with the French Army towards the end of the 1940s, and Zahal procured its first consignment in 1954. In the fight now facing it, to make matters worse, the AMX/13 was deprived of its ability to manoeuvre, which enhanced the advantages of the T/55. The AMX/13's weight is less than half that of the T/55, and its gun cannot pierce the T/55. The AMXs were both outgunned and unable to use their superior ability to manoeuvre.

Zeev's order to open fire was given when the lead Egyptian tank was 100 metres from the defensive position. The second tank was 170 metres away, the third 250 metres. Everyone fired, with machine guns and guns. Zeev actually saw two shells strike the first tank and bounce off it in a shower of sparks. Without losing his presence of mind, he ordered his AMXs to try and hit the T/55s on their sides or from behind.

"Marganit. This is Zarzir. Under heavy pressure from T/55s. Over," Zeev radioed to the 'M' Brigade commander.

"Tirah. This is Marganit. Zarzir battalion under heavy attack by T/55s. Over," the 'M' Brigade commander reported to General Tal who was then with S/10. Tal received the message a moment after Colonel Shmuel's Pattons had arrived, after a reconnaissance jeep had been sent to guide them in with flares.

General Tal heard the sounds of battle on his radio and saw the flashes and the bursts of flame. He immediately ordered the 'M' Brigade commander to dispatch a company of Sherman tanks from his 2nd Tank Battalion and also ordered Zeev to break off contact with the enemy and to withdraw one and a half kilometres. At the same time he ordered Colonel Shmuel to send a company of Centurions to the aid of the heavily pressed battalion in order to reinforce it in preparation for the morning. Colonel Shmuel ordered S/10 to send a company, and Major Shamai Kaplan set out with his company of Centurions. They had to cover more than forty kilometres.

"Zarzir. This is Marganit. Fold up one bound back. I am sending you a Sherman company. Over," Colonel Men radioed Zeev. It was a Sherman company with improved engines and guns which had set out to join M/100.

Zeev issued orders to his battalion to break off contact and start withdrawing, but then immediately changed his mind and decided to return to his original positions. The ranges were very short, but the AMXs had begun to manoeuvre and to get into firing positions where they were able to hit the T/55's sides. The lead Egyptian tank which had done so much damage to the battalion, had already been hit on its right side and there the shell had penetrated. The second Egyptian tank was not moving behind the first, but was attempting to outflank M/100 from the left, from where it fired several shells into the midst of the position, causing considerable damage. The AMX which fired at it first, hit its hull, but the armour-piercing shell merely bounced off it. The AMX then tried to outflank the T/55 and managed to hit it a second time, in its track, but still the T/55 did not stop. Finally the AMX managed to outflank the T/55 squarely and from a range of forty metres sent a shell through its side. The T/55 caught fire.

Zeev's decision not to fall back under the Egyptian pressure seemed to instil his men with a new spirit. His stubbornness, together with the proof that an AMX could knock out the T/55s from the side, encouraged the men of his battalion and probably amazed the Egyptians. Another two T/55s were hit on their sides, and their crews jumped out and fled into the sands. The sight of the fleeing tank crews caused the rest of the column considerable concern; it halted and the T/55s took up positions along the road and the sandy edges, now and then moving into firing positions, firing a round and falling back.

When the company of Shermans arrived, it found M/100 standing fast, prepared and ready for battle. At first sight the leaguer looked a shambles. Vehicles, half-tracks and even AMXs were burning. Charred and damaged corpses were trapped in the flaming wreckage, and it was not even possible to extricate their bodies. The Sherman battalion's second-in-command, Haim Tamir, who had come with the Sherman company, immediately went forward to observe the Egyptian tank positions. They went up to a distance of only one and a half kilometres, and when the jeep came into sight, it was hit and Haim Tamir lost a leg.

The Shermans had come straight from another battle and each tank had only a few shells left. Nevertheless they opened fire. At the same time an Israeli plane put in an appearance and swooped down on the Egyptian tanks, which withdrew

225

to a distance of five kilometres. Here they awaited developments after having failed to break through the division.

"Zarzir. This is Marganit. A Centurion company is on its way to you. Over," the 'M' Brigade commander informed Zeev.

"Marganit. This is Zarzir. Query. Is the company under my command? Over."

"Zarzir. This is Marganit. Negative. Over."

A short while later Zeev was receiving Major Shamai Kaplan on his radio: "Zarzir. This is Shamai. I'm on my way to you. Where are the Egyptian tanks? Over."

"Shamai. This is Zarzir. I shall brief you personally. Not by radio. Out."

The Centurions soon joined the beleagured position, Shamai Kaplan leading the company. Zeev climbed into the Centurion and drove with Shamai to an observation point, from where he explained the situation. He then returned to his battalion while Shamai advanced with his company. Zeev had received instructions not to follow the Centurion company, but that Shamai's radio contact with command headquarters would be via M/100's radio.

Shamai, however, was soon out of good radio reception range, and Zeev started to feel worried. He clambered into his command half-track and drove forward rapidly in order to reduce the range; when at last he contacted Shamai on the radio he told him: "Don't move out more than ten kilometres from our positions."

But Shamai drove on, at the head of his Centurions.

By morning it had become obvious that the three divisions were no longer up against an organised enemy, and General Tal decided to advance as speedily as possible in the direction of the Suez Canal. At first he had wished to leave 'S' in the Bir Gafgafa area and advance with 'M', but after the losses 'M' had suffered, he found it best to fully organise 'S' and dispatch it, properly equipped and supplied, to reach the canal in one sweep. At his orders group, still at Jebel Khutumia, Tal assigned the objectives: 'S' to the canal; 'M' the capture of the Bir Gafgafa airfield with artillery support, and the securing of the division's left flank; T/01 as the division's reserve; T/01 now had one Patton company. Israel Force was to advance to the junction of the Kantara road and the lateral axis running parallel to the canal, connecting the Kantara road with that of Ismailia. The evening before, while General Tal had been following 'S' Brigade's assault in the Ml'ez, Colonel

Raphoul had contacted him to inform him that he had no further assignments in the Gaza Strip, and that he was longing to get back to General Tal. The two men had agreed that Colonel Raphoul would contact southern command and ask to be attached to Division Tal. His request had been granted and on Thursday at 1130 hours Colonel Raphoul and his 'Z' Brigade had linked up with Israel Force which from then on was under his command.

While 'S' was being re-equipped for its advance to the canal, General Tal received a message from Lieutenant-Colonel Zeev, Shamai had gone beyond the radio receiving range, and contact with him had been lost. "Dear God", the general said. He instructed Colonel Shmuel to halt all preparations and to race west with the entire brigade to link up with the lone company. Colonel Shmuel, who had been at his side, needed no explanations. He understood at once what the general was worried about: The possibility that Shamai's company would find itself in the middle of a large Egyptian tank force which they knew was in the area.

Colonel Shmuel ordered S/10 to move at once – it had been the first to complete refuelling – and he himself led it at top speed towards Ismailia and Shamai. But the axis was blocked with 'M' Brigade's supply trucks carrying ammunition and fuel. The heavy vehicles lumbered along at a maddeningly slow pace and Shmuel was obliged to dismount from his command half-track to clear them off the road so that the Centurions could get through.

The orders given to Shamai by Lieutenant-Colonel Gabriel had been not to advance beyond the M/100 positions. But when Shamai had gone up to the observation point with Zeev and seen no enemy in sight, he had apparently decided to advance as far as he possibly could. He had eight Centurions with him, their crews all war-seasoned warriors; Shamai's company had seen more action than any other of 'S' Brigade's companies, with the exception of Ein-Gil's.

"Shamai Stations. This is Shamai," Major Shamai Kaplan was now saying over the company radio. "We are advancing towards the Suez Canal. We will advance until we make contact; then we'll see what happens. We shall advance in a swift column along the road, but before every crest the first three tanks will disperse and climb to observation positions. If the coast is clear we shall continue in column formation. If we sight the enemy, we fight. Move now. Follow me. Over."

227

Shamai's Centurion was scarred from battles at the frontier, from the break-through at Khan Yunis, from the heavy fighting at the Rafa Junction, Sheikh Zuweid, the Jiradi, from the blocking operations at El-Arish and Jebel Libni. Skirting plates over the tracks were perforated, the armour on the turret was lacerated and the stowage boxes in the turret were split and cracked. Shamai himself was grey with fatigue and dirt, his shirt torn, his hands bandaged; but he stood erect in the commander's cupola, at the head of his company so that all his men could see him. The black, narrow asphalt road spread on its bed of sand was badly pitted and scarred so that in several places the road-bed could be seen. Sand dunes stretched away on both sides of the track as far as the eye could see, soft and deep and probably impassable to tanks. On the way they had seen many enemy trucks which had gone off the road in their desperate attempt to escape Zahal's planes and had sunk in the sands. He would have to take care not to disperse his company too far from the road.

The road wound ahead of them to the top of a hill, and soon they were nearing its crest. "Shamai Stations. This is Shamai. We are approaching the crest. Advance in operational formation, one force covering the other. We will climb to observation positions."

The first three tanks dispersed over an area of a hundred metres, one tank on Shamai's right and the other on his left, Shamai himself remaining on the road. "Shamai Stations. This is Shamai. I can see several tanks. Nothing serious. We shall destroy them and advance."

The Centurions' fire was rapid and accurate. The first shots hit three T/55s which were in hulldown positions but were targets enough for the company's gunners. The three tanks then formed up again in the column, Shamai's at the head, then the rearguard of the company, under the command of Lieutenant Yoab, rejoined the column after destroying two T/55s which they had spotted on the flanks.

"Shamai Stations. This is Shamai. I think that is all for this ridge. Until the next one everything seems quiet. A beautiful panorama. Move now, follow me. Out."

Another crest was reached, the company dispersed again, and more T/55s were destroyed. Then they resumed their rapid progress, advancing in column along the narrow road. "Shamai Stations. This is Shamai. We are advancing in the direction of the Suez Canal, which might be the end of the war. We'll finish it ourselves and go home."

228

The road seemed to stretch endlessly through its sea of sand. The company was already fifteen kilometres from the M/100 positions. The next fold in the terrain was sighted and reached. Again Shamai ordered the company to disperse, and again the first three tanks moved into observation positions, with their commander at the head. Looking back for a moment Shamai noticed that one tank was not moving. "Samik," he called to its commander, "what's the matter?"

"I've no clutch, Sir."

"We won't leave you behind. Don't worry."

Seven tanks were now on the move. In the last few days the Centurions had proved themselves to be a brilliant tank. Shamai's company was proud of them, calling them "the perfect tanks". Their steel had saved innumerable lives and they carried on even though they should have been given their customary check-ups and periodical maintenance long ago. The company resumed its advance along the road in column formation.

"We shall be the first to reach the canal, Dan Meridor," Shamai said, and at that moment a shell struck his cupola.

"Shamai. This is Zarzir," Lieutenant-Colonel Zeev called over his radio to Shamai Kaplan. He had been trying to catch up with the company in his half-track, and radioing constantly to Shamai to warn him not to advance further and not to get out of radio range.

"Shamir. This is Zarzir," he called for the umpteenth time.

"Zarzir. This is Shamai's 2iC. Over," Lieutenant Yoab replied.

Zeev was delighted that at last he had caught up with the company and made radio contact with it, but was disconcerted to get a reply from the second-in-command. "Shamir. This is Zarzir. Why does the 2iC reply? Over."

"Zarzir. This is Shamai's 2iC. The company commander has been killed. Over."

The company had driven straight into an ambush set by a battalion of T/55s. The Egyptian tanks had been hidden in very good firing positions, at short range. The first shell had struck Shamai's Centurion, destroying the 0.5 Browning machine gun and striking the top of the cupola. A large splinter cut through Major Shamai, killing him instantly. Shamai's tank crew did not lost their presence of mind and withdrew immediately. The second shell struck the third tank in the column; its commander, Sergeant Giora Shklarchik, was about to give a fire correction to his gunner when he felt a heavy blow and saw black smoke rising from his tank. At first he did not realise what had happened, but understood when he saw that the loader was wounded and heard the gunner yell: "Giora, we've been hit!" The three of them climbed from the tank, their weapons in their hands, then called to the driver to get out of his compartment. There was no reply, and they saw that the tank had received two direct hits, one in the front. The tank continued to circle round and round, then began to slide down the incline, for it had been standing exactly on the crest. When the driver had been hit, his foot had slipped off the brake. The three crew members ran after the Centurion until it came to a stop. They opened the driver's hatch and found him dead.

There was no more than two or three minutes of confusion. Lieutenant Hanoch, whose Centurion was one of the first three, immediately realised that the company commander had been killed and that the company was heading for an ambush. He ordered his driver to make a sharp right turn, into the valley, then located the enemy tanks and ordered a rapid dispersal. He then passed the command over to the company 2iC, Lieutenant Yoab, who was with the Centurions in the rear.

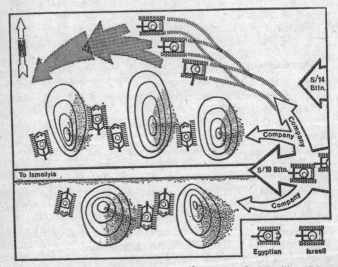

10   'S' Brigade's 'steamroller' action (8 June) on the Ismailia axis.

A fierce battle now developed, at ranges from 400 to 1300 metres, the six Centurions fighting an enemy force which was both numerically superior and better positioned. Shamai's Centurion returned to the fray after the crew, with the help of Sergeant Zadok, had extricated Major Shamai Kaplan from the tank and placed him on a half-track which hastened to the rear with the body. Sergeant Wahaba was now the tank commander.

The half-track with Major Shamai Kaplan's body raced to the battalion aid post, flashing past the smoking remains of tanks and the burnt out chassis of vehicles on either side of the road. At the aid post, Shamai was wrapped in a blanket and his personal possessions collected; in his wallet they found a poem he had copied out during the days of preparation and waiting: "Never again shall our necks be offered like sheep to the slaughterer. If we must die, then let us die in battle."

While the half-track was still racing to the rear, the six Centurions fought on until they had wiped out the ambush and destroyed ten T/55s. When the battle was over the company gathered on the road and awaited the arrival of S/10. The men of the company were informed of their commander's death and they wept.

Colonel Shmuel arrived at the head of his brigade to rescue Shamai's company a short while after Shamai's death. He was informed that the strength of the Egyptian armour blocking the route to the Suez Canal was the size of a brigade and immediately decided to destroy it with a brigade-scale steamroller movement.

The Egyptian tanks were positioned on both sides of the road, facing it and concealed by the twists and turns of the sandy terrain from anyone coming from the east towards the canal. Ostensibly, Colonel Shmuel's plan seemed to suit the Egyptian commander. The brigade was to walk into the mouth of the trap, with one company outflanking the ambush from the north and striking at it. S/10 drove down the road and into the ambush, one company dispersed to the left of the road and one company to the right, in a frontal attack; S/14 drove behind it in two columns through the sands to the right of the road; one company of Centurions outflanked the Egyptians in a wide arc north of the road, about one kilometre from it, thus placing themselves behind the Egyptian tanks emplaced to the north of the road and in front of those to the south.

The Egyptian tanks occupied positions along a stretch of seven kilometres in very sandy terrain, and hardly expected a company to outflank them from terrain which was frankly thought to be impassable. It required superb driving not to sink in the deep, soft sands. The Egyptian officers must have been overjoyed to see the brigade walking into their ambush, but they had scarcely corrected their first shots when the company on their flank struck. S/10 then drove up to the next mound, taking another step in its steam-roller system. Again the Egyptians were delighted at the frontal attack and returned the Centurions' fire as they came driving in, only to be struck at once more from the flank. For five hours the steam-roller advanced down the road, purposefully and calmly, destroying some seventy Egyptian tanks, most by the outflanking company. 'S' suffered no losses.

It was already evening and S/10 needed refuelling. Four Mystères flew overhead and Colonel Shmuel requested them to attack the Egyptian defence zone which was located twenty-five kilometres from Ismailia. One of the Mystères flew down the length of the Ismailia road and found more concentrations of Egyptian armour on it. Colonel Shmuel decided to continue his sweep forward, advancing with the S/14 Patton Battalion.

"Tirah. This is Shamir. Request permission to advance. Over."

"Shamir. This is Tirah. Advance and get permission every five kilometres," replied General Tal.

Israel Force, now commanded by Colonel Raphoul, also went into action against enemy paratroops and tanks which were endeavouring to push them back. Raphoul set out for the outskirts of Kantara at the head of the Patton company which was leading the rest of the force, but an hour after assuming command of Israel Force, he received a head wound from a bullet. He was immediately flown by helicopter to a hospital in Israel, while Colonel Israel took over command. His force had been attacked by Egyptian bombers the previous day and his main problem was to marshal and equip his detachment for one more full-scale attack. Even ammunition for the tanks was in short supply. During the battle for Kantara the commander of the Patton company was wounded, but by 1800 hours on Thursday, 8 June, Colonel Israel could report to General Tal that Kantara had been taken.

During the same evening a helicopter landed near General Tal's command group in Bir Gafgafa, bringing with it the deputy chief-of-staff, General Haim Bar-Lev and the general officer southern command, General Yeshayahu Gavish. Bar-Lev suggested to Tal that 'S' Brigade speed up its advance, and General Tal explained to him that on the Ismailia axis dozens of Egyptian tanks were arrayed in fighting formation and displaying stubborn resistance. He also said that he was not willing to incur heavy losses and was therefore directing the battle as a long-range fire assault, managing at the same time to inflict heavy losses on the enemy. 'S' Brigade's steamroller tactics had cost it only two tanks and two men killed.

"But if there are political considerations or any other reasons which necessitate a speedy advance to the canal I will do it at once." At that moment two enemy bombers appeared above General Tal's command group. Most of those present dispersed, throwing themselves down in the sands far from the command half-tracks, whose forest of aerials towering above them made them easily identifiable, but the generals continued their talk as though nothing had happened.

"The chief-of-staff, Talik, is interested in both these things. We want to get to the Suez Canal as quickly as possible, but at the same time we must avoid heavy losses," replied General Bar-Lev.

The decision was left to General Tal, and he chose to advance cautiously and slowly. The general's helicopter took off and Division Tal formed up. But then the transistor radio, which had accompanied the division throughout the campaign, brought the news from New York that the Egyptian government was ready for a cease-fire. General Tal now understood that there was sound and valid reasons for occupying positions along the length of the canal as rapidly as possible, and he ordered Colonel Shmuel to dispatch his reconnaissance force towards the canal at high speed. Even so the general took precautions to save lives. His orders to Colonel Shmuel were that if the reconnaissance party met with no resistance it was to continue to advance, with the brigade following in its wake. However, should it come up against large and stubborn enemy resistance, the general himself would decide whether or not to launch a night offensive.

General Tal was here faced with one of his most difficult moments of the war. On the one hand he wanted to get to the canal quickly, on the other he feared a trap of numerically superior Egyptian forces; hence his decision to send 'S' Brigade's reconnaissance company ahead, as a trial balloon. He knew that it was a cruel decision to take, to assign to the much pummelled and pounded reconnaissance company so grave and dangerous a task at the final stage of the war. If in fact the Egyptians had prepared a trap, the reconnaissance company could be completely wiped out.

Colonel Shmuel understood General Tal's dilemma and fully grasped its implications. He, too, realised that there was a possibility of the reconnaissance company being wiped out. He decided to augment the team: six of Ein-Gil's Pattons and a battery of self-propelled artillery were added to the reconnaissance company. Because there was nothing further he could do to aid the company, he decided to throw in his lot with it and accompany his men on their hazardous mission. He was already seated in his command half-track and about to order the column to move, when General Tal got wind of it and forbade Colonel Shmuel to join them.

"Shamir. This is Tirah. You will not join the reconnaissance company. Over," the general said over the division's wavelength.

Colonel Shmuel acknowledged the order, but with obvious reluctance, and the general understood Colonel Shmuel's predicament. His men would not understand why he had changed his mind. General Tal got on to the brigade's radio network and repeated his order to the colonel, so that every officer in the brigade was now aware that his change in plan had been upon his express orders. Soon the company, under the command of Captain Ori, was ready to set out. They would be the first men to reach the canal.

"Sir," said Lieutenant Yossi B., "I'd like to join them."

"O.K. Yossi," the colonel agreed, "take my jeep and get moving."

The battle group set off on its mission. Each time Captain Ori, who was leading the column, saw a suspicious shadow, he flashed a small torch to the rear and a tank with a projector lit up the suspect area. The commander of Kahalany's company, Lieutenant Ilan, would then move over to the flank and direct the tank's gun.

"Fire! Out!" Lieutenant Yossi B. called over the radio.

Thus they continued to advance, a flash of the torch, then the beam of light from the projector. The Egyptian tanks retreated rapidly, and the jeep carrying Captain Ori and Lieutenant Yossi, followed by the six Pattons of Lieutenant Ein-Gil's company, chased after them, with now and then the projector lighting up an area and a Patton setting fire to an Egyptian tank.

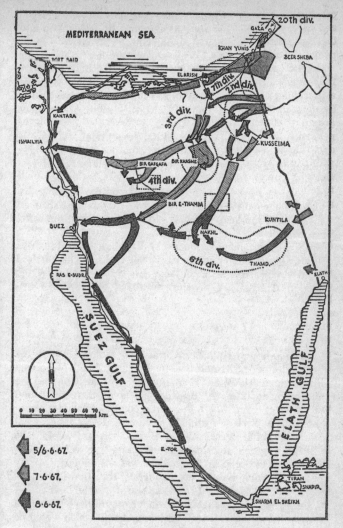

11 *Zahal's advances across Sinai (7–9 June).*

At midnight they reached their objective. Captain Ori saw an Egyptian sentry signalling to him with a flashlight to hurry up and get across the canal before the bridge was removed.

235

Beside him was an Egyptian tank. In a flash Ein-Gil grasped the situation. Swinging his Patton round he brought it into a firing position against the Egyptian tank.

"Fire!" he commanded, and became the last to fire at an Egyptian tank on the east bank of the Suez Canal. The time was 0030 hours, Friday 9 June 1967. A few hours later the Kantara and Ismailia forces linked up at the Firdan Bridge, and Division Tal was united along the length of the Suez Canal.

Only then did the division stop for breath and rest a while after having fought its way through the desert for one long continuous day during which the sun had risen and set several times. And here for the first time the tank crews bathed their feet, swollen now in their Type 2 Armoured Corps boots, which till then they had not removed. They bathed them in the waters of the Suez Canal. Yossi B. jumped into the canal in his overalls.

In Sinai, nine hundred and fifty Egyptian tanks fought a considerably smaller number of Israeli tanks. Eight hundred and fifty tanks, hit or abandoned, were left behind by the Egyptian Army. Tal's division destroyed ten Egyptian brigades.

CHAPTER TWENTY-SIX

It was 0200 hours, Thursday 8 June 1967. Colonel Albert, the commander of 'A' Armoured Brigade and Lieutenant-Colonel Biro, commander of A/112 Sherman Tank Battalion and the unit commanders of 'A' Brigade met at northern command headquarters, from where they proceeded to Givat Ha'em to observe the Syrian fortified positions at Na'amush and Zaoura. If Zahal attacked Syria, Biro's Shermans would have to break through formidable fortifications in very difficult terrain, and the brigade commander was searching for a way to avoid tackling Kala'a, the strongest fortication in his sector. He wanted to get to it from the rear, from the direction of Zaoura, which meant that the battalion would have to make a left turn before Sir Adib village, along a trail which would be difficult to find during the battle.

When Colonel Albert and Biro were at Givat Ha'em looking out over the Syrian terrain, Zahal's divisions in Sinai had already reached the Suez Canal and the Egyptian delegate to the United Nations, bursting into tears, had announced his government's readiness to accept a cease-fire agreement. The

Gaza Strip, too, had been taken. The eastern sector of Jerusalem, the Judaean and Samarian hills and the Jordan valley, had been captured from the Jordanian Legion which had fled across the Jordan River, and the government of Jordan was also ready to accept a cease-fire agreement. If the fighting stopped now Syria would emerge from the war as the only participant Arab country to retain its territory intact and its army untouched, and would be able to continue shelling the settlements of the Galilee, as she had done only the previous Monday, and carry out its project of diverting the sources of the Jordan River.

The hills of Judaea and Samaria and the Jordan valley had fallen in less than two and a half days in a war which had started on Monday afternoon and had ended before midnight on the Wednesday. Paratroop and armoured brigades had fought that war: the Harel Brigade under Colonel Uri Ben-Ari had decided the battle for Jerusalem when in less than twelve hours it had taken up positions on the Jerusalem–Ramallah road, at Tel el-Pul, and from there raced to Jericho; Colonel Moishe's armoured brigade had captured Jenin, fighting one of the fiercest battles of the Six Days War against the Jordanian battalions of Patton tanks; Colonel Uri's armoured brigade had taken the town of Nablus. The capture of the hills of Judaea and Samaria and the Jordan valley were not part of the war for survival, as was the case with Egypt. In a way the battle for the Old City of Jerusalem and the Mount was a continuation of the War of Independence nineteen years ago. The retaking of the Land of the Bible for the first time in two thousand years became overnight the battle cry in a historic campaign to regain the Land of the Fathers. The Western (Wailing) Wall and the Temple Mount had been returned to Israel by what seemed almost the hand of the Messiah.

Jerusalem and the Western Wall intoxicated the Jews of Israel, compressing in a moment a historical span of thousands of years of dispersion and exile of a people with no consistent national existence into one continuous national life. It was as though two thousand years had become one short, fleeting moment in the life of the Jewish people, when the Western Wall, the Temple Mount and the Old City of Jerusalem were returned to them.

But in the north, at the foot of the Golan Heights, joy was mingled with misgivings. The Syrian Army remained undefeated by Zahal, a fact the Syrians constantly made claim to and which served to enhance their confidence in the chances of an Arab victory. If in this third military encounter to break out since Israel's establishment, the Syrians were not soundly thrashed, the border settlements in the foothills of the Golan mountains could expect a future filled with hardships and suffering. In the national exhilaration over the Western Wall and the Temple Mount, in the rejoicing at the historical significance of the war, the problems of actual physical existence in the north of Israel still stood out in all their chilling starkness. The delay in the campaign against Syria was due to considerations of foreign policy, and in particular to relations between Israel and the Soviet Union, who had recently become the protector and supporter of the Syrian government. The Soviet Union had threatened to sever diplomatic relations with Israel.

"Wait patiently," Lieutenant-Colonel Biro told his men at battalion headquarters, to where he had returned from Givat Ha'em. "If we go for Syria, you'll know soon enough, don't worry." The men of his battalion counted the minutes to what seemed the war's end. They had been the last to be mobilised, and now they were worried that the part they would be asked to play in the Six Days War would be insignificant.

Biro was born on 4 December 1927 in the town of Arad in Rumania, in the southern part of Transylvania. After the outbreak of the second world war, Transylvania was annexed by Hungary, and Biro's family was rounded up and sent to Auschwitz.

One day Biro came back from work to the living quarters in a hut in the camp. It was snowing, the inmates of the camp were hungry and impatiently waiting for their evening meal. The hut commander was a German, a Communist. He distributed the food – a thick muddy soup which he ladled into the prisoners' tin plates. Food was distributed by numbers, every day starting with a different one, as the last ones in the queue were served the sediment, which was richer than the soup on top.

Biro, near the front of the queue, waited for the hut commander to call his number, but when his turn came the commander grasped his arm and pushed him away. "You, stand aside!" he told Biro.

The boy was terrified. He saw the cauldron emptying and felt the pangs of hunger. But his fear was stronger, and he did not even bother to think about the cause of his being deprived

238

of his meal. Far more important was what was going to happen to him; was it true, as the gypsies in the camp were always saying, that in Auschwitz there was a section for mass slaughter by gas and other means?

When Biro had arrived at Auschwitz he weighed sixty kilos. Now he was nearer forty. He had noticed that the thin ones were sent elsewhere. He was trembling.

"You!" the hut commander called, "come here!"

Biro approached with shaking knees. The queue was coming to its end. The cauldron was almost empty. Then Biro felt his tin plate being taken away. He saw the hut commander scraping the bottom of the cauldron with his ladle, in the sediment. He poured a ladle-full on to the plate and then a second one. On Biro's plate was the richest meal he had seen for a long time.

"You probably don't remember, boy. But today's the 4th of December. You're seventeen today. I hope next year you'll be free at home with your family. Next," the hut commander said.

Biro remembered his seventeenth birthday very well. He had not forgotten that German hut commander; nor did he forget the blacksmith from Cologne.

He was working at the I.G. Farben Works at Monowicz, near the camp. It was a large chemical plant which extracted subsidiary products from coal. One hundred thousand men worked there, the majority from Auschwitz. Biro, who had learned the locksmith's trade in Hungary, was made apprentice to a German blacksmith from Cologne whose job it was to instal and repair tools the workers needed. Biro was told to call him "Herr Meister". Like all the German personnel there, the blacksmith ate at eight o'clock in the morning and at one o'clock midday. The workers who came from the camp were given no food, and the German personnel was strictly forbidden to give them any of theirs.

Biro would sit on a stool and watch the blacksmith at his workbench eating out of his box. The Meister would open the drawer of his workbench a little, curse the baker for burning the bread, and with his penknife slice off chunks of bread which would fall into the open drawer. Then he would peel his apple, dropping the thick spiral into the drawer. Sometimes he would even drop pieces of meat into the drawer, as if by accident. When he had finished his meal, he would push the drawer shut with his foot, stretch himself and say: "Alex, I'm going for a walk. Tidy up here. And clean out the drawers."

But these were exceptions. Every evening when he returned to the camp from work, Biro would be terrified that he had lost weight. The prisoners had to shower every evening, and when they walked into the showers, stark naked, the Germans would separate those sentenced to die at Birkenau and those sentenced to live tomorrow in the camp.

Biro was terribly afraid, but never became faint-hearted or apathetic. Some prisoners preferred death. But Biro wanted to live, and his fear of death gave him the energy to work to the last ounce of his strength. If he stopped working he would be burnt, he never stopped repeating to himself.

At 0530 there was a morning parade, and from there the prisoners were marched in threes to work. Some instinctive, extraordinary power would force him off the planks he slept on, help him pull himself together, dress himself in his rags and report for parade. A band played as they marched to work. Sometimes Biro still hears it.

One morning he got up after several attempts to climb off his bunk and stand on his feet. He reached the "Appellplatz" with his last remaining strength. The section commander was a German criminal who wore a green triangle on his uniform. He was huge and very powerful. Biro's tottering gait was not to his liking. He slapped him across the face. Biro woke up in hospital.

Auschwitz created an atmosphere of delusions: Let's get through today, tomorrow may be better. Biro hoped the day would come when he would get out of Auschwitz. But every day he saw prisoners suddenly throw themselves on the electrified fence and die.

Occasionally the optimistic prisoners would exchange ideas about what they would eat once they were free. Such discussions were a source of hope, of entertainment, of argument. Biro was always consistent. "When I get out I want a big loaf of black bread and to eat as much of it as I like. But I shall also have a rifle with a bayonet, so people will be afraid of me." Lieutenant-Colonel Biro told his subordinates that what he said then has pursued him ever since. "Bread and a gun equals survival."

He was taken ill with pneumonia, with brought on pleurisy. He weighed less than thirty-five kilos when the Red Army liberated them.

On the morning of Friday 9 June, everybody listened in to the news over the transistor radios. The armoured infantry battalion's second-in-command, Major Moshe Haviv, was also listening. Immediately after the news he sat down to write a postcard home.

"Dear Gila,

"I was so pleased to speak to you yesterday. This morning the radio announced the possibility of a cease-fire, which has upset our plans. It will be a shame if the Syrians get off scot-free.

Lots of kisses to everyone.

Yours,

Mosh."

He had just dropped the postcard into the letter-box of the settlement near where the battalion was stationed, when the order was received: "Get ready to move!" The order flashed through the brigade like an electric spark. There was a feeling of satisfaction, perhaps even of joy.

Major Moshe Haviv knocked on the door of Abraham Banion's house. Banion was a member of the settlement at whose house the battalion headquarters had held several meetings. "Madam," Major Haviv said to the landlady, when she opened the door, "could we use your house for just one last short meeting before we leave?"

This was the armoured infantry battalion's last orders group. When it ended, Major Haviv climbed into his command half-track and ordered the driver to advance towards the Golan Heights. There were five men in the half-track, which now moved forward at the head of the column towards Kfar Szold and Givat Ha'em. From their elevated positions the Syrians could see the brigade's movements, and immediately they opened up with an artillery bombardment on the advance axes, with their long-barrelled 135mm Czech guns and 120mm heavy mortars.

It was strange for the men in Haviv's half-track to be going to war, after having already accepted the fact that it was all over. The previous evening the five of them had held a banquet; the driver planned to open a restaurant, and as an introduction had wanted to show off his culinary abilities. He had cooked, roasted, fried, and the verdict had been that it was a dinner which would be remembered for many years.

Now he said to his friends in the half-track. "Well, we'll do our best, and what will be, will be." The time was 1000 hours.

Dr. Gluck was looking for the brigade medical company, but it was difficult to locate it in the middle of an advancing armoured brigade, along narrow and bombarded axes. The officers of the brigade whom he asked for the whereabouts of the medical company did not even hear his question; they were busy hugging each other and shouting: "We're off to the Golan Heights!" He came across a medical company belonging to an infantry brigade, in Kibbutz Hagoshrim. The company commander begged Dr. Gluck and his medical orderly, Ronnie, to stay with him. He pointed to the green lawns of the kibbutz, to the swimming pool. "What's wrong with this, Gluck?"

The idea appealed to Dr. Gluck, and for a moment he almost decided to accept the invitation and join the infantry brigade. In the commotion going on along the roads it was doubtful whether he would ever find his own company; all around was the noise of tanks and half-tracks and the smoke of exploding shells and mortars. But something nudged Dr. Gluck, telling him that he must take his place with his own brigade. The medical officer lent him a jeep and he drove off in search of his company. Ahead of him stretched a long line of Sherman tanks.

In the lead tank, standing up in the cupola, rotund and moustached, was Lieutenant-Colonel Biro. Next to him drove Major Mokady in his half-track. Mokady immediately recognised the doctor (who had joined his company early in the campaign on a daring recce patrol), but he had no time to reply to the doctor's questions and certainly not to direct him to the brigade medical company, whose whereabouts he did not know.

"What's going on there?" growled Lieutenant-Colonel Biro in his deep voice, annoyed at the delay.

"It's the doctor and the medical orderly looking for the medical company," Major Mokady replied.

"Doctor? Orderly?" Biro boomed with satisfaction. "Tell them to join us. The battalion will need them."

Dr. Gluck and Ronnie climbed on to one of the battalion aid post's two half-tracks.

"Move, now, follow me, out!" called Biro to his tanks.

Dr. Leron, the battalion medical officer, was surprised to see Gluck climb into his half-track. "What are you doing here, Gluck?"

"Come to join you, Leron."

"Who's pregnant?"

The news had got around that Gluck was a gynaecologist in civilian life. Gluck grimaced.

"Right. Well, welcome aboard," said Dr. Leron, "but we'd better separate. You go in the evacuation half-track."

The bombardment was now deafening. "Ronnie, I'd give a ton of gold at this moment for a steel helmet," said Gluck. In their hurry they had left their equipment with the infantry brigade medical company. Someone in the battalion gave them tank helmets, and these helped to lessen the noise of the bombardment, but they were no protection against splinters. It was impossible for the men in the evacuation half-track to hear each other talking. Danny, the medical orderly attached to the evacuation party, passed a rolled-up note to Dr. Gluck. It was "A Prayer on Going into Battle", distributed by the Army Rabbinate. This was Friday, and later on the armoured companies would go into battle on the Sabbath. On top of Givat Ha'em, one of the men of the Army Rabbinate offered sweet wine in a beaker to those going to war, for the Kiddush (the sanctification of the Sabbath Day).

"Doctor! Doctor!" an excited soldier shouted, running up to the evacuation half-track, "Casualties!"

The column's advance slowed down for a while. Dr. Gluck wanted to get up but his legs would not obey him. He ordered himself to get up, but his legs were like lead. The heavy mortar bombardment was all around them, and the one thing he was terrified of was mortars. The shriek of the shells paralysed him.

Logic persuaded him to stay put. Where could he possibly attend to the wounded? Here, on this bombarded, screaming hill? And all around him there were the jams characteristic of a first move into battle, so that even if he did manage to treat the wounded, where could he possibly evacuate them to? Forward was out of the question, and the rear was no better.

All this took a split second; deep inside him the voice which said "Get up" gained control. Gluck sprang up from his seat and ran with the soldier who had come to call him. A shell had hit the aid-post half-track, which Gluck had so recently vacated, and Dr. Leron, the medical orderly, the radio-operator and the driver had all been injured. Gluck looked around him and spotted a United Nations Truce Observation position, with its sand-bags walling the trench near it.

"Over there!" he yelled.

They carried the wounded to the sandbagged position.

"Doctor! Wounded!" another shout was heard.

Two half-tracks had been hit one after the other by mortars which had fallen straight on them. One was the armoured

243

infantry battalion's second-in-command's Major Moshe Haviv. A 120mm mortar shell had exploded inside the half-track and blown up its five occupants. The half-track was burning furiously and its ammunition had begun to explode. There was nothing Dr. Gluck could do for the occupants of these two half-tracks, for they had received direct hits. He was the only doctor in the area, and he began to attend to the wounded which were brought to him in the sand-bagged position. One of the first was Dr. Leron, who was injured in his leg. "May I have some morphine, doctor," Dr. Leron asked, and then added, as though jokingly, "And you had better take over command."

The knowledge that he was the only medical officer in the area imbued Dr. Gluck with a feeling of responsibility which drove out of his mind all thought of fear. He busied himself with the wounded which began to arrive in numbers, paying no attention to the shelling.

"Why the hell have you set up shop here?" an angry voice demanded. It was the brigade commander, Colonel Albert.

"There's no other place, Sir," replied Dr. Gluck.

Colonel Albert looked around for somewhere to station his forward command group, but Givat Ha'em was being too heavily shelled. The best was to advance. "Forward", he ordered the driver of his command half-track. The half-track returned to the advance axis, bypassing the armoured vehicles moving along it and just missing the minefields laid along both sides. Dr. Gluck watched as the brigade commander drove off and vanished into the battle. Then he went back to attend to the wounded.

The tank battalion commanded by Biro had already crossed the Syrian frontier.

'A' Brigade's assignment was to break through to Givat Ha'em, to capture the Zaoura defence positions, link up at the Mass'ada road and be ready to advance towards Kuneitra. As it was to be a daylight action, the lead force would be tanks, Biro's A/112 Battalion. Biro's assignment was to capture the Na'amush defence position and the area above the Zaoura defence position. Tank Force 'B', not under his command, was given the task of capturing the upper Zaoura defences; the armoured infantry battalion was to capture the lower Zaoura positions.

Anyone standing in the Jordan valley and looking up at the Golan Heights, is obliged to bend back his head and stretch his neck. In many places they stand up like a wall. The Heights have few openings, and even those it has, mostly ravines, do not permit easy ascent. These facts force motorised columns on the Golan Heights to keep to the few asphalt roads and tracks, and of course on these the Syrians had constructed their main defence positions. In fact the Golan Heights are anyway a natural fortress, and the Syrians had made them truly formidable. The rocky terrain was completely covered with gun positions, bunkers, minefields, dragon teeth, anti-tank ditches and army camps, most of which were housed in buildings whose basements were used as firing positions. There were also the large artillery concentrations and tanks. There was just one section which was not almost completely impassable and this was the area between Kfar Szold and the Syrian defence position at Tel Azzaziat. Here the mountain wall was not so steep and the basalt rocks less dense; the general officer northern command, General David Elazar, had selected this area for the break-through which would lead them on to the Syrian Patrol Road linking the Syrian positions, and along it to Zaoura.

The Syrian Patrol Road linked the positions at Tel Azzaziat, Gur el-Askar, Na'amush, Ukda, Sir Adib and Kala'a, in a line which hugged the escarpment and, therefore, rose gradually to Kala'a. At Kala'a, which straddled the road to Kuneitra, the Syrians had built one of their strongest fortifications. The plan was to avoid a frontal engagement with Sir Adib and Kala'a. Hence it was decided that the tank force would travel 1800 metres along the Patrol Road, leave the road after the Ukda positions, send off a strong blocking force towards Ukda-Sir Adib, get on to the oil pipeline track (midway between Sir Adib and Zaoura) and capture Zaoura. With the occupation of Zaoura the attacking force would find itself at the back of Kala'a, which would make the advance to Kuneitra much easier.

To get on to the oil pipeline track, the tank force had to follow the track which links it up with the Patrol Road before it reaches Ukda. As the track passed through a field which had been sown and harvested, thus making it extremely difficult to find, Danny, a native of the Galilee, had been assigned to Major Mokady's reconnaissance company as the guide. Danny's job was to locate the track in good time, so that Biro's tank could swing off to the left before reaching Sir Adib and exposing themselves to the Syrian guns of Kala'a. This was a very difficult job.

The Syrian artillery bombardment had already started when the brigade advanced in the direction of Givat Ha'em. The first to cross were the scouts, in a jeep and a half-track, commanded by Major Mokady. When they had discussed the plan of attack, Colonel Albert, the brigade commander, had thought it best to select a small scouting party, eight at the most, which, if necessary, would guide the entire brigade to the Patrol Road. Colonel Albert had even considered the possibility of the scouts proceeding on foot, poking about in the rocky terrain to find the track for the advance axis. He did not want the reconnaissance company to lead the brigade, reckoning that in all probability they would be completely wiped out. He had also decided that the scouting party would be a volunteer force.

Following the scouting party's jeep and half-track came Lieutenant-Colonel Biro's battalion, led by Nati's company. Nati rode in the first tank, Biro occupied the fifth tank in the column.

The tanks passed through the pathway made in the minefields by the engineering units, got on to the Patrol Road and advanced along it southwards. Apparently the air raids on the enemy defence positions, provided by northern command on Colonel Albert's request, had weakened the Syrians' fighting spirit; the first position, Gur el-Askar, put up no opposition. Nati's tanks fired at it and continued to advance, with the scouting party returning to lead the way. At Na'amush, the second defence position, Nati dispersed one tank platoon, which covered the company's advance and with the rest of his company took it in a quick sweep. Major Mokady's reconnaissance company now moved to behind the first five tanks, next to Biro's tank.

At Na'amush Nati's company should have changed over with Ilan's which was supposed to take the lead for the next bound. But Ilan's company was finding the way difficult along the basalt rock and had been delayed. It was about a kilometre behind Nati's company, while Nati was advancing in full swing and had already passed Na'amush. The first two enemy positions had not put up strong resistance, their main fire having been machine guns and grenades. Only at Na'amush had they encountered an anti-tank gun, and that had been destroyed at a range of 400 metres before it had had time to fire a round. Nati's company had so far suffered no casualties.

"No problems. It's like an exercise. Request permission to

proceed. Over," Nati radioed.

"Nati. This is Biro. Proceed. Roger. Over," Biro replied.

The first tanks, however, had no sooner passed Na'amush when they were exposed to the position at Ukda, which began to fire at them. In some respects the route here was like a surprise-packet, of the type when one opens the packet only to find another inside, which is unwrapped to reveal yet another. But here the order was reversed. The first packet was the smallest, the last the biggest. No sooner had the force passed Gur el-Askar, when it came up against Na'amush. After Na'amush was Ukda, even larger. Nati decided that he would have to take Ukda in column formation, as the terrain ruled out dispersing and no manoeuvering could be done.

After Na'amush the tank battalion was supposed to turn left, on to the track which would connect them with the oil pipeline road and to Zaoura. As the enemy fire poured down on them from Ukda, a heated dispute was developing in the scouts' jeep. Major Mokady, who had studied his map in every detail and measured each millimetre, held that the narrow pathway they had just spotted was actually the track they should take, but Danny, the Galilee-born scout, relying more on his instincts and his knowledge of the country, argued that they had not yet reached the turning point and should continue along the Patrol Road.

"Biro. This is Nati. Where do we turn left? Over," Nati asked Lieutenant-Colonel Biro as he busied himself directing the fire against the Ukda position. The tanks were advancing, and it was not possible to stop them, as they would become sitting targets, and Biro was pushing and goading his men all the time to advance quickly and vigorously, so as not to break the momentum of the attack.

"Nati. This is Biro. I'll check at once. Over," Biro replied.

Nati heard Biro radio to the scout party in the jeep to ask them where the turning point was.

"Biro. This is Mokady. The left turn is here. The trail is on our left. Over," said Major Mokady.

"Biro. This is Danny. The left turn is not here. The trail is further up. We must continue along this road. Over," said Danny.

The discussion was being held under intense and close-range fire, and before Biro had time to reply, Nati had been drawn, as if by some powerful magnet, towards the fire which was pouring down on his company. For some reason Nati relied more on Danny, though perhaps there was no option but to

247

deal first with Ukda, a company defence position on the first level of the Golan wall, rising some five hundred metres above Kfar Szold.

The Patrol Road bypasses Ukda to the left. Biro now ordered Nati to traverse his guns to the right and to open fire as they sped past the position. He wanted speed and penetration in depth and he did not even bother to enter the position to mop it up, but moved on. Only later did the brigade engineers' unit go in to mop it up.

As the tanks passed Ukda, a new position was revealed to them, containing tanks and anti-tank guns, and buildings whose ground floors were fortified firing positions. On the map a good road is marked which leads to Zaoura, and as they left Ukda behind, Biro spotted what looked like a good road. This decided him that the new position which had come into view was Zaoura, the position he had to capture to command the area above it.

"Nati. This is Biro. Knock the tanks out first. Over," he ordered Nati, and immediately asked the artillery liaison officer to lay down a barrage on Zaoura.

"On where?" the artillery officer radioed back.

"Artillery bombardment on Zaoura," said Biro.

"But we've been shelling Zaoura all the time," the artillery officer replied.

"Where are you laying it? I don't see any bombardment!"

Biro raised his field glasses to his eyes. The defence position which he now saw enlarged through his glasses showed no signs of being under artillery attack.

"Give me the map reference," said the artillery officer.

It soon became clear that Biro had mistaken Sir Adib for Zaoura. Wishing to correct his error at once and return to find the left-hand turn to Zaoura, he radioed Eppi ordering him to take his company and look for the trail which would lead them there. But Eppi did not receive the message. He was racing forward following the battalion commander, and hence the entire battalion was pulled forward after Nati who was now storming Sir Adib.

And this was how the battalion reached the positions it had wanted so much to avoid. However, when Sir Adib came into view there was no option – or so its commanders thought – but to take it. Resistance, as expected, was much stronger than at the previous defence positions. The surprise-packet was getting bigger and bigger. Anti-tank guns roared, scoring several direct hits on Biro's Shermans. Nevertheless Nati, at

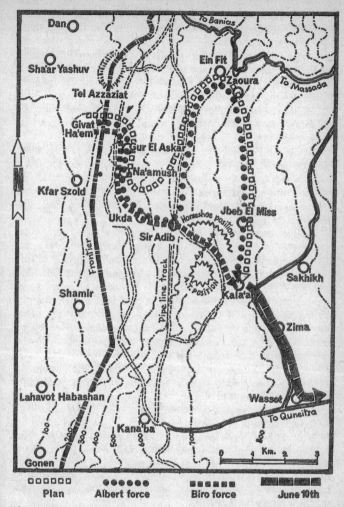

□□□□□□	●●●●●●	■■■■■	▬▬▬▬
Plan	Albert force	Biro force	June 10th

12 'A' Brigade's break-through at the Golan Heights (9 June).

the head of his company, succeeded in reaching the defences.
They were obliged to advance straight along the road as Biro's
explicit orders had been not to deviate from the advance axis,
because the area was rock-strewn and mined. Nati and his

company engaged the anti-tank guns and destroyed them, and soon the vanguard of the company, with Nati in the lead tank, had already passed Sir Adib. A platoon commander was hit by mortar splinters and seriously wounded, then Biro's tank touched an electric pole, and a mortar shell sliced off its aerial. The battalion commander was slightly wounded by splinters which caught him in the face. Over the tank's intercom Biro enquired whether anyone had been hurt. They said, no, but the gunner saw Biro's injured face and asked if it was not best he be evacuated.

"Stalin and Hitler couldn't do me in. You think these Syrians can?" was his answer. At that moment he spotted a tomato plant, heavy with ripe tomatoes. "One minute," he called to the crew. He vaulted from the tank, picked a handful of the tomatoes and clambered back into the tank, distributing them among the crew.

Back at the battalion radio he urged the other companies to get to Sir Adib and join the battle. He himself had spent all his personal ammunition; he had tossed his grenades into the communication trenches, and when none were left, carried on with smoke grenades. One such smoke grenade he threw into a bunker and a platoon of frightened Syrian soldiers rushed out. Of the ten magazines he was carrying, seven were already empty. The scouts' jeep, travelling close by his tank, passed by a ravine, only twenty metres away, which was covered with camouflage netting. Major Mokady suspected it and ordered Israel to toss a grenade on to the netting. Israel threw the grenade straight in, and there was an enormous explosion, bringing a hail of dust and pebbles on to the occupants of the jeep. The net-covered ravine had concealed a high explosives dump.

Half of Nati's company had already passed Sir Adib. Nati still believed that he would now come upon the track to Zaoura, but instead he saw in front of him another Syrian stronghold, formidable and menacing. From the position jutted two extensions which hugged the road from both sides. Lieutenant-Colonel Biro, who was still at Sir Adib, asked him over the radio if he knew where he was.

"Not opposite Zaoura, Sir," Nati replied. "I think it must be Kala'a. It's a strong, high fortification, and two wings stretch out on either. . . ."

Biro relied on his good gunner. He had just spotted two anti-aircraft guns aiming directly at him. "Gunner, H.E. (High Explosive Shell). Anti-aircraft on the left. Fire!" The gunner promptly hit one of the guns, sending it flying; the crew of the other fled.

Biro left Sir Adib behind and began the advance towards Kala'a. Soon the fortress was looming up in front of him. He ordered Nati's company to disperse, then studied carefully the ridge to the left of the road on which were Syrian tank positions. It was essential to take that ridge before anything else, whether they attacked or withdrew. He was about to give the order when a burst of machine gun fire streaked across his face from left to right. A stream of blood spurted from his cheek and throat as from a burst pipe, and his jaw swung hideously on a lump of flesh.

Biro re-entered the turret, and with his hand signalled to the gunner to tie up his jaw with his first-aid bandage. He laid a heavy hand on the shoulder of the signals officer, Yuval Ben-Artzi, who was with him in the tank, to tell him not to report that he was injured, and then signalled that he wished to write. The gunner gave him a water-flask, and Biro rinsed his mouth with water, which was like fire in his mouth. Red water poured from his perforated throat and wet his shirt. Yuval gave him a notebook and pen and Biro began issuing his orders in writing. He passed his notes on to Yuval who radioed them to the battalion in the name of the commander. The first order was to Ilan's company, to capture the ridge on the left. He next requested an intensification of the artillery barrage on Kala'a and was told, via Yuval, that the artillery was now firing its last salvoes. Biro asked the brigade commander for air support, and this was promised him.

Biro realised that there was no other way but to attack Kala'a. Most of the battalion had already passed Sir Adib, and to withdraw, he thought, would not be possible without heavy losses. But he could not go on. His body was being drained of blood, and helplessly he sank to the floor of the tank. The signals officer, Yuval Ben-Artzi, ordered the driver to return at once to Sir Adib,, and from there the driver radioed to the reconnaissance jeep carrying Major Mokady and Israel.

The gunner and Yuval helped Biro out on to the deck. He was very heavy, as he was incapable of supporting himself, but when he saw his men his pride overcame his weakness and by himself he jumped from the deck of the tank to the ground, then climbed into the jeep and sat in the seat next to the driver, straight as a rod.

At the orders group he had joked with Major Mokady: "If

I get a packet, you take over command." But now he wrote him a note. "Tell Nati to take command and to continue the assault on Kala'a. Out."

Biro knew the battalion was in a difficult situation, and that only a fighting commander would be able to extricate it. He was relying on Nati, whom he had nurtured for three years, but when Major Mokady radioed Nati to take command, he received no answer. A Syrian tank had hit Nati's tank with an armour-piercing shell and blown off the commander's hatch. The communications system had been damaged and Nati had dived down into the tank to attend to it. Major Mokady immediately took over command of the battalion. "Turn left," he ordered the tank driver.

Danny, the scout, accompanied Biro in the jeep to guide it to the battalion's aid post. Throughout the journey the lieutenant-colonel sat up straight in the jeep, which bounced and jerked on the basalt rocks. At the aid post, still located near the United Nations Truce Observation position on Givat Ha'em, Dr. Gluck had his hands full. Biro was still hoping that he would be able to return to his battalion, but when Dr. Gluck untied the bandage and saw the injuries, he ruled out such a possibility. Biro was bleeding profusely, and his breathing was becoming more laboured by the minute. Two bullets had penetrated his left cheek, smashed his jaw in four places, torn out five teeth and come out through his throat below the windpipe. Gluck swabbed the blood from his mouth with cotton-wool and rebandaged the jaw to keep it in place. He bandaged it tightly, with Biro indicating to him with his eyes when it was tight enough.

"Sir, will you please lie down on a stretcher," Dr. Gluck requested.

Lieutenant-Colonel Biro shook his head. He would drive to hospital in the jeep.

"Sir, do you feel fit enough to sit in a jeep and ride over such rocky terrain?"

Biro nodded his head.

Gluck helped him back into the jeep and fixed the safety belt. "Good luck, Sir."

Biro raised his arm and the jeep began its journey down the sloping, churned-up hill of Givat Ha'em.

"A lion," Dr. Gluck said to himself.

CHAPTER TWENTY-SEVEN

Major Mokady wanted to adhere to the original plan and cancel the attack on Kala'a. He was afraid that the entire battalion would be slaughtered.

It was past 1300 hours. The battalion had now been in the thick of the battle for three hours, along steep basalt terrain which was a mass of flames. Artillery shells, air bombardments, tank guns and the bursts of machine gun fire had set alight the stubble and the weeds and, of course, the ammunition and fuel dumps. Blood red smoke whirled over the battle field, adding to the terror of the place.

"Pull left," Major Mokady called over the radio to the company commanders. "Pull left. Pull left. Pull left."

He guided his tank towards a track he had spotted and which he believed would lead to the oil pipeline track and on to Zaoura. He wanted to direct the battalion to it. But soon he came up against two more Syrian defence positions, one parallel to his line of advance and the other, at a range of 400 metres, opposite him. The first position opened up with anti-tank fire, and an armour-piercing shell struck the differential. The blazing shell whipped through the carter, the oil burst into flames, and the motor went dead. In a moment the tank was filled with white, choking smoke.

"Fire!" Major Mokady ordered the gunner. The gun was aimed at the position opposite. The gun fired one shell and stopped; the loader did not know how to release the locking device and put it back into operation, for the signals officer, Yuval Ben-Artzi, had taken the place of the loader, and his knowledge of the gun was elementary.

Major Mokady made up his mind to fight the enemy position in front with his 0.5 Browning. But to operate the Sherman's machine gun at short ranges with maximum efficiency, one must expose oneself outside the turret. Major Mokady pulled himself out of the tank and began firing, knowing full well that he was taking a grave risk, that there was practically no hope of his not being hit.

"Nati. This is Mokady. Take command. Over," Major Mokady said over the radio. He had been wounded almost immediately. A bullet had hit him in the chest, and he could feel his strength deserting him. "Nati. This is Mokady. Take command. Over," he called and called.

But from Nati came no reply. Major Mokady, who had

been almost completely outside the turret, fell from the tank, and Yuval Ben-Artzi rose to take over the machine gun. He fired at the enemy position until he too was hit. He fell back into the tank and there he died.

The battalion commander was wounded and evacuated, the acting commander, Major Mokady, wounded and dying. Who would take over command? There was no reply from Nati.

"Nati. This is Mokady. Take command. Over. . . ." Major Mokady said with his dying breath.

The oil in the carter had cooled and the driver managed to restart the tank's engine. He drove the tank about a hundred and fifty metres down an incline, but then it stopped again in a cleft. There the driver and gunner deserted the tank. Major Mokady did not move. He was dead.

At last Nati managed to repair the communications system in his tank. He heard: "Nati. Take command. Over." He did not know from whom the order had come but he immediately understood that something had happened to Biro, and the blood rushed to his head. Actually it had been Major Amnon at brigade headquarters, who had received all the radioed commands, including Mokady's final call, and had kept calling to Nati to take over command. Nati had a desperate battle in store.

The first thing he did was to line up his radio. He connected all the battalion's companies to his own network and then connected himself to the brigade network. He next informed Colonel Albert that he had taken over command of A/112. Colonel Albert was on his way to Sir Adib, and had actually met Lieutenant-Colonel Biro on the way down to the aid post. At Sir Adib, Colonel Albert realised that it would not be possible to break off contact with the enemy without incurring heavy losses, that they would have to push ahead and carry out the original plan with part of the force, while A/112 continued to fight for Kala'a. He ordered Nati to pursue the assault while he, in the command half-track, at the head of the second tank force and the armoured infantry battalion, turned left at the spot Major Mokady had earlier found in his search for the way to Zaoura. Kala'a was now the objective. 'A' Brigade advanced upon it in two heads, the one commanded by Nati engaging it directly, the other under the command of the brigade commander, Colonel Albert, which would attack Kala'a from the rear as soon as it had completed its main assignment – the capture of the Zaoura fortifications.

Only twenty minutes had passed since Lieutenant-Colonel

Biro had been wounded.

Zaoura and Kala'a, which were the major dispositions on the mountain plateau in 'A' Brigade's sector, were a combination of village and fortress. The village of Kala'a stands on a high plateau on the Golan Heights, and whoever holds the plateau can reach Damascus easily. The road leading from Sir Adib to Kala'a first descends steeply, forming what is known as a sihpon, then climbs abruptly, turning right at the summit, from where the gradient is easier, then turning left then right again until it enters the village.

At the bottom of the siphon the Syrians had built a row of concrete dragon teeth, forming an anti-tank barrier. The only way through was the road and the tanks could negotiate the dragon teeth only by manoeuvering backwards and forwards. But this did not end the difficulties of the attacking force. From the north side, on the left of the Kala'a road, rose horseshoe shaped crests upon which the Syrians had built defence positions armed with anti-tank guns and tanks. Near Kala'a the anti-tank guns were particularly numerous. Besides these there was a Syrian tank force on the mountain side at Jebeb el-Mis, part of which had already set out to reinforce the horse-shoe defence position, and from the south, on the right of the road, which is separated from Sir Adib by a chasm, rose a crest as flat as a table on which were anti-tank guns and tanks. At Kala'a itself tanks and anti-tank guns, concealed among the houses, were trained on the road which dipped and climbed the V-shaped sihpon. As if all this was not enough, the Syrians had constructed concrete pillboxes along the way, whose heavy machine guns poured out a thick hail of fire.

When Nati took over command he had twenty-one Shermans in three companies under him. The rest had either been hit or had touched off mines or had met with mechanical difficulties and could not advance. Nati changed his tank which had had its commander's hatch blown off and its radio damaged. He was obliged to fight on several fronts, and the pillboxes were engaging him more than he wanted. He ordered his Shermans, which were equipped with new French guns, to destroy the pillboxes and they began to pound them at ranges of 400 and 600 metres.

His main battle, however, was against the enemy's tanks and anti-tank guns. While Biro had still been in command, Nati had taken on three tanks which had been firing on him from the right, from the table-top enemy position, and had

255

scored direct hits, putting all three out of action. Then he had hit two tanks in Kala'a, while Lieutenant Ilan's company had advanced on the horse-shoe shaped crest to the left, enabling Nati's company to advance past the concrete dragon teeth, to destroy the tanks positioned on the horse-shoe and to intercept the Syrian tank which had left Jebeb el-Mis to reinforce the horse-shoe positions.

The battle arena was a mass of fire and smoke, and the air was filled with flying bullets and shells. The cloud of war hung low over the area, and in Nati's heart one ambition was burning: to carry out the battalion commander's order to take the position. From the concrete dragon teeth roadblocks at the boundary of Sir Adib to the elevated Kala'a fortress was a distance of 1800 metres. He had to battle for every metre.

When Nati had ordered Ilan's company to assault the horse-shoe on the left and the assault had succeeded, Ilan had been in a position to cover the advance of Nati's and Eppi's companies towards the dragon teeth roadblock at the bottom. But while taking the position, Ilan's tank had skidded down the decline. He had taken over another tank whose commander had been wounded during the assault.

Nati now requested additional artillery support and began to correct the artillery fire, while also dispatching his tanks through the roadblock. He asked for air support, but suddenly his radio stopped again. He could hear nothing through his earphones. Shaking the control box he discovered that it was soaked. It was blood, but where it had come from to cause the short-circuit he had no idea. Then he became aware of a sharp pain. A bullet had ploughed a wide furrow through his scalp. In the heat of the battle he had not felt anything but the blood which had flowed into the control box had silenced his radio. Later Nati discovered that he had also been hit by splinters in his back and hands. While he was still examining the radio for the cause of the breakdown, an anti-tank gun on the north side of Kala'a scored a direct hit on his tank's differential, and the steering system stopped functioning. Nati ordered the tanks near him to destroy the anti-tank gun which had hit him, but then two were spotted, one sticking out and the other withdrawn. Shell after shell was fired at the obtrusive one, until it was noticed that accurately aimed shells were hitting the tanks trying to manoeuvre through the dragon teeth. Nati realised that the obtrusive gun was a dummy. He ordered his gunner to divert his shots and the active gun was destroyed.

Under cover of a smoke screen Nati left his second tank and climbed into his third, a platoon commander's. He now ordered Ilan's company to come down from the horse-shoe on to the road leading to Kala'a, and ordered Eppi's company to take its place to cover the advance of the other two companies. Then the two companies covered Eppi's company as he descended to the road to join them for the climb to Kala'a. Nati's orders were that everyone whose tank was fit was to take part in the charge which would break through the obstacles and get them to Kala'a; those whose tanks were immobile were to fire their guns and machine guns to cover the assaulting tanks. Of his twenty-one tanks, ten passed the roadblock to make the assault and eleven stayed behind, covering the ten.

Ilan's company passed the roadblock first. Ilan advanced in the first tank against withering fire, Nati dispatching the tanks after him one by one to avoid congestion at the roadblock. Radio contact between the tanks was poor, as most of the assaulting tanks had been damaged, and Nati was obliged to shout to them through cupped hands. Ilan's tank, in the lead, was immediately hit. It burst into flames and Ilan jumped down, wounded in the scrotum. The loader too managed to get clear, but the men in the hull, the machine-gunner and the driver, were trapped in the burning tank, the gun blocking their exits. Through a hail of machine gun bullets the injured Ilan went back, climbed the burning tank and traversed the gun to enable his men to crawl out. Ilan staggered away and took refuge under an abandoned Syrian truck.

Nati did not stop to evacuate the wounded, but continued his attack on Kala'a. At the roadblock Sergeant Vardi was wounded in the face. He shouted into the radio to Nati that he could not see and was unable to manoeuvre his tank through the dragon teeth. Nati turned to him and was shocked. The sergeant's face had been ravaged by splinters so that it looked like a raw steak. From his tank, by radio, Nati guided the blind Vardi, who listened and repeated the directions to his driver who was manoeuvering through the roadblock. Then Nati radioed Vardi to follow behind him; it was impossible to evacuate him. Suddenly the sergeant happily announced that he could see again. The blood on his face had congealed and, as though through the holes in a rubber mask, he was able to peer.

"Can you carry on, Vardi?" Nati asked.

"Hundred per cent, Nati. Everything's O.K.", the sergeant

replied and was again in command of his tank.

Two more tanks had been hit by anti-tank guns and the situation now was that seven tanks were advancing up one arm of the V towards Kala'a, while along the other arm, on the Sir Adib side, the immobile tanks covered the seven's advance. The commander of the lead tank was Alfred, followed by Eppi, Eli, Nahum, Nati, Sergeant Vardi and another tank which had been hit.

Alfred now ordered his driver to proceed through a difficult passage in first gear. As they slowed down Alfred was hit in the head by a bullet and the driver received no further orders from him. He continued in low gear, and the two tanks behind him were obliged to shift to first as well, sticking close behind. Nati ordered the tanks to spread out, and the three rear tanks (the seventh had fallen back) advanced fifty metres behind the first three.

Over his radio Nati heard that seven Syrian tanks had left Quasset, on the Heights, to reinforce Kala'a. At first he wanted to order his tanks to race forward and occupy positions on the commanding ridge before the enemy, who were still at a lower level, could get up there, but by now his first three tanks were no more than twenty metres from the entrance to the village.

Alfred, leading the climbing column, still stood erect in his tank, his hands resting on the turret ring, exposed and vulnerable. Not a word came from him over the radio. The frightening realisation came to Nati that a dead man was leading the attack on Kala'a. Then a shell struck Alfred's tank. It exploded with such force that the turret was torn out. It shot up into the air and landed upside down on the ground with a loud crash. The Syrians had concealed a tank inside a one-storey house of basalt rock and were aiming through the window at Nati's tanks which were struggling at the village entrance. For a long time the source of the fire could not be discovered, because the aperture of the window was dark and the muzzle obscure.

Nati ordered Eppi to bypass Alfred's tank, and the second tank raced forward, but this tank, too, was hit and caught fire. Eppi, who by sheer good luck was only slightly wounded, managed to jump down from his tank and evade the shooting. Eli's tank, the third in the column, drove around Eppi's burning vehicle, raced forward, reached the first houses in the village, and then received a direct hit. Smoke rose up from it and there was an explosion, but the tank did not catch fire.

Of the fifteen crewmen in the three tanks (the Sherman has a crew of five), seven had been killed and eight wounded. The wounded crawled to cover.

Three tanks entered Kala'a, with the Syrian headquarters camp and their defence positions ranged across a large square on the other side of the village. Nati's radio contact with the two remaining tanks was poor. He could hear their commanders well, but they could not hear him, and he had to issue his commands by shouts and flags, and even to draw close to the tank when he wished to speak to its commander. He now ordered Sergeant Vardi to drive up to the left between the houses and find the source of the fire which had already destroyed three tanks. Vardi told his driver to turn left and they began to pass in front of the houses. His tank was hit in the rear by a bazooka missile and immediately burst into flames, but its crew managed to escape and take cover. Now at last the source of the shooting was discovered. The last two active tanks in Nati's force fired armour-piercing shells into the house and silenced the Syrian tank.

They had finally reached Kala'a, but they desperately needed to stop for a moment and catch their breath, and Nati was dismayed to see three Syrian tanks, two SU/100s and a T/34, on the road opposite him. Apparently they were the vanguard of the reinforcement of seven tanks the Syrians had dispatched to Kala'a. He immediately ordered his driver and the commander of the second tank, Nahum, to hide the two tanks in the shadows of the houses. He was not in any condition to wage a new battle. He repeated his request to the brigade commander for air support and received a reply, in a calm voice, that there were no planes available at the moment, but that all was being done to give him air support quickly.

Sergeant Vardi rounded up the wounded who could walk and led them to Nati's tank. Here they were given grenades and Uzzi submachine guns collected from the two sound tanks and ordered to comb the buildings, as rifle and machine gun fire was still being aimed at them, particularly at Lieutenant Eppi and his wounded men who had taken cover in a ditch. Nati could not permit the fit members of his crews to run to the ditch to extricate the wounded from it. They would almost certainly be killed. Over the radio the brigade commander told him that he would soon be reaching Kala'a from the rear.

"Sir, I repeat my request for planes," said Nati.

"There are none now," Colonel Albert said, "you must wait a little while."

"Sir, if you don't send planes for me now, you'll never see me again."

"Have patience, Nati. We're already past Zaoura and have a fierce battle on our hands for upper Zaoura, but we'll finish them off. We'll soon reach Kala'a from the rear."

"Sir, planes!"

"Nati, we're getting to you. It's only a matter of time. Hold on and wait patiently."

Nati knew that after dark his men and their two tanks would be easy prey to the Syrians. When night fell, air support would no longer be of any help. It was already 1800 hours and would soon be dark. He was greatly alarmed for his men and now that he had stopped fighting he began to feel afraid. He assembled the pathetic remnants of his force in a house near which the two tanks were parked. Now and then rifle and machine gun fire was heard, aimed at the wounded in the ditch.

And then, a few minutes before dusk, the planes arrived. Nati had no means of communicating with them, nor of indicating his position. The pilots could not distinguish between Nati's tanks and those of the Syrians, and were forced to make several dry runs over Kala'a. Their appearance greatly encouraged Nati and his men and frightened the Syrian tank crews, who started to withdraw in their tanks towards the outskirts of Kala'a. Then Nahum found the last smoke grenade and with it he indicated the location of his two tanks. It was a broad enough hint for the pilots. They swooped down upon the withdrawing Syrian tanks. Nati now gave the order to fire, and the two gunners hit two Syrian tanks. The rest were set ablaze by the gunners of the force under the command of the brigade commander, Colonel Albert, who finally reached Kala'a at 1830 hours.

Night was now falling; the last rays of the setting sun lit up Kala'a. On one side most of the brigade under Colonel Albert's command began to enter, while on the other waited the two tanks with the wounded and survivors of Biro's battalion. Both sections of the brigade had to link up, but Nati and his men were afraid that the brigade's tank crews would mistake them for Syrians. It was difficult to tell the difference in the twilight. Nati had no means of identification left, and his radio calls remained unanswered. The danger was very great, as Colonel Albert's force was still engaged with the Syrian tanks. Colonel Albert, however, told his intelligence officer to advance in the command half-track to the centre of the village and wave his maps. He was spotted by Nati and his men waiting at the other end of the village, and only then did the little groups emerge from the houses and the ditches to meet the forward command group. The relief felt by Nati and his men expressed itself in tears.

After four hours at Givat Ha'em Dr. Gluck decided to advance his post nearer to the battle and moved it up to the Na'amush defence position. The position was under fire which gradually became more and more desultory, and a stream of wounded began to arrive. While attending to the wounded, Gluck and his assistants had to mop-up the bunkers; for that was the character of the war here – the tanks cut through but did not consolidate. Every now and then one of the medical orderlies would fire his Uzzi or throw a hand grenade at one of the trenches which was firing at the aid post.

Then Dr. Gluck saw Ilan, his trousers bloodstained below the belt. Gluck removed Ilan's trousers and saw that he had been hit by splinters. His scrotum was cut open and his testicles dangled, exposed..

A soldier at war is terrified of two things, thought Dr. Gluck: of blindness and the loss of potency. "This is out of the question," said Dr. Gluck to himself. "It's not right. I simply cannot allow it. Not me." In the defence position, strewn with dead bodies and enveloped by the stench of death, Dr. Gluck attended to life. He was determined to repair the scrotum at once and give it back its anatomical shape. Regardless of the terrible operating conditions, the disturbances from the bothersome trenches, his unclean surgical instruments and filthy hands, it was best to operate quickly and not to send the lad down in such a condition on the long journey to hospital, for who was to know what might happen before he reached there, if he did.

It took fifteen minutes to complete his treatment; Ilan was fully conscious throughout.

"Will I be able to have children, doctor?" Ilan asked.

"Certainly you will. Everything's all right."

Dr. Gluck gave Ilan a shot of morphine to alleviate the pain.

"Where are we now, doctor? Advancing?"

"And how."

"Have we reached Kala'a?"

But Dr. Gluck had no idea where Kala'a was. He knew

nothing of battle plans. He did not even know he was in Na'amush until he was told. He was to discover where Kala'a was only when he went up there with his aid post at 1900 hours, where the wounded had been collected. Here Dr. Gluck was brought to a seriously wounded soldier. A shell splinter had broken his neck. By the light of the vehicles' headlights he began to operate on him, but the man died under his hands. The soldier's friends who watched the operation, could not believe it.

"But he spoke only a few minutes ago!"

EPILOGUE

'A' Brigade smashed the Syrian wall. Through the cracks it made, other armoured brigades poured in, while more brigades broke through at different places. An infantry brigade fought a fierce battle for the lower defence positions of the Golan Heights. The northern command wanted to secure a maximum of axes to the heights, for the transportation of the supply echelons and fighting forces. The next day, Saturday, 10 June, Zahal forces dispersed throughout the Golan Heights. The cease-fire came into force the same day, and thus ended the war known as the Six Day War. The victory was great, so great that it was incredible.

Nobody knew what to do with this victory, least of all the government. Nobody had any plans prepared for such an outcome and for the occupied territories and their inhabitants. Israel's joy was not because its dreams and ambitions had been realised, nor was it because this was the war to end all wars, it was the joy at staying alive, of surviving, and of pride in the strength of Zahal. There was no hysteria, no Victory Balls. People did not dance in the streets, public houses did not serve free drinks to the masses, and lovely young girls did not climb on tanks to kiss the soldiers and stick flowers in their hair. The joy was a domestic one. In a short while the reserves had returned home, released with the same speed that they had been conscripted. They returned home, to their families and jobs.

The very first event was a three days' mourning period. Memorial ceremonies were held at the military cemeteries in Be'eri, Jerusalem and Afula, where each gathering was addressed by a representative of the Bereaved Parents Association – an institution which, alas, is becoming more and more a part of Israeli life – who proffered condolences to the bereaved parents, to the widows and orphans who had lost their dear ones in 1967. Those who in 1956 had received condolences from parents who had lost their sons in 1948, now tried to soothe and console those whom the war of 1967 had embittered. Parents whose sons had fallen in reprisal operations, in the Water War or on reconnaissance patrols along the borders, now tried to find words to comfort the new members of the Association, repeating the same words they themselves had heard in 1948: Let us find solace in the independence of Israel. Words which at first offer meagre consolation, but which over the years, as the first agony of loss is dulled, become a cause for pride.

At Be'eri cemetery General Tal passed between the fresh graves of the Armoured Corps dead. Many of his friends were buried there, fallen in 1948, in 1956, in 1967 and in the intervening years. He paused in front of the graves of Lieutenant-Colonel Ehud Elad, of Major Shamai Kaplan and of Captain Ilan Yakuel. Here was Ilan Yakuel who had planned to travel overseas, to contemplate the ways of the world. He would never leave his homeland now. In another part of the cemetery stood Lieutenant-Colonel Oshri, a platinum disk under the skin of his reddish head shielding his brain where a splinter had smashed his skull. Not far from him an amputee and a cripple met their battlefield friends and compared impressions. Colonel Shmuel, Major Haim, Lieutenant Yossi B. and others stood next to the grave of Lieutenant-Colonel Ehud Elad, promoted posthumously. With them was Hava, her red eyes dry. "He was a tiger," was all Colonel Shmuel said in consolation, and that he repeated again and again. "He was a tiger."

At the cemeteries in Afula and Haifa Colonel Albert stood in front of the graves of his men. Two future battalion commanders of his brigade were buried here. Major Moshe Haviv was buried in Afula in a communal grave with his men in the half-track, who in war had become eternally united, body and soul, in the flames of the blazing half-track. Major Mokady was buried in Haifa. His funeral had been delayed, because for several days his body had not been found.

On the Mount of Peace in Jerusalem, the Minister of Defence, Major-General Moshe Dayan, lamented the dead, as in the past he had lamented many of his friends and soldiers. His one eye sparkled with a powerful lust for life, his other eye was extinguished and dead. At times it seems Dayan is the

263

symbol of Israel, for whose existence life and death have formed a close partnership. Israel is ready to die in her struggle to live, and it is from this readiness that she draws her courage.

On Thursday 8 June, the day Major Shamai Kaplan was killed, the authorities were instructed not to inform Nava of his death. It was thought wisest to consult her doctor first, as she was expecting to give birth. The doctor recommended that she should not be told. But Nava sensed that something was wrong. Shamai would have telephoned, written a letter, sent regards. She was staying with Shamai's parents in Ramat Gan, and every day she had said to his mother, "I don't understand, Shamai would have written." Shamai knew she was staying with his parents and he, who was so devoted to his family, had not written? or telephoned? or sent a message? Why, he used to telephone from the field every day to ask if Nava had given birth and had asked to be informed by an announcement in the press or by radio, via Armoured Corps headquarters.

Nava waited patiently for the postman. When Sunday dragged by without a line from Shamai, her fears mounted. On Monday, 12 June, the postman's ring was late. She had a long and difficult wait, and when he came there was still nothing for her. Nava thought she would go out of her mind. She went to wash her face in the bathroom, and then she heard her sister and sister-in-law ask the children who were out in the garden to play further away from the house. Looking out, she saw her sister and sister-in-law talking to an officer from the Armoured Corps and her doctor. They entered the apartment, and then she knew.

At the end of the seven days of mourning for Shamai, while General Tal and all his friends stood before his grave in Be'eri cemetery, Nava gave birth to a girl and called her Shamit.

A short while later Captain Avigdor Kahalany's doctors permitted him to leave his bed to attend the circumcision of his newborn son. His burns had been most serious, and the doctors were amazed he had survived. But for his strong will to live, they told his friends, he would not have lived. It was a miracle.

Captain Kahalany was wheeled in a chair to his firstborn son's circumcision, and General Tal, Colonel Shmuel, Lieutenant-Colonel Haim and Major Ori pushed the chair.

On introducing his son to the ancient covenant of Abraham, Kahalany gave him the name Dror, which means Freedom.

SPHERE SOLE AGENTS

Africa: Ethiopia: G. P. Giannopoulos,
Kenya, Uganda, Tanzania, Zambia,
Malawi: Thomas Nelson & Sons Ltd.,
Kenya; South Africa, Rhodesia:
Thomas Nelson & Sons (Africa) (Pty) Ltd.,
Johannesburg: Ghana, Nigeria,
Sierra Leone: Thomas Nelson & Sons Ltd.,
Nigeria; Liberia: Wadih M. Captan;
Angola, Mozambique: Electroliber
Limitada, Angola;
Zambia: Kingstons (North) Ltd.
Australia: Thomas Nelson (Australia) Ltd.
Austria: Danubia-Auslieferung
Bahamas: Calypso Distributors Ltd.
Belgium: Agence et Messageries de la Presse, S.A.
Bermuda: Baxters Bookshop Ltd.
Brazil: Francisco Romana & Cia. Ltda., Rio de Janeiro
Canada: Thomas Nelson & Sons (Canada) Ltd.
Carribean: Roland I. Khan (Trinidad)
Denmark: Danske Boghandleres Bogimport a/s
France: Librairie Estrangere, Hachette
Germany: Distropa Buchvertrieb
Gibraltar: Estogans Agencies Ltd.
Greece: Hellenic Distribution Agency Ltd.
Holland: Van Ditmar
Hong Kong: Western Publications Distribution Agency
(H.K.) Ltd.
Israel: Steimatzky's Agency Ltd.
Iran: I.A.D.A.
Iraq: Dar Alaruba Universal Distribution Co.
Italy: Agenzia Internazionale di Distribuzione
Kuwait: Farajalla Press Agency
Lebanon: The Levant Distributors Co.
Malaysia, Singapore and Brunei: Marican & Sons (Malaysia) (Sdn) Berhad
Malta: Progress Press Co. Ltd.
New Zealand: Hodder & Stoughton Ltd.
Portugal: Electroliber Limitada
South America: Colombia: Libreria Central
Chile: Libreria Studio
Mexico and Central America: Libreria
Britanica
Peru: Librerias ABC
Venezuela: Distribuidora Santiago
Spain: Comercial Atheneum
Sudan: Sudan Bookshop
Sweden: Importbokhandeln
Switzerland: Friedr. Daeniker
Thailand: The Pramuansarn Publishing House
Turkey: Librairie Hachette